MW00474941

Exploring
THE GOSPEL
OF LUKE

THE JOHN PHILLIPS COMMENTARY SERIES

Exploring

THE GOSPEL OF LUKE

An Expository Commentary

JOHN PHILLIPS

kregel
PUBLICATIONS

Grand Rapids, MI 49501

Exploring the Gospel of Luke: An Expository Commentary

© 2005 by John Phillips

Published in 2005 by Kregel Publications, a division of Kregel, Inc., P.O. Box 2607, Grand Rapids, MI 49501.

Scripture quotations are from the King James Version of the Holy Bible.

Library of Congress Cataloging-in-Publication Data
Phillips, John.
    Exploring the gospel of Luke: an expository commentary / by John Phillips.
        p.   cm.
Includes bibliographical references.
    1. Bible N.T. Luke—Commentaries. I. Title.
BS2595.53.P45 2004
226.4'077—dc22   2004019272

ISBN 978-0-8254-3377-1

Printed in the United States of America

09 10 11 / 6 5 4

Contents

Complete Outline

9

   b. The problem (1:7)
   c. The place (1:8–10)
    (1) The minister within (1:8–9)
    (2) The multitude without (1:10)
   d. The panic (1:11–12)
    (1) The apparition (1:11)
    (2) The apprehension (1:12)
  2. The stirring prophecy of the angel (1:13–17)
   a. John's coming foretold (1:13–14)
    (1) A prayer answered (1:13a)
    (2) A prospect announced (1:13b–14)
   b. John's character foretold (1:15)
   c. John's career foretold (1:16–17)
  3. The sobering prediction of the angel (1:18–25)
   a. The angel's astonishment (1:18–20)
   b. The angel's accuracy (1:21–25)
    (1) Concerning the priest's speechlessness (1:21–22)
    (2) Concerning the priest's son (1:23–25)
 B. The birth of Jesus announced (1:26–55)
  1. The annunciation (1:26–38)
   a. The angel's descent (1:26–29)
   b. The angel's disclosure (1:30–38a)
    (1) The revelation (1:30–33)
    (2) The realization (1:34)
    (3) The ramification (1:35–37)
     (a) The plan (1:35)
     (b) The proof (1:36)
     (c) The power (1:37)
    (4) The resignation (1:38a)
   c. The angel's departure (1:38b)
  2. The adjustment (1:39–45)
   a. The counsel Mary required (1:39–40)
   b. The confirmation Mary received (1:41–45)
    (1) The instant sign (1:41a)
    (2) The inspiring Spirit (1:41b–45)
  3. The anthem (1:46–55)
   a. A personal note (1:46–49)

b. A practical note (1:50–53)

c. A prophetical note (1:54–55)

Section 2: The Advent (1:56–3:22)

A. The comings (1:56–2:52)

1. The coming of John (1:56–80)

a. The departure of Mary (1:56)

b. The deliverance of Elizabeth (1:57–66)

(1) The coming of the neighbors (1:57–58)

(a) The birth recorded (1:57)

(b) The bliss recorded (1:58)

(2) The crisis of the name (1:59–66)

(a) The name decided (1:59)

(b) The name disputed (1:60–61)

(c) The name determined (1:62–66)

i. The priest's assertion (1:62–64)

ii. The people's astonishment (1:65–66)

c. The declaration of Zacharias (1:67–79)

(1) Words about Jesus (1:67–69)

(a) The Spirit of God (1:67)

(b) The Son of God (1:68–69)

i. A redeeming Messiah (1:68)

ii. A royal Messiah (1:69)

(2) Words about Jewry (1:70–75)

(a) Scripture (1:70–73)

(b) Service (1:74)

(c) Sanctification (1:75)

(3) Words about John (1:76–79)

(a) His calling (1:76a)

(b) His commission (1:76b–79)

i. As Messiah's herald (1:76b)

ii. As Messiah's helper (1:77–79)

a. Rebuking the sinner (1:77–78a)

b. Revealing the Savior (1:78b–79)

d. The development of John (1:80)

2. The coming of Jesus (2:1–52)

a. The birth (2:1–20)

(1) The powers of this world (2:1–7)
(2) The princes of that world (2:8–14)
   (a) The herald from on high (2:8–12)
      i. Whom he sought (2:8–9)
      ii. What he said (2:10–12)
         a. The salvation (2:10)
         b. The Savior (2:11)
         c. The sign (2:12)
   (b) The hosts from on high (2:13–14)
(3) The people of their world (2:15–20)
   (a) The response of the shepherds (2:15–16)
   (b) The reaction of the shepherds (2:17–19)
      i. Their tidings told (2:17–18)
         a. The wideness of their witness (2:17)
         b. The wonder of their witness (2:18)
      ii. Their tidings treasured (2:19)
   (c) The return of the shepherds (2:20)
b. The Babe (2:21–38)
   (1) The presentation of Jesus in the temple (2:21–24)
      (a) The naming of the Lord (2:21)
      (b) The nature of the law (2:22–24)
   (2) The proclamations about Jesus in the temple (2:25–38)
      (a) The words of the prophet Simeon (2:25–35)
         i. The man (2:25–26)
            a. His character (2:25)
            b. His conviction (2:26)
         ii. The moment (2:27–28)
            a. The Spirit in his heart (2:27)
            b. The Savior in his arms (2:28)
         iii. The message (2:29–35)
            a. A message for mankind (2:29–32)
               1. Concerning the Savior (2:29–30)
               2. Concerning the salvation (2:31–32)
            b. A message for Mary (2:33–35)
               1. Awe (2:33)
               2. Awareness (2:34–35)
      (b) The words of the prophetess Anna (2:36–38)

    c. The Boy (2:39–52)
      (1) Where He lived (2:39–40)
        (a) The place (2:39)
        (b) The plan (2:40)
          i. His growth (2:40a–b)
          ii. His grace (2:40c)
      (2) What He loved (2:41–50)
        (a) His Father's building (2:41–47)
          i. What they supposed (2:41–44)
            a. Jerusalem (2:41–42)
              1. The annual visit to Jerusalem (2:41)
              2. This anniversary visit to Jerusalem (2:42)
            b. Jesus (2:43–44)
              1. A missing Christ (2:43)
              2. A missed Christ (2:44)
          ii. Where they searched (2:45–46a)
          iii. What they saw (2:46b–47)
        (b) His Father's business (2:48–50)
      (3) What He learned (2:51–52)
        (a) His submission described (2:51)
        (b) His stature described (2:52)
          i. Selfward (2:52a)
          ii. Godward (2:52b)
          iii. Manward (2:52c)
B. The commencement (3:1–22)
  1. John the Baptist's teaching (3:1–20)
    a. His sudden arrival (3:1–6)
    b. His spectacular appeal (3:7–18)
      (1) Those coming to his crusade (3:7–9)
      (2) Those convicted by his crusade (3:10–14)
      (3) Those confused by his crusade (3:15–18)
        (a) Their speculations aired (3:15)
        (b) Their speculations answered (3:16–18)
          i. The ministry of John exemplified (3:16)
          ii. The ministry of John explained (3:16b–17)
          iii. The ministry of John expanded (3:18)
    c. His subsequent arrest (3:19–20)

(1) Herod's wickedness condemned (3:19)

(2) Herod's wickedness climaxed (3:20)

2. John the Baptist's testimony (3:21–22)

   a. Its success (3:21a)

   b. Its successor (3:21b–22)

     (1) The Son of God (3:21b–c)

     (2) The Spirit of God (3:21d–22)

Section 3: The Ancestry (3:23–38)

A. His age (3:23a)

B. His ancestors (3:23b–38)

   1. The footnote about Joseph (3:23b)

   2. The forebears of Jesus (3:24–38)

     a. The royal line (3:24–31)

       (1) The silent years: Jesus to Zerubbabel (3:24–27a)

       (2) The secret years: Zerubbabel to David (3:27b–31)

     b. The religious line: David to Abraham (3:32–34a)

     c. The racial line (3:34b–38)

       (1) Back to a time before the Flood: Abraham to Noah (3:34b–36a)

       (2) Back to a time before the Fall (3:36b–38)

         (a) To the human father of the race (3:36b–38a)

         (b) To the heavenly Father of the race (3:38b)

Section 4: The Adversary (4:1–13)

A. The Spirit forces Satan to fight (4:1)

B. The Savior forces Satan to flee (4:2–13)

   1. The temptation of Jesus (4:2–12)

     a. The forty days (4:2)

     b. The final day (4:3–12)

       (1) The temptation along the line of the will of God (4:3–4)

         (a) The lure extended (4:3)

           "You are famished. Do what I say, and you can instantly have the sustenance you so obviously need."

         (b) The lie exposed (4:4)

       (2) The temptation along the line of the worship of God (4:5–8)

         (a) The lure extended (4:5–7)

"You have failed. Do what I say, and you can instantly have the scepter you so obviously need."

   (b) The lie exposed (4:8)

   (3) The temptation along the line of the Word of God (4:9–12)

       (a) The lure extended (4:9–11)

"You are forgotten. Do what I say, and you can instantly have the success you so obviously need."

       (b) The lie exposed (4:12)

   2. The triumph of Jesus (4:13)

PART 3: EVENTS RELATING TO THE SAVIOR'S CAREER (4:14–21:38)

Section 1: The Work in Galilee: His Anointing in Focus (4:14–9:50)

   A. The work is commenced (4:14–5:17)

   1. He comes to be the Savior (4:14–15)

   2. He claims to be the Savior (4:16–5:17)

       a. The Scripture itself attests the claim (4:16–30)

           (1) The setting (4:16–20)

               (a) The Lord's coming to Nazareth (4:16a)

               (b) The Lord's custom at Nazareth (4:16b–20)

           (2) The sermon (4:21–27)

               (a) The proclamation (4:21–22)

               (b) The provocation (4:23–27)

                   i. The Lord's bluntness (4:23–24)

                   ii. The Lord's Bible (4:25–27)

                       a. The case of Elijah and the destitute widow (4:25–26)

                       b. The case of Elisha and the desperate leper (4:27)

           (3) The sequel (4:28–30)

               (a) Their fury (4:28)

               (b) Their folly (4:29)

               (c) Their failure (4:30)

       b. The Savior Himself attests the claim (4:31–5:15)

           (1) He commands the demons (4:31–37)

               (a) The move (4:31a)

               (b) The message (4:31b–32)

               (c) The man (4:33–34)

  (d) The miracle (4:35–37)
    i. The Lord's rebuke (4:35)
    ii. The Lord's reputation (4:36–37)
      a. How it was spoken about (4:36)
      b. How it was spread abroad (4:37)
 (2) He cures the sick (4:38–44)
  (a) The disciple (4:38–39)
    i. Simon's residence (4:38a)
    ii. Simon's relative (4:38b–39)
  (b) The diseased (4:40)
  (c) The demoniacs (4:41)
    i. The Lord's power (4:41a)
    ii. The Lord's policy (4:41b)
  (d) The desert (4:42)
    i. The Lord's quest described (4:42a)
    ii. The Lord's quiet disturbed (4:42b)
  (e) The departure (4:43–44)
    i. The great imperative (4:43)
    ii. The great impact (4:44)
 (3) He controls the fish (5:1–11)
  (a) The request (5:1–3)
  (b) The reward (5:4–10)
    i. Peter's pride (5:4–7)
    ii. Peter's penitence (5:8–9)
      a. His confession (5:8)
      b. His confusion (5:9)
    iii. Peter's partners (5:10a)
    iv. Peter's prospect (5:10b)
  (c) The result (5:11)
 (4) He cleanses the leper (5:12–15)
  (a) The case (5:12)
  (b) The cure (5:13)
    i. The touch (5:13a)
    ii. The transformation (5:13b)
  (c) The command (5:14)
  (d) The consequences (5:15)
c. The Spirit Himself attests the claim (5:16–17)

(1) Witnessing to the Lord's private life (5:16)

(2) Witnessing to the Lord's public life (5:17)

B. The work is criticized (5:18–6:11)

  1. The silent criticism (5:18–26)

    a. Problems (5:18–24)

      (1) The material problem (5:18–19)

        (a) A helpless cripple (5:18)

        (b) A hindering crowd (5:19)

      (2) The moral problem (5:20)

      (3) The mental problem (5:21–24)

        (a) How Jesus faced their silent criticism (5:21–22)

          i. How their minds were reacting to Jesus (5:21)

          ii. How their minds were read by Jesus (5:22)

        (b) How Jesus fought their silent criticism (5:23–24)

          i. The way He asked His question (5:23)

          ii. The way He answered His question (5:24)

            a. The Lord's comment (5:24a)

            b. The Lord's command (5:24b)

    b. Praise (5:25–26)

  2. The spoken criticism (5:27–6:5)

    a. Because He ignored their religious prejudices (5:27–32)

      (1) Levi's call (5:27–28)

      (2) Levi's companions (5:29)

      (3) Levi's critics (5:30–32)

    b. Because He ignored their religious practices (5:33–39)

      (1) A needling challenge (5:33–35)

        (a) The question asked (5:33)

        (b) The question answered (5:34–35)

          i. The then and the there (5:34)

          ii. The here and the now (5:35)

      (2) A needed change (5:36–39)

        (a) He takes us into the workshop (5:36)

        (b) He takes us into the wineshop (5:37–39)

          i. The matter of storing the wine (5:37–38)

          ii. The matter of sampling the wine (5:39)

    c. Because He ignored their religious pretences (6:1–5)

      (1) A Sabbath law (6:1)

(2) A Scripture lesson (6:2–4)

    (a) The question asked of Him (6:2)

    (b) The question asked by Him (6:3–4)

(3) A sovereign Lord (6:5)

3. The subversive criticism (6:6–11)

  a. The man (6:6–7)

    (1) The Sabbath (6:6a)

    (2) The synagogue (6:6b)

    (3) The snare (6:7)

  b. The Master (6:8–9)

    (1) Confronting His critics (6:8)

    (2) Confounding His critics (6:9)

  c. The miracle (6:10–11)

    (1) A deliberate healing (6:10)

    (2) A diabolical hatred (6:11)

C. The work is climaxed (6:12–9:50)

1. A dependent Savior (6:12–16)

  a. Depending on the faithfulness of His Father (6:12)

  b. Depending on the faithfulness of His friends (6:13–16)

    (1) The men: what they were (6:13)

      (a) Chosen men (6:13a)

      (b) Changed men (6:13b)

    (2) The men: who they were (6:14–16)

2. A dynamic Savior (6:17–9:17)

  a. Dynamic in His words (6:17–49)

    (1) What the multitudes sought (6:17–19)

      (a) The tremendous nature of the crowds (6:17a)

      (b) The terrible nature of their condition (6:17b–18a)

      (c) The triumphant nature of their cure (6:18b–19)

    (2) What the Master said (6:20–49)

      (a) Unusual beatitudes (6:20–23)

        i. A difficult outlook (6:20–22)

          a. Those of His people who are disadvantaged (6:20–21a)

          b. Those of His people who are distressed (6:21b)

          c. Those of His people who are detested (6:22)

        ii. A different outcome (6:23)

(b) Unusual barriers (6:24–26)
    i. The woes expressed (6:24–26a)
        a. Those who are prosperous in life (6:24–25a)
        b. Those who are pleased with life (6:25b)
        c. Those who are popular in life (6:26a)
    ii. The woes explained (6:26b)
(c) Unusual behavior (6:27–49)
    i. Toward our foes (6:27–29)
        a. The principle of love (6:27–28)
          1. To those who detest us (6:27)
          2. To those who degrade us (6:28a)
          3. To those who despoil us (6:28b)
        b. The practice of love (6:29)
          1. The man who strikes at us (6:29a)
          2. The man who steals from us (6:29b)
    ii. Toward our fellows (6:30–40)
        a. A great expectation (6:30)
        b. A great essential (6:31)
        c. A great explanation (6:32–38)
          1. The comparison (6:32–34)
          2. The contrast (6:35–38)
            (i) The divine nature (6:35–36)
            (ii) The divine negative (6:37a)
            (iii) The divine necessity (6:37b–38)
        d. A great example (6:39–40)
          1. The lost are lost (6:39)
          2. The Lord is Lord (6:40)
    iii. Toward our faults (6:41–45)
        a. The matter of criticism (6:41–42)
        b. The matter of corruption (6:43–45)
    iv. Toward our faith (6:46–49)
        a. The test of a confessed faith (6:46)
        b. The triumph of a correct faith (6:47–48)
        c. The tragedy of a counterfeit faith (6:49)
b. Dynamic in His works (7:1–17)
  (1) Distance could not thwart Him (7:1–10)
    (a) The setting (7:1)

  (b) The soldier (7:2–8)
    i. His servant (7:2)
    ii. His supporters (7:3–5)
    iii. His sincerity (7:6–8)
      a. What He realized (7:6a)
      b. What He requested (7:6b–8)
        1. A word of confession (7:6b–7a)
        2. A word of confidence (7:7b)
        3. A word of comparison (7:8)
  (c) The Savior (7:9)
    i. His reaction (7:9a)
    ii. His rebuke (7:9b)
  (d) The sequel (7:10)
 (2) Death could not thwart Him (7:11–17)
  (a) The Lord's coming (7:11–12)
  (b) The Lord's compassion (7:13–15)
    i. His pity (7:13)
    ii. His power (7:14–15)
  (c) The Lord's compatriots (7:16–17)
    i. A word about Jesus (7:16)
    ii. A word about Judea (7:17)
c. Dynamic in His ways (7:18–35)
 (1) Perfecting John's faith (7:18–23)
  (a) A word from John the Baptist (7:18–20)
    i. What he had heard (7:18)
    ii. What he had hoped (7:19–20)
  (b) A word for John the Baptist (7:21–23)
    i. What Jesus did (7:21)
    ii. What Jesus declared (7:22–23)
      a. A word of assessment (7:22)
      b. A word of assurance (7:23)
 (2) Praising John's faithfulness (7:24–35)
  (a) John as a fearless man (7:24–25)
    i. Not to be shaken by the wind (7:24)
    ii. Not to be shaped by the world (7:25)
  (b) John as a faithful messenger (7:26–29)
    i. John and his calling (7:26–28)

     a. The promised prophet (7:26–27)

     b. The proper perspective (7:28)

    ii. John and his career (7:29)

    iii. John and his critics (7:30–35)

     a. Their rejection of John (7:30)

     b. Their rejection of Jesus (7:31–35)

  d. Dynamic in His walk (7:36–8:3)

   (1) Accepting the hospitality of Simon (7:36–50)

    (a) The sinful woman (7:36–38)

     i. Where she came: an indication of her courage (7:36)

     ii. Why she came: an indication of her contrition (7:37–38)

    (b) The scornful Pharisee (7:39–47)

     i. A look at his expression (7:39–43)

      a. His inward assessment (7:39)

       1. Contempt for the sinner (7:39a)

       2. Contempt for the Savior (7:39b)

      b. His outward assurance (7:40–43)

     ii. A look at his exposure (7:44–47)

      a. A lesson in contrasts (7:44–46)

       1. Contrition (7:44)

       2. Consecration (7:45)

       3. Coronation (7:46)

      b. A lesson in conversion (7:47)

    (c) The saving Christ (7:48–50)

     i. A word about forgiveness (7:48–49)

      a. What Jesus forgave (7:48)

      b. Why Jesus forgave (7:49)

     ii. A word about faith (7:50)

   (2) Accepting the help of some (8:1–3)

    (a) Proclamation (8:1)

     i. The tour (8:1a)

     ii. The tidings (8:1b)

     iii. The Twelve (8:1c)

    (b) Provision (8:2–3)

     i. Why the women went (8:2a)

   ii. Who the women were (8:2b–3a)

   iii. What the women wanted (8:3b)

 e. Dynamic in His wisdom (8:4–21)

  (1) Understanding the hearts of men (8:4–18)

   (a) A parable about fruitbearing (8:4–15)

    i. Jesus and the multitude (8:4–8)

     a. The sower (8:4–5a)

     b. The seed (8:5b)

     c. The soil (8:5c–8)

      1. The roadside soil (8:5c)

      2. The rocky soil (8:6)

      3. The ruined soil (8:7)

      4. The receptive soil (8:8)

    ii. Jesus and His men (8:9–15)

     a. An exclusive company (8:9–10)

     b. An expanded company (8:11–15)

      1. The problem soil (8:11–14)

       (i) The demonic factor (8:11–12)

       (ii) The disappointment factor (8:13)

       (iii) The deterrent factor (8:14)

      2. The productive soil (8:15)

   (b) A parable about lightbearing (8:16–18)

    i. The illustration (8:16)

    ii. The illumination (8:17–18)

     a. Everything revealed (8:17)

     b. Everyone responsible (8:18)

  (2) Understanding the heart of Mary (8:19–21)

   (a) The coming of His mother (8:19–20)

   (b) The comment of the Master (8:21)

 f. Dynamic in His will (8:22–9:17)

  (1) The stilling of the tempest (8:22–25)

   (a) The simple suggestion (8:22–23a)

   (b) The stormy sea (8:23b–c)

   (c) The stricken seamen (8:24a)

   (d) The sudden stillness (8:24b)

   (e) The sovereign Savior (8:25)

    i. The fact of their faith challenged (8:25a)

(3) The subjection of the tomb (8:40–56)
   (a) A distracted father (8:40–42)
   (b) A diseased woman (8:43–48)
      i. Her condition (8:43)
      ii. Her cure (8:44)
      iii. Her confession (8:45–48)
         a. A special touch (8:45–46)
            1. What the Lord discerned (8:45a)
            2. What the Lord declared (8:45b–46)
         b. A splendid testimony (8:47)
         c. A spiritual truth (8:48)
   (c) A dead child (8:49–56)
      i. The message (8:49–50)
      ii. The mourners (8:51–53)
         a. Their removal (8:51)
         b. Their ridicule (8:52–53)
(4) The sending of the Twelve (9:1–10)
   (a) The Twelve (9:1–6)
      i. Their might (9:1)
         a. Over demons (9:1a)
         b. Over disease (9:1b)
      ii. Their message (9:2)
      iii. Their money (9:3)
      iv. Their method (9:4–5)
         a. When they were received by men (9:4)
         b. When they were rejected of men (9:5)
      v. Their move (9:6)
         a. Their systematic plan (9:6a)
         b. Their successful preaching (9:6b)
   (b) The tetrarch (9:7–9)
      i. Why he wondered (9:7–9a)
         a. His doubts (9:7–8)
         b. His dismay (9:9a)
      ii. What he wanted (9:9b)
   (c) The tidings (9:10)
      i. The report (9:10a)
      ii. The retreat (9:10b)

(5) The spreading of the table (9:11–17)

    (a) The crowds (9:11)

        i. Their spiritual hunger (9:11a)

        ii. Their special healing (9:11b)

    (b) The crisis (9:12–13a)

    (c) The Christ (9:13b–17)

        i. The protest (9:13b–14a)

        ii. The preparation (9:14b–15)

        iii. The provision (9:16–17)

            a. Plenty for all of those many mouths (9:16–17a)

            b. Plenty for all of the Master's men (9:17b)

3. A divine Savior (9:18–45)

  a. His deity is declared (9:18–27)

    (1) The Lord and His prayer (9:18a)

    (2) The Lord and His person (9:18b–21)

    (3) The Lord and His passion (9:22)

    (4) The Lord and His perspective (9:23–26)

        (a) Life's priority—a cross (9:23)

        (b) Life's profit—or loss (9:24–26)

    (5) The Lord and His promise (9:27)

  b. His deity is demonstrated (9:28–45)

    (1) Glory on the mount (9:28–36)

        (a) The heavenly vision (9:28–29)

            i. The setting for the Transfiguration (9:28)

            ii. The splendor of the Transfiguration (9:29)

        (b) The holy visitors (9:30–31)

            i. Their coming (9:30)

            ii. Their conversation (9:31)

        (c) The human vagary (9:32–33)

            i. What was seen (9:32)

                a. Their awakening (9:32a)

                b. Their awareness (9:32b)

            ii. What was said (9:33)

                a. The fading presence (9:33a)

                b. The foolish proposal (9:33b)

        (d) The highest validation (9:34–36)

    (2) Grace in the valley (9:37–45)

(a) The people (9:37)
(b) The problem (9:38–41a)
    i. Of the possessing demon (9:38–39)
    ii. Of the powerless disciples (9:40)
    iii. Of the perverse dispensation (9:41a)
(c) The power (9:41b–45)
    i. The power seen (9:41b–43a)
    ii. The power suspended (9:43b–45)
        a. A warning now communicated to the disciples (9:43b–44)
        b. A warning not comprehended by the disciples (9:45)

4. A discerning Savior (9:46–50)
  a. Believers within the group criticized (9:46–48)
    (1) The question raised (9:46)
    (2) The question resolved (9:47–48)
      (a) The child displayed (9:47)
      (b) The challenge delivered (9:48)
  b. Believers without the group criticized (9:49–50)

Section 2: The Way to Golgotha: His Adversaries in Focus (9:51–21:38)

A. The scholastic approach (9:51–10:42)
  1. The Savior sets His face (9:51)
    a. A critical moment (9:51a)
    b. A critical move (9:51b)
  2. The Savior sends His followers (9:52–10:24)
    a. The dispensational question (9:52–56)
      (1) The messengers (9:52–53)
        (a) Dispatched by Jesus to the Samaritans (9:52)
        (b) Despised as Jews by the Samaritans (9:53)
      (2) The mistake (9:54–56)
        (a) The indignation of James and John (9:54)
        (b) The ignorance of James and John (9:55–56)
          i. The Lord's displeasure (9:55–56a)
            a. Their ignorance of the Spirit (9:55)
            b. Their ignorance of the Savior (9:56a)
          ii. The Lord's departure (9:56b)

        a. A refuge for now (10:34b)

        b. A resource for now (10:35a–b)

           1. An adequate price provided (10:35a)

           2. An adequate person provided (10:35b)

      iii. As to the prospect (10:35c–d)

        a. A time inferred (10:35c)

        b. A truth inferred (10:35d)

    (3) A lethal probe (10:36–37)

      (a) The question of discerning what is revealed (10:36–37a)

      (b) The question of doing what is required (10:37b)

  4. The Savior sees His friends (10:38–42)

    a. Martha's house (10:38)

    b. Martha's hospitality (10:39–40)

      (1) A word about her sister (10:39)

      (2) A word about her service (10:40a)

      (3) A word about her spirit (10:40b)

    c. Martha's haste (10:41)

      (1) She was being too busy (10:41–42a)

      (2) She was being too bossy (10:42b)

B. The slanderous approach (11:1–28)

  1. A suggestion that was unprincipled (11:1–14)

    a. Declaring the person of God the Father (11:1–13)

      (1) A request (11:1–4)

        (a) The request made (11:1)

        (b) The request met (11:2–4)

          i. The Father's person (11:2a)

          ii. The Father's place (11:2b)

          iii. The Father's purity (11:2c)

          iv. The Father's purpose (11:2d)

          v. The Father's provision (11:3)

          vi. The Father's pardon (11:4a)

          vii. The Father's protection (11:4b)

      (2) A revelation (11:5–13)

        (a) Based on the behavior of a friend (11:5–10)

          i. A word picture (11:5–8)

          ii. A warm pledge (11:9–10)

            a. The contrast revealed (11:9)

        b. The contrast repeated (11:10)

     (b) Based on the behavior of a father (11:11–13)

        i. The behavior of a human father (11:11–12)

           a. He will not mock with a stone (11:11a)

           b. He will not mock with a serpent (11:11b)

           c. He will not mock with a scorpion (11:12)

        ii. The behavior of the heavenly Father (11:13)

  b. Demonstrating the power of the Holy Spirit (11:14)

    (1) The miracle of the Master (11:14a)

    (2) The marveling of the multitude (11:14b)

 2. A suggestion that was unpardonable (11:15–28)

  a. The Lord exposes the nonsense of the suggestion (11:15–22)

    (1) He read their evil thoughts (11:15–16)

    (2) He ridiculed their evil thoughts (11:17–19)

    (3) He repudiated their evil thoughts (11:20–22)

      (a) The true source of His power (11:20)

      (b) The tremendous scope of His power (11:21–22)

  b. The Lord exposes the nature of the suggestion (11:23–28)

    (1) A principle (11:23)

    (2) A parable (11:24–26)

      (a) The restlessness of an exorcised spirit (11:24a)

      (b) The return of an exorcised spirit (11:25b–26)

        i. What it discovers (11:25b)

        ii. What it does (11:26)

    (3) A proclamation (11:27–28)

C. The sophisticated approach (11:29–52)

 1. In public: the hardness of the people of Israel (11:29–36)

  a. The signs (11:29–32)

    (1) The sign of the convicting seer (11:29–30)

    (2) The sign of the conscientious sovereign (11:31)

    (3) The sign of the converted sinners (11:32)

  b. The sermon (11:33–36)

    (1) The illustration (11:33–34)

      (a) The lamp and its purpose (11:33)

      (b) The light and its power (11:34)

    (2) The application (11:35–36)

      (a) A threatening possibility (11:35)

        (b) A thrilling potentiality (11:36)

   2. In private: the hypocrisy of the peers of Israel (11:37–52)

     a. An unspoken criticism of His manners (11:37–38)

     b. An outspoken criticism of their motives (11:39–52)

       (1) Woes upon the formal traditionalists (11:39–44)

         (a) Washing up the dishes (11:39–41)

         (b) Working in the dark (11:42–43)

         (c) Walking on the dead (11:44)

       (2) Woes upon the false teachers (11:45–52)

         (a) The challenge (11:45)

         (b) The charge (11:46–52)

           i. The curse of their loaded demands (11:46)

           ii. The curse of their lauded dead (11:47–51)

             a. Their continuing folly (11:47–48)

               1. Enhancing the sepulchers of the prophets (11:47)

               2. Endorsing the slayers of the prophets (11:48)

             b. Their crowning folly (11:49–51)

               1. A new generation of prophets (11:49a)

               2. A new generation of persecutors (11:49b–51)

                 (i) The final heralds rejected (11:49b)

                 (ii) The full harvest reaped (11:50–51)

           iii. The curse of their locked doors (11:52)

D. The systematic approach (11:53–13:9)

   1. Total warfare on their part (11:53–54)

     a. The provocation (11:53)

     b. The purpose (11:54)

   2. Terrible warnings on His part (12:1–13:9)

     a. Against concealment (12:1–3)

       (1) The crowd (12:1a)

       (2) The command (12:1b–3)

         (a) Beware of the leaven (12:1b)

         (b) Be aware of the light (12:2–3)

     b. Against cowardice (12:4–12)

       (1) A great plea (12:4–7)

         (a) Fear of persecution (12:4)

         (b) Fear in perspective (12:5–7)

    i. The power of God (12:5)

    ii. The pity of God (12:6–7)

  (2) A great pledge (12:8–9)

  (3) A great peril (12:10)

  (4) A great principle (12:11–12)

 c. Against covetousness (12:13–21)

  (1) An appeal (12:13–14)

   (a) A materialistic request (12:13)

   (b) A majestic reply (12:14)

  (2) An application (12:15–21)

   (a) The precept (12:15)

   (b) The parable (12:16–20)

    i. The man and his money (12:16–17)

    ii. The man and his mistakes (12:18–20)

     a. Mistaking his bankbook for his Bible (12:18)

     b. Mistaking his body for his soul (12:19)

     c. Mistaking time for eternity (12:20)

   (c) The point (12:21)

 d. Against care (12:22–32)

  (1) Our material problems (12:22–31)

   (a) The first emphasis (12:22–28)

    i. The principle stated (12:22–23)

    ii. The principle studied (12:24–28)

     a. Look at the fowls (12:24)

     b. Look at the facts (12:25–26)

     c. Look at the flowers (12:27–28)

      1. The loveliness they display (12:27)

      2. The lesson they declare (12:28)

   (b) The further emphasis (12:29–31)

    i. A question of proportion (12:29)

    ii. A question of perspective (12:30)

    iii. A question of priorities (12:31)

  (2) His millennial program (12:32)

   (a) A little flock (12:32a)

   (b) A loving Father (12:32b)

   (c) A large future (12:32c)

 e. Against complacency (12:33–13:9)

(1) The simple command (12:33–34)
 (a) Living for the right world (12:33)
 (b) Loving in the right way (12:34)
(2) The Second Coming (12:35–48)
 (a) Waiting for the Lord (12:35–36)
  i. An impressive readiness for His return (12:35)
   a. Loins girded: working for Him (12:35a)
   b. Lamps glowing: witnessing for Him (23:35b)
  ii. An immediate response at His return (12:36)
   a. Where He went (12:36a)
   b. What He wants (12:36b)
 (b) Watching for the Lord (12:37–40)
  i. A great promise (12:37)
  ii. A great preparedness (12:38–39)
   a. As to the nearness of His coming (12:38)
   b. As to the nature of His coming (12:39)
  iii. A great principle (12:40)
 (c) Working for the Lord (12:41–48)
  i. The question asked (12:41)
  ii. The question answered (12:42–48)
   a. The wise servant (12:42–48)
   b. The wicked servant (12:45–58)
    1. His skepticism (12:45a)
    2. His sinfulness (12:45b–c)
     (i) His abuse of power (12:45b)
     (ii) His absorption with pleasure (12:45c)
    3. His sentence (12:46–48)
     (i) The false servant (12:46)
     (ii) The forgetful servant (12:47)
     (iii) The feeble servant (12:48)
(3) The stormy canvas (12:49–59)
 (a) The Master's warning to His men (12:49–53)
  i. The coming curse (12:49)
  ii. The coming cross (12:50)
  iii. The coming cost (12:51–53)
   a. How widespread the coming divisions would be (12:51)

    b. How woeful the coming divisions would be
     (12:51–52)
   (b) The Master's warning to the multitude (12:54–59)
     i. Their blindness to what was apparent (12:54–56)
     ii. Their blindness to what was approaching
      (12:57–59)
      a. The Law called in (12:57–58a)
      b. The line crossed over (12:58b–59)
  (4) The stern conclusion (13:1–9)
   (a) Needed repentance (13:1–5)
     i. The question of a national disaster (13:1–3)
     ii. The question of a natural disaster (13:4–5)
      a. A faulty conclusion (13:4)
      b. A firm contention (13:5)
   (b) National repentance (13:6–9)
     i. The barren tree (13:6)
     ii. The bitter truth (13:7)
     iii. The borrowed time (13:8–9)
      a. A new opportunity (13:8–9a)
      b. A needful overthrow (13:9b)
E. The sermonic approach (13:10–30)
 1. A sympathetic Christ (13:10–13)
  a. The synagogue (13:10a)
  b. The Sabbath (13:10b)
  c. The sufferer (13:11)
  d. The summons (13:12a)
  e. The Savior (13:12b–13a)
  f. The sequel (13:13b)
 2. A sanctimonious critic (13:14–16)
  a. His hairsplitting (13:14)
  b. His hypocrisy (13:15–16)
 3. A sobered crowd (13:17–30)
  a. How they were cheered (13:17)
   (1) The humbling of the critics (13:17a)
   (2) The happiness of the crowd (13:17b)
  b. How they were challenged (13:18–30)
   (1) His parables (13:18–21)

(a) The abnormal mustard (13:18–19)

(b) The adulterated meal (13:20–21)

(2) His progress (13:22)

(3) His pronouncement (13:23–30)

(a) The question asked (13:23)

(b) The question answered (13:24–30)

    i. A warning for the Hebrews (13:24–28)

      a. Belated anxiety (13:24–27)

        1. Wrong about the time (13:24–25)

        2. Wrong about the truth (13:26–27)

          (i) What they fancied (13:26)

          (ii) What they found (13:27)

      b. Bitter anguish (13:28)

        1. The reality of it (13:28a)

        2. The reason for it (13:28b)

    ii. A welcome for the heathen (13:29–30)

      a. A process (13:29)

      b. A principle (13:30)

F. The scare approach (13:31–35)

1. A warning (13:31–32)

  a. The warning received by Jesus (13:31)

  b. The warning rejected by Jesus (13:32)

2. A woe (13:33–35)

  a. The fatal denunciation of Jerusalem (13:33)

  b. The factual description of Jerusalem (13:34)

  c. The fearful destruction of Jerusalem (13:35a)

  d. The final destiny of Jerusalem (13:35b)

G. The subtle approach (14:1–35)

1. An invitation to dinner (14:1–24)

  a. The table was spread (14:1a)

  b. The trap was sprung (14:1b–4)

  c. The tables were turned (14:5–24)

    (1) Their secret attitude exposed (14:5–6)

      (a) The searching question (14:5)

      (b) The sudden quietness (14:6)

    (2) Their social attitude exposed (14:7–11)

      (a) His perception (14:7)

        (b) His parable (14:8–10)

            i. The proud man humbled (14:8–9)

            ii. The prudent man honored (14:10)

        (c) His point (14:11)

    (3) Their selfish attitude exposed (14:12–14)

        (a) The banquet (14:12–13)

            i. The guests they would choose (14:12)

            ii. The guests they should choose (14:13)

        (b) The blessing (14:14)

    (4) Their spiritual attitude exposed (14:15–24)

        (a) A great supper (14:15–17)

            i. The remark of the listener (14:15)

            ii. The response of the Lord (14:16–17)

        (b) A great sin (14:18–20)

            i. The man who was too big (14:18)

            ii. The man who was too busy (14:19)

            iii. The man who was too blissful (14:20)

        (c) A great search (14:21–23)

        (d) A great summary (14:24)

  2. An invitation to discipleship (14:25–35)

    a. The appeal (14:25–32)

      (1) Court the cross (14:25–27)

        (a) The great imperative (14:25–26)

        (b) The great impossibility (14:27)

      (2) Count the cost (14:28–32)

        (a) Like a man preparing to build (14:28–30)

        (b) Like a monarch preparing for battle (14:31–32)

    b. The application (14:33–35)

      (1) An intimation (14:33)

      (2) An illustration (14:34)

      (3) An invitation (14:35)

H. The sarcastic approach (15:1–32)

  1. The people (15:1–2)

    a. The publicans and sinners (15:1)

    b. The Pharisees and scribes (15:2)

  2. The parables (15:3–32)

    a. The lost sheep (15:3–7)

        (1) The wandering sheep (15:3–4a)

        (2) The wonderful shepherd (15:4b–7)

           (a) The search (15:4b–5)

           (b) The song (15:6–7)

               i. The human song (15:6)

               ii. The heavenly song (15:7)

    b. The lost silver (15:8–10)

        (1) Distress (15:8a)

        (2) Diligence (15:8b)

        (3) Delight (15:9–10)

    c. The lost sons (15:11–32)

        (1) The scandalous son (15:11–24)

           (a) The far horizons (15:11–16)

           (b) The father's house (15:17–24)

               i. What the prodigal decided (15:17–19)

                  a. He thought of his father's goodness (15:17)

                  b. He thought of his father's grace (15:18–19)

                     1. His plan (15:18)

                     2. His penitence (15:19)

               ii. What the prodigal discovered (15:20–24)

                  a. A gracious father (15:20–22)

                  b. A glorious feast (15:23)

                  c. A great forgiveness (15:24)

        (2) The sanctimonious son (15:25–32)

           (a) His simple discovery (15:25–27)

           (b) His sinful displeasure (15:28)

           (c) His surly disposition (15:29–30)

               i. His self-righteousness (15:29a)

               ii. His secret regrets (15:29b)

               iii. His sinful resentment (15:30)

           (d) His seeming decision (15:31–32)

               i. How he was loved (15:31)

               ii. How he is left (15:32)

I. The scoffing approach (16:1–17:10)

    1. The love of money (16:1–13)

        a. A difficult story (16:1–8)

           (1) The accusation of the steward (16:1–2)

          (2) The action of the steward (16:3–7)

          (3) The approbation of the steward (16:8)

              (a) His logic applauded (16:8a)

              (b) The lesson applied (16:8b)

     b. A definite statement (16:9–13)

          (1) A question of money (16:9)

              (a) Using it to make friends here (16:9a)

              (b) Using it to make friends hereafter (16:9b)

          (2) A question of management (16:10–12)

          (3) A question of masters (16:13)

2. The laugh of mockery (16:14)

3. The Law of Moses (16:15–18)

     a. The essential nature of the Law (16:15–16)

          (1) A question of human values (16:15)

          (2) A question of heavenly values (16:16)

     b. The eternal nature of the Law (16:17)

     c. The ethical nature of the Law (16:18)

4. The lap of misery (16:19–31)

     a. Two deaths (16:19–22)

          (1) The fortunes of the two men (16:19–21)

              (a) Abundant wealth (16:19)

              (b) Abject want (16:20–21)

          (2) The funerals of the two men (16:22)

     b. Two destinies (16:23–31)

          (1) The tranquility of the one (16:23)

          (2) The torment of the other (16:24–31)

              (a) His sudden belief in prayer (16:24–26)

                 i. What the lost man desired (16:24)

                 ii. What the lost man discovered (16:25–26)

              (b) His sudden belief in preaching (16:27–31)

                 i. His request voiced (16:27–28)

                 ii. His request vetoed (16:29–31)

5. The life of ministry (17:1–10)

     a. Its special relationship (17:1–2)

          (1) The objects of His curse (17:1–2a)

          (2) The objects of His care (17:2b)

     b. Its spiritual resources (17:3–6)

(1) Forgiveness (17:3–4)

(2) Faith (17:5–6)

    (a) The request (17:5)

    (b) The reply (17:6)

c. Its specific responsibilities (17:7–10)

  (1) What the Lord dramatized (17:7–9)

    (a) The responsibilities of the servant (17:7)

    (b) The rights of the squire (17:8)

    (c) The rationale of the Savior (17:9)

  (2) What the Lord demands (17:10)

J. The selfish approach (17:11–19)

  1. The meeting (17:11–12)

    a. The Lord (17:11)

    b. The lepers (17:12)

  2. The Master (17:13–14a)

    a. The cry (17:13)

    b. The command (17:14a)

  3. The miracle (17:14b)

  4. The man (17:15–19)

    a. How he praised the Lord (17:15–16)

      (1) His wonder (17:15a)

      (2) His will (17:15b)

      (3) His worship (17:16)

    b. How he pleased the Lord (17:17–19)

      (1) What grieved the Savior (17:17–18)

      (2) What gladdened the Savior (17:19)

K. The snobbish approach (17:20–19:27)

  1. The demanding attitude (17:20–18:8)

    a. The character of the kingdom (17:20–21)

      (1) An abrupt request (17:20a)

      (2) An abrupt reply (17:20b–21)

        (a) A representative national view (17:20b–21a)

        (b) A revolutionary new view (17:21b)

    b. The coming of the kingdom (17:22–18:8)

      (1) A day of visitation (17:22–37)

        (a) The rejection in view (17:22–25)

          i. The Second Coming (17:22–24)

          ii. The suffering Christ (17:25)

      (b) The return in view (17:26–32)

          i. A return of the days of Noah (17:26–27)

          ii. A return of the days of Lot (17:28–32)

            a. A careless world (17:28–29)

            b. A clear warning (17:30–32)

      (c) The Rapture in view (17:33–37)

          i. The reality of the Rapture (17:33–36)

            a. A midnight rapture in view (17:33–34)

            b. A morning rapture in view (17:35–36)

          ii. The result of the Rapture (17:37)

    (2) A day of vengeance (18:1–8)

      (a) The purpose of the parable (18:1)

      (b) The pieces of the parable (18:2–5)

          i. The wicked judge and his impiety (18:2)

          ii. The widowed Jewess and her importunity (18:3)

          iii. The worldly judgment and its implication (18:4–5)

      (c) The point of the parable (18:6–8)

          i. The compassion of God (18:6–8a)

          ii. The coming of Christ (18:8b)

2. The disdainful attitude (18:9–30)

  a. The man who disdained the prayer of a publican (18:9–14)

    (1) A parable of prayer (18:9)

    (2) A principle of prayer (18:10–14)

      (a) Two men (18:10)

      (b) Two minds (18:11–14)

          i. The Pharisee and his righteousness (18:11–12)

            a. His pride (18:11)

            b. His presumption (18:12)

          ii. The publican and his repentance (18:13–14)

            a. His abasement (18:13)

            b. His absolution (18:14)

  b. The men who disdained the challenge of a child (18:15–17)

    (1) The intention of the mothers (18:15a)

    (2) The interference of the men (18:15b)

    (3) The invitation of the Master (18:16–17)

  c. The man who disdained the demands of discipleship
    (18:18–30)
    (1) The ruler (18:18–23)
      (a) The question (18:18–19)
      (b) The quotation (18:20–22)
        i. The five commandments (18:20)
        ii. The false claim (18:21–22)
          a. The claim put forth (18:21)
          b. The claim proven false (18:22)
    (2) The reality (18:24–27)
      (a) What Jesus saw (18:24a)
      (b) What Jesus said (18:24b–27)
        i. A revolutionary remark (18:24b–25)
        ii. A rationalistic reaction (18:26–27)
    (3) The reward (18:28–30)
      (a) The comment (18:28)
      (b) The compensation (18:29–30)
 3. The derogatory attitude (18:31–19:27)
  a. The shadow of the Savior's passion (18:31–34)
    (1) The inevitable (18:31–33)
      (a) Warnings from the Scripture (18:31)
      (b) Warnings from the Savior (18:32–33)
    (2) The incredible (18:34)
  b. The showing of the Savior's power (18:35–43)
    (1) The man's plight (18:35)
    (2) The man's plea (18:36–42)
    (3) The Master's plan (18:43)
      (a) How it was rebuked (18:36–39)
        i. His discovery (18:36–37)
          a. The passing crowd (18:36)
          b. The passing Christ (18:37)
        ii. His decision (18:38)
        iii. His discouragement (18:39a)
        iv. His determination (18:39b)
      (b) How it was rewarded (18:40–42)
        i. The call (18:40–41)
        ii. The cure (18:42)

c. The shining of the Savior's presence (19:1–27)
  (1) False ideals are exposed (19:1–10)
      (a) The place (19:1)
      (b) The publican (19:2–4)
          i. Who he was (19:2)
          ii. What he wanted (19:3–4)
      (c) The prospect (19:5–6)
          i. Jesus came (19:5a)
          ii. Jesus called (19:5b–6)
              a. The imperative requirement (19:5b)
              b. The immediate response (19:6)
      (d) The people (19:7)
      (e) The promise (19:8)
      (f) The pardon (19:9)
      (g) The program (19:10)
  (2) False ideas are exposed (19:11–27)
      (a) What was thought (19:11)
      (b) What was taught (19:12–27)
          i. The journey (19:12–14)
              a. The purpose of it (19:12)
              b. The preparation for it (19:13–14)
                  1. Those who helped him (19:13)
                  2. Those who hated him (19:14)
          ii. The judgment (19:15–27)
              a. The judgment of his friends (19:15–26)
                  1. The faithful servants (19:15–19)
                      (i) The one with the larger ability
                          (19:15–16)
                      (ii) The one with the lesser ability
                          (19:17–19)
                  2. The faulty servant (19:20–26)
                      (i) His confession (19:20–21)
                          (a) His folly (19:20)
                          (b) His fear (19:21)
                      (ii) His conviction (19:22–23)
                          (a) The unanswerable quotation
                              (19:22)

                    (b) The unanswerable question (19:23)

               (iii) His condemnation (19:24–26)

                    (a) What he lost at last (19:24–25)

                    (b) What he learned too late (19:26)

          b. The judgment of his foes (19:27)

L. The straightforward approach (19:28–20:19)

   1. Coronation (19:28–44)

     a. Jerusalem's crowning day (19:28–40)

       (1) The coming (19:28–29)

         (a) The plan (19:28)

         (b) The pause (19:29)

       (2) The colt (19:30–38)

         (a) It was redeemed (19:30a)

         (b) It was released (19:30b–34)

         (c) It was ruled (19:35–38)

            i. The Lord was exalted (19:35–36)

            ii. The Lord was extolled (19:37–38)

       (3) The critics (19:39–40)

         (a) The demand (19:39)

         (b) The denial (19:40)

     b. Jerusalem's coming doom (19:41–44)

       (1) A weeping Savior (19:41–42)

         (a) The burden of Jesus (19:41)

         (b) The blindness of Jerusalem (19:42)

       (2) A woeful sight (19:43–44)

         (a) The calamity (19:43–44a)

            i. The siege of Jerusalem (19:43)

            ii. The sack of Jerusalem (19:44a)

         (b) The cause (19:44b)

   2. Confrontation (19:45–48)

     a. Traffic in the temple (19:45–46)

       (1) The sanctuary cleansed (19:45)

       (2) The Scripture confirmed (19:46)

     b. Teaching in the temple (19:47–48)

       (1) The persistence of His teaching (19:47a)

       (2) The popularity of His teaching (19:47b–48)

       (a) How the masters of Israel resented it (19:47b)

       (b) How the masses of Israel received it (19:48)

3. Condemnation (20:1–19)

  a. How they wickedly assailed His authority (20:1–8)

     (1) The delegation (20:1)

     (2) The demand (20:2–4)

     (3) The dilemma (20:5–6)

     (4) The decision (20:7)

     (5) The denial (20:8)

  b. How they wickedly asserted their authority (20:9–19)

     (1) The vineyard (20:9)

     (2) The violence (20:10–12)

       (a) The first messenger sent (20:10)

       (b) The further messenger sent (20:11)

       (c) The final messenger sent (20:12)

     (3) The visitor (20:13–15a)

       (a) The coming of the heir (20:13)

       (b) The crime of the husbandmen (20:14–15a)

     (4) The verdict (20:15b–16)

       (a) Death (20:15b)

       (b) Disinheritance (20:16a)

       (c) Dismay (20:16b)

     (5) The villains (20:17–19)

       (a) The warning of the Savior (20:17–18)

       (b) The wickedness of the Sanhedrin (20:19)

M. The seductive approach (20:20–21:38)

  1. The plot of the adversaries exposed (20:20–21:4)

    a. They question Him (20:20–40)

      (1) An attempt to catch Him with the law of the land (20:20–26)

        (a) What they asked (20:20–22)

          i. The trap set (20:20)

          ii. The trap sprung (20:21–22)

        (b) What He answered (20:23–26)

          i. His perception (20:23)

          ii. His pronouncement (20:24–25)

     a. How vivid it was (20:24)

     b. How valid it was (20:25)

    iii. His perfection (20:26)

   (2) An attempt to catch Him with the law of the Lord (20:27–40)

    (a) The skeptics (20:27)

    (b) The Scripture (20:28)

    (c) The story (20:29–32)

    (d) The sting (20:33)

    (e) The Savior (20:34–40)

     i. A word about this world (20:34)

     ii. A word about that world (20:35–36)

      a. A new social order is there (20:35)

      b. A new spiritual order is there (20:36)

     iii. A word about their world (20:37–38)

      a. He denies their false premise (20:37a)

      b. He disproves their false premise (20:37b–38)

       1. The biblical text (20:37b)

       2. The biblical truth (20:38)

    (f) The sequel (20:39–40)

  b. He quells them (20:41–21:4)

   (1) Their beliefs challenged (20:41–47)

    (a) How He confounded them (20:41–44)

     i. What the scribes said (20:41)

     ii. What the Scripture said (20:42–43)

     iii. What the Savior said (20:44)

    (b) How He condemned them (20:45–47)

     i. Openly (20:45)

     ii. Overwhelmingly (20:46–47)

      a. What the scribes desired (20:46)

      b. What the scribes devoured (20:47a)

      c. What the scribes deserved (20:47b)

   (2) Their behavior challenged (21:1–4)

    (a) How the wealthy gave (21:1)

    (b) How the widow gave (21:2–4)

     i. What Jesus saw (21:2)

     ii. What Jesus said (21:3–4)

          a. A proper perspective about giving (21:3)

          b. A proper perception about giving (21:4)

              1. Giving out of abundant prosperity (21:4a)

              2. Giving out of abject poverty (21:4b)

2. The plan of the ages exposed (21:5–38)

   a. Events leading up to the collapse of Jerusalem (21:5–24)

     (1) A question of pride (21:5–7)

       (a) The limited view of the crowd (21:5)

       (b) The larger view of the Christ (21:6–7)

     (2) A question of prophecy (21:8–24)

       (a) A preliminary view of subsequent events (21:8–11)

          i. False christs (21:8)

          ii. Fearful crises (21:9–11)

              a. National calamities (21:9–10)

              b. Natural calamities (21:11)

       (b) A protracted view of sequential events (21:12–24)

          i. Beware of intolerant adversaries (21:12–19)

              a. Persecution (21:12)

              b. Prosecution (21:13–15)

              c. Provocation (21:16–17)

                 1. From family (21:16a)

                 2. From friends (21:16b)

                 3. From foes (21:17)

              d. Preservation (21:18–19)

          ii. Beware of invading armies (21:20–24)

   b. Events leading up to the coming of Jesus (21:25–38)

     (1) The signs (21:25–26)

       (a) In the celestial sphere (21–25a)

       (b) On the terrestrial sphere (21:25b–26a)

          i. Perplexity on earth (21:25b)

          ii. Panic on earth (21:26a)

       (c) In the infernal sphere (21:26b)

     (2) The Son (21:27)

     (3) The sermon (21:28–36)

       (a) The challenge (21:28–33)

       (b) The charge (21:34–36)

          i. To our personal life (21:34–35)

          ii. To our prayer life (21:36)

(4) The Savior (21:37–38)
  (a) His program (21:37)
  (b) The people (21:38)

PART 4: EVENTS RELATING TO THE SAVIOR'S CROSS (22:1–24:53)

Section 1: The Table (22:1–38)
A. The last Passover (22:1–18)
  1. The date (22:1)
  2. The Devil (22:2–6)
    a. The foes of Jesus (22:2)
    b. The fall of Judas (22:3–6)
      (1) His dreadful surrender (22:3)
      (2) His demonic suggestion (22:4)
      (3) His deliberate sale (22:5)
      (4) His diabolical secret (22:6)
  3. The decision (22:7–13)
    a. What the Lord resolved (22:7–8)
    b. What the Lord revealed (22:9–11)
    c. What the Lord received (22:12–13)
  4. The desire (22:14–18)
    a. His assertion (22:14–15)
    b. His assurance (22:16–18)
B. The last provision (22:19–20)
  1. His body (22:19)
  2. His blood (22:20)
C. The last protests (22:21–38)
  1. The disclosure (22:21–23)
  2. The dispute (22:24–30)
    a. The disciples and their conflict (22:24)
    b. The disciples and their conversion (22:25–27)
      (1) The Lord's explanation (22:25–26)
        (a) Lordship as exhibited in human kingdoms (22:25)
        (b) Lordship as exhibited in His kingdom (22:26)
      (2) The Lord's example (22:27)
    c. The disciples and their coronation (22:28–30)
      (1) Recognition (22:28)
      (2) Reward (22:29–30)

        (a) A great assignment (22:29)
- i. A place at His table (22:29a)
- ii. A position over the tribes (22:29b)

        (b) A great assurance (22:30)

3. The deceiver (22:31–34)
   a. Magnificent concern (22:31a)
   b. Malicious cruelty (22:31b)
   c. Meaningful compassion (22:32)
   d. Mistaken conviction (22:33)
   e. Marvelous comprehension (22:34)
4. The dispensation (22:35–38)
   a. The challenge (22:35)
   b. The change (22:36–38)
      (1) The rule (22:36a)
      (2) The reason (22:37)
      (3) The response (22:38)

Section 2: The Tears (22:39–53)

A. The agony of Jesus (22:39–46)
   1. Gethsemane (22:39)
   2. Guidance (22:40)
   3. Grief (22:41–42)
      a. The distance (22:41)
      b. The desire (22:42)
   4. Grace (22:43)
   5. Groans (22:44)
   6. Guilt (22:45–46)
B. The arrival of Judas (22:47–53)
   1. The betrayal in the garden (22:47–48)
   2. The battle in the garden (22:49–53)
      a. A display of disappointing weakness (22:49–51)
         (1) Peter's simple reaction (22:49–50)
            (a) His carnal weapon (22:49)
            (b) His clumsy work (22:50)
         (2) Christ's sublime reaction (22:51)
      b. A display of despicable worldliness (22:52–53a)
      c. A display of demonic wickedness (22:53b–c)

Section 3: The Trials (22:54–23:25)
  A. The trial before the Hebrew priests (22:54–71)
    1. Jesus is denied (22:54–62)
      a. Peter's terror (22:54)
        (1) What inspired it (22:54a)
        (2) What indicated it (22:54b)
      b. Peter's trial (22:55–60a)
        (1) Peter accommodated by the world (22:55)
        (2) Peter accused by the world (22:56–60a)
          (a) The accusation of the maid (22:56–57)
          (b) The accusation of the men (22:58–60a)
            i. Peter linked with the Lord's people (22:58)
            ii. Peter linked with the Lord's person (22:59–60a)
      c. Peter's tears (22:60b–62)
        (1) Peter's Gabbatha (22:60b–61)
        (2) Peter's Gethsemane (22:62)
    2. Jesus is derided (22:63–65)
      a. Badgered by the men of Israel (22:63a)
      b. Beaten by the men of Israel (22:63b)
      c. Blindfolded by the men of Israel (22:64)
      d. Blasphemed by the men of Israel (22:65)
    3. Jesus is divine (22:66–71)
      a. The morning light (22:66)
      b. The moral night (22:67–71)
        (1) The confrontation (22:67–70)
          (a) His positional identity: "Are You the Christ?" (22:67–69)
            i. The Lord exposed their disbelief (22:67)
            ii. The Lord exposed their determination (22:68)
            iii. The Lord exposed their destiny (22:69)
          (b) His personal identity: "Are You the Son of God?" (22:70)
        (2) The condemnation (22:71)
  B. The trial before the heathen procurator (23:1–25)
    1. Pilate's political dilemma (23:1–12)
      a. A lethal lie (23:1–5)
      b. A legal loophole (23:6–12)
        (1) What Pilate discovered (23:6)
        (2) What Pilate decided (23:7–11)

          (a) Jesus referred to Herod (23:7)
          (b) Jesus received by Herod (23:8–10)
             i. What Herod hoped (23:8)
             ii. What Herod heard (23:9–10)
          (c) Jesus ridiculed by Herod (23:11a)
          (d) Jesus returned by Herod (23:11b)
       (3) What Pilate did (23:12)
    2. Pilate's personal dilemma (23:13–25)
      a. Roman justice demonstrated (23:13–15)
       (1) How Pilate restated the charge (23:14a)
       (2) How Pilate rejected the charge (23:14b–15)
         (a) His considered verdict (23:14b)
         (b) His confirmed verdict (23:15)
      b. Roman justice distorted (23:16–21)
       (1) The formal decision of the judge (23:16–17)
         (a) To punish an innocent man (23:16)
         (b) To pardon an innocent man (23:17)
       (2) The furious dissent of the Jews (23:18–21)
         (a) Their demonstration (23:18–19)
            i. The man they hated (23:18)
            ii. The man they hailed (23:19)
         (b) Their demand (23:20–21)
            i. The concern of the magistrate (23:20)
            ii. The cry of the mob (23:21)
      c. Roman justice denied (23:22–25)
       (1) The last stand (23:22)
       (2) The last straw (23:23)
       (3) The last step (23:24–25)
         (a) The crowd satisfied (23:24)
         (b) The convict saved (23:25a)
         (c) The Christ surrendered (23:25b)

Section 4: The Tree (23:26–49)

  A. Jesus on the way to the cross (23:26–33)
    1. The foreign conscript (23:26)
    2. The fickle crowd (23:27)
    3. The future calamity (23:28–31)

        a. The Lord's pity (23:28)

        b. The Lord's prophecy (23:29–31)

            (1) A coming disaster (23:29)

                (a reference to the Roman war coming in their lifetime)

            (2) A coming despair (23:30–31)

                (a reference to the Roman world coming in the last times)

                (a) The Lord's prediction (23:30)

                (b) The Lord's point (23:31)

    4. The friendless convicts (23:32)

    5. The fearful crime (23:33)

B. Jesus and the work of the cross (23:34–49)

    1. The Mediator (23:34)

    2. The mockers (23:35–38)

        a. The Hebrews: They mocked Him as Savior (23:35)

        b. The heathen: They mocked Him as sovereign (23:36–38)

            (1) Their mocking tribute (23:36)

            (2) Their mocking taunt (23:37)

            (3) Their mocking title (23:38)

    3. The malefactors (23:39–43)

        a. The reviling malefactor (23:39)

        b. The repentant malefactor (23:40–43)

            (1) What He rebuked (23:40)

            (2) What He realized (23:41)

            (3) What He requested (23:42)

            (4) What He received (23:43)

    4. The miracles (23:44–49)

        a. What they attested (23:44–46)

        That Jesus was:

            (1) The light of the sun (23:44–45a)

            (2) The lord of the sanctuary (23:45b)

            (3) The life of the soul (23:46)

        b. What they accomplished (23:47–49)

            (1) Conversion (23:47)

            (2) Conviction (23:48)

            (3) Contemplation (23:49)

Section 5: The Tomb (23:50–56)
  A. The sepulcher prepared (23:50–54)
      1. The lovely man (23:50–52)
          a. Joseph's calling (23:50a)
          b. Joseph's character (23:50b)
          c. Joseph's conviction (23:51–52)
      2. The loving ministry (23:53–54)
          a. The tenderness is emphasized (23:53a)
          b. The tomb is emphasized (23:53b–c)
              (1) Its security (23:53b)
              (2) Its sanctity (23:53c)
          c. The time is emphasized (23:54)
  B. The spices prepared (23:55–56)
      1. The women watched (23:55)
      2. The women worked (23:56a)
      3. The women waited (23:56b)

Section 6: The Triumph (24:1–49)
  A. Events at the empty tomb (24:1–12)
      1. The vacant tomb (24:1–3)
          a. The ministry that propelled them (24:1)
          b. The mystery that perplexed them (24:2–3)
              (1) The barrier removed (24:2)
              (2) The body removed (24:3)
      2. The vital truth (24:4–8)
          a. The men (24:4–5a)
          b. The message (24:5b–8)
              (1) A message of rebuke (24:5b)
              (2) A message of resurrection (24:6a)
              (3) A message of remembrance (24:6b–8)
                  (a) When the Lord had spoken (24:6b)
                  (b) What the Lord had said (24:7–8)
      3. The verbal tidings (24:9–11)
          a. The return (24:9a)
          b. The report (24:9b–10)
              (1) Those who received it (24:9b)
              (2) Those who relayed it (24:10)

        c. The ridicule (24:11)

     4. The visual test (24:12)

        a. Peter's discovery (24:12a–c)

        b. Peter's departure (24:12d)

B. Events on the Emmaus road (24:13–35)

     1. The two disciples and their blighted hopes (24:13–24)

        a. The sad steps they took (24:13–17)

           (1) Their sorrowful communion (24:13–14)

           (2) Their stranger companion (24:15–17)

        b. The sad story they told (24:18–24)

           (1) The question of Cleopas (24:18)

           (2) The question of Christ (24:19–24)

               (a) Their tragic bereavement (24:19–20)

               (b) Their tangled beliefs (24:21)

               (c) Their total bewilderment (24:22–24)

                   i. The unbelievable news (24:22–23)

                  ii. The unbelievable negative (24:24)

     2. The two disciples and their burning hearts (24:25–27)

        a. How the Lord convicted them (24:25–26)

        b. How the Lord convinced them (24:27)

     3. The two disciples and their blessed home (24:28–32)

        a. What they suggested (24:28–29)

        b. What they saw (24:30–31)

        c. What they said (24:32)

     4. The two disciples and their breathless haste (24:33–35)

        a. The news confirmed (24:33–34)

        b. The news conveyed (24:35)

C. Events in the Upper Room (24:36–53)

     1. Jesus in the midst (24:36–49)

        a. Peace proclaimed (24:36–37)

           (1) The simple greeting (24:36)

           (2) The supposed ghost (24:37)

         b. Peace provided (24:38–49)

           (1) Bodily proof (24:38–43)

               (a) Personal identification (24:38–40)

               (b) Practical illustration (24:41–43)

           (2) Biblical proof (24:44–48)

(a) The proof of His sayings (24:44a)
(b) The proof of Holy Scripture (24:44b–49)
    i. Their understanding quickened for them (24:45–46)
    ii. Their undertaking quoted to them (24:47–49)
2. Jesus on the mount (24:50–53)
    a. The last blessing (24:50)
    b. The life beyond (24:51)
    c. The lasting bliss (24:52–53)

PART 1

Introduction
Luke 1:1–4

Paul's second missionary journey brought him to Troas. He was perplexed. Doors were closed against him everywhere and he did not know which way to turn. Ancient Troy was not far away, however, so Troas was a place to dream dreams. It conjured memories of marching men, strategies of war, Helen and the Greeks, and the fabled Trojan horse.

So Paul slept, and in his sleep the world of nearby Macedonia and Greece ruled his dreams. He saw a man, a Greek, a man from Macedonia, a European. "Come on over and help us," the man said.

Paul awoke! Europe—that was it! Of course! Now he knew what to do. Moreover, Paul's assurance was soon confirmed. Whom should Paul see next but a man from Macedonia in the flesh. And one he seemingly knew, no less—Dr. Luke! He was a friend from college days in Tarsus, perhaps, or Antioch.

All we know of Luke is found in the "we" passages that begin right here (Acts 16:10–17; 20:5–15; 21:1–18; 27:1–28:16); in three other places, where Paul mentions him by name (Col. 4:14; 2 Tim. 4:11; Philem. 24); and in Acts 1:1–3, where he identifies himself as the author of the gospel of Luke and the book of Acts.

He joined Paul at Troas but remained at Philippi until Paul arrived back there some six or seven years later, toward the end of Paul's third missionary journey. He accompanied Paul to Jerusalem and seems to have remained in Palestine during the two years that Paul was imprisoned at Caesarea. Doubtless, he took advantage of this period to continue his personal investigation of the gospel story.

From his evident familiarity with matters relating to ships and the sea, some people have inferred that he had been at one time a ship's doctor. He seems to have been a native of Antioch, and some people think that he was a brother of Titus. He might have been that "true yokefellow" whom Paul addressed in his letter to the Philippians (Phil. 4:3). He was true to Paul to the end.

By the time Luke wrote, the gospel was spreading rapidly. Paul marched boldly into city after city. Everywhere he left converts and churches fired with his own passion for souls. As a result, Gentile converts were pouring into the church. The need for an authentic version of the gospel to be written in stylish Greek and based on a careful and systematic investigation of the facts was growing. Luke was the Holy Spirit's choice; he had the training, the temperament, and the time. He had an artistic flair about him that enabled him to produce two of the most beautiful books in the world, full of compassion and inspired by the Spirit of God.

Section 1: Luke's Declaration (1:1–2)

"Many have taken in hand to set forth in order a declaration of those things which are most surely believed among us," Luke says. An enormous amount of material was available—good and bad, true and false, authentic and apocryphal.

Many people had tried their hand at sorting things out and setting them down. But the Spirit of God passed over them all and settled on Luke and gave him spiritual discernment to sort out the facts from the fables and the falsehoods. Both Paul and Peter were able to give Luke accurate information. We can be sure that he talked to everyone of those people who had some splendid story to tell but also those who had just some scrap of information to share.

Certain facts of the faith had already been settled because the salient facts were already known. Jesus of Nazareth was no ordinary man; He was the incarnate Son of God. He entered into human life by way of a virgin's womb. He lived a supernatural and sinless life. He taught truth in a pungent, undiluted, memorable way. He triumphed over demons, disease, and death. He died an atoning death upon a Roman cross. He was buried. He rose from the dead three days later and then ascended bodily into heaven. He now sits at God's right hand in heaven as our Advocate with the Father, anticipating His bodily return to establish His kingdom on earth.

Section 2: Luke's Determination (1:3a–b)

He mentions his *sources.* He says that he had "perfect understanding of all things." Much of this understanding was based on conversations and interviews with people who had known the Lord Jesus. They had memorized His teaching. They had seen His miracles. They had stories to tell of His wisdom, love, and power. Then, too, Luke surely studied Mark's gospel, already in circulation. (Some 320 of Mark's 661 verses—nearly half of Mark's gospel—are found in Luke's gospel.) He surely must have met Mary and the Lord's brothers; the various apostles and disciples; Philip the Evangelist; Martha, Mary, and Lazarus; and many others, most of whom would share with this personable companion of Paul their personal memories of Jesus.

Then, too, he received firsthand direct divine revelation from the Holy Spirit.

Luke says that he had perfect understanding "from the very first." The Greek word here can be translated "from above." It is translated that way elsewhere (John 3:31; 19:11).

Luke also mentions his *system*. He was determined to put his mass of material "in order." The word he used suggests chronological sequence. Nothing about this great enterprise was going to be haphazard. He was going to be meticulous in his handling of the facts as they emerged.

Section 3: Luke's Dedication (1:3c–4)

The finished work Luke dedicated to one whom he calls "most excellent Theophilus" (1:3). The name itself was common enough in the Roman world. It meant "beloved of God." The man was probably a high-ranking official. Luke used the title several times to denote high Roman officials, such as Felix and Festus (Acts 23:26; 24:3; 26:25). Theophilus seems to have been a Gentile convert to Christianity. We are not told why Luke was so solicitous of him as to address both of his books to him.

Possibly, Luke settled down to his great task while Paul was a prisoner at Caesarea. In that case, we can picture Luke's submitting page after page to Paul for his comments. Paul was Luke's mentor, and Luke's thoughts reflect Paul's thoughts. Like Paul, Luke makes much of such words as *faith, repentance, mercy,* and *forgiveness*. Paul had investigated thoroughly the story of Jesus for himself—first as the archenemy of Christianity and then as one of the chosen apostles.

Perhaps Paul and Luke compared notes and commented on each other's sources. Perhaps that is why early Christian writers—such as Tertullian, Irenaeus, Origen, Jerome, and Eusebius—link this gospel so closely with not only Luke but also Paul.

PART 2

Events Relating to the Savior's Coming

Luke 1:5–4:13

Section 1: The Announcements (1:5–55)
  A. The birth of John announced (1:5–25)
      1. The sudden presence of the angel (1:5–12)
          a. The people (1:5–6)

Luke's writing includes both a touch of artistry and the very evident influence of his medical background. "Herod, the king of Judaea," he writes; then, alongside that name of horror, he puts "a certain priest named Zacharias, of the course of Abia." Could the contrast be greater—the one a monster of iniquity, the other a man of integrity? It is the skilled touch of the artist to put two such men in the same sentence. One of these men was a vicious prince; the other man was a virtuous priest. One was a man of extraordinary talent, drive, and wickedness; the other was a retiring and godly old man. One of them hated God; the other loved Him. One was a man who murdered his sons, his own favorite wife, and countless other victims as well; the other was a gentle minister of the sanctuary. One was an Idumean, a descendent of Esau; the other was a Jew, a descendent of Jacob, Esau's twin. One was a foreign-born usurper; the other was a native-born citizen of Israel. One was a member of an alien and hostile race; the other was a Levite, the tribe that furnished Israel with its priests. One man gave Israel a scorpion's nest of sons to plague and torment them, the other gave Israel a son, set apart from birth to become the God-sent herald of the Messiah. One was "Herod, the king of Judaea" (thanks to the Romans); the other was "a certain man named Zacharias, of the course of Abia."

The sacred historian ignores the haughty Herod, whose reign of terror and whose death in torment are adequately chronicled elsewhere, and concentrates on the humble priest. He belonged to the course or division of Abia (Abijah), the eighth of two dozen such courses. The course was changed weekly, beginning each Sabbath. After the Babylonian captivity, only four courses came back to the Promised Land (Ezra 2:36–39; Neh. 7:39–42; 12:1–21). The missing courses were filled by the priests who actually did return.

Zacharias was married to a descendent of Aaron, Israel's first high priest (1:5). To be not only a priest but also married to the daughter of a priest was considered a great honor.

Luke tells us that "they were both righteous before God, walking in all the commandments and ordinances of the Lord blameless" (1:6). Their lives were peaceable and quiet. They probably had little excitement. The old priest, however, had one thing to which he looked forward with great anticipation—his turn was coming to minister in the sanctuary.

b. The problem (1:7)

One thing saddened this godly couple; they were childless. Moreover, their case was hopeless. "Elisabeth was barren," Luke says, "and they both were now well stricken in years." Among the Jews, "the commencement of old age" occurred when a person became sixty-five. At seventy, he was said to have reached "hoary-headed age." After eighty, he was said to be "well stricken in years." In their barren old age, the godly couple often might have taken hope from Abraham and Sarah, from Manoah and his wife, and from vexed and anguished Hannah. We can picture Zacharias and Elizabeth musing on these Old Testament characters and fanning their slumbering hopes. "Perhaps God is saving us for something special. Perhaps He has an Isaac, a Samson, or a Samuel for us!"

c. The place (1:8–10)

At last, the month of the year arrived when the course of Abia had the service of the sanctuary, and for the first and last time the lot fell on Zacharias to go into the Holy Place of the temple and to burn incense on the golden altar.

He chose two friends to be his helpers. Through the great door of the temple, they went to find themselves surrounded by the golden splendor of the sanctuary and the brilliant colors of the veil. One of his friends removed the remnants of the previous day's offering and reverently backed out of the Holy Place. Then his other priestly friend approached the golden altar and carefully covered its grid with burning coals taken from the great brazen altar where the sacrificial animals were burned. He, too, retired. Zacharias was left alone.

He drew near to the golden altar behind which was the veil. Well did Zacharias know what was beyond the veil—the sacred ark of the covenant with its mercy seat where God had sat enthroned between the cherubim in happier times.

The moment had come. Zacharias advanced and put incense on the fiery coals. Clouds of pungent perfume arose. Its fragrance would cling to him and advertise to everyone that he had been very near to God, whose awesome majesty filled that place.

Outside, the multitudes of the people were praying, anticipating at any moment the return of Zacharias. They were a religious people (1:10), zealous for the law, attentive to the rites and rituals that Moses had commanded. Their ranks included the true, believing remnant of Israel. Little did even these devout worshipers guess what was delaying their priest.

d. The panic (1:11–12)

In the Holy Place, his duties discharged, the old man prepared to back out of the sanctuary. Then he saw him! Beside the golden altar was a shining angel. Zacharias was standing on the right side of the altar. The angel stood on the south side, between the altar and the golden lamp stand. The priest was suddenly afraid.[1] He had been brought face-to-face with a messenger from another world.

2. The stirring prophecy of the angel (1:13–17)
a. John's coming foretold (1:13–14)

"Fear not!" The angel's first words hushed the mounting terror that took possession of the old man. "Thy prayer is heard; and thy wife Elisabeth shall bear thee a son, and thou shalt call his name John." Many a time this aging couple had besieged heaven for a son, but their prayers seemingly had been ignored. Perhaps even as he went about his once-in-a-lifetime duties in the Holy Place, standing by the golden altar burning incense, watching the perfumed cloud ascend, he whispered, "Oh God, if only I had a son!"

"Thy prayer is heard!" He could hardly believe his ears. A son! To be called "John" (Jehochanan—"Jehovah shows favor!" or "God is gracious!"). The fifteen-hundred-year reign of the Law was about to be replaced by an age of grace.

"Thou shalt have joy and gladness; and many shall rejoice at his birth" (1:14). With these words a gap of four hundred years of silence on the part of God was broken. There had been four centuries of war and woe. Poor little Israel had been kicked back and forth like a football in the ceaseless struggles between Syria and Egypt for power. The fearful days of Antiochus had come and gone, days of oppression not to be exceeded in horror and terror until the coming of the Antichrist. Finally, the Jews had struck back and gained a measure of independence, but then the Romans—and Herod—had come.

---

1. Luke seems to have been particularly interested in angels (Luke 1:26; 2:9, 13, 21; 12:8; 15:10; 16:22; 22:43; 24:4, 23).

And now John, the herald of the Messiah, was to come, bringing joy and gladness for the old priest and his wife and rejoicing for the nation—and then Jesus was to come!

b. John's character foretold (1:15)

He would be great in the eyes of men and in the sight of God. The angel prescribed total abstinence from wine and strong drink. He was to be filled with the Spirit from his mother's womb. The hallmarks of his life—from his conception to his execution by Herod—would be personal holiness, moral authority, and spiritual power.

c. John's career foretold (1:16–17)

The Old Testament had ended with a promise. The Lord would come, but before that, Elijah would come (Mal. 4:5–6). Then the nation would be confronted with the Christ.

The angel said concerning John, "And many of the children of Israel shall he turn to the Lord their God. And he shall go before him in the spirit and power of Elias [Elijah], to turn the hearts of the fathers to the children, and the disobedient to the wisdom of the just; to make ready a people prepared for the Lord." The angel's words were a quotation from the Old Testament (Mal. 3:1; 4:5–6). The expression *spirit and power of Elias* can be rendered "the powerful spirit of Elijah." Elisha received a double portion of that spirit (2 Kings 2:9–14). Elisha performed exactly twice as many miracles as Elijah did.

John, by contrast, with a purely spiritual ministry, performed no miracles at all (John 10:41). John's ministry was wholly spiritual and was in all ways subservient to that of Christ.

The actual fulfillment of Malachi's prophecy concerning Elijah was twofold: it had an initial partial fulfillment in the ministry of John the Baptist, and it will have a further fuller fulfillment in the days of the Antichrist (Matt. 11:7–15; 17:1–13; John 1:19–27; Rev. 11:1–14). Note that one of these two future witnesses will undoubtedly be Elijah, returned to complete his earthly life and armed, as before, with many mighty miracles; the other witness is probably Enoch, likewise returned to finish his earthly life and ministry.

3. The sobering prediction of the angel (1:18–25)
   a. The angel's astonishment (1:18–20)

The old priest, dumbfounded by both the messenger and the message, finally found his tongue: "Give me a sign. We are both very old, my wife and I," he said.

Now it was the angel's turn to be astonished. No one had ever doubted his word before. So this old man wanted a sign, did he? Then he'd give him a sign! "I am Gabriel," he said, "that stand in the presence of God; and am sent to speak unto thee, and to show thee these glad tidings." It would never have occurred to Gabriel to doubt for a moment the word of God. "You want a sign, do you? Well, a sign you shall have. Because of your unbelief, you will be dumb until your son is born."

And so it was. Thus, this old priest might have come out of the temple with a tongue set aflame to herald the good news that the promised forerunner of Christ was soon to be born. Instead, he was tongue-tied for the next nine months.

   b. The angel's accuracy (1:21–25)

The herald angel vanished. The old priest, shaken and shamed, stood in the Holy Place wrapped in silence. He bowed and backed himself out of the sanctuary. Now faith and joy unspeakable filled his soul. We must not be hard on this old man; we too are prone to unbelief. Besides, his reputation for goodness had preceded him into heaven.

Meanwhile the worshipers waited with growing unease at the delay. After all, it didn't take that long to sprinkle a handful of incense on the altar (1:21).

Suddenly, Zacharias appeared and took his stand at the top of the steps that led from the Porch to the Court of the Priests. He must now give the priestly benediction (Num. 6:24–26). Certain psalms must be sung, and the drink offering must be outpoured. Instead of performing these normal functions, however, he stood before the people dumb and silent (1:22), gesturing to indicate his affliction. It dawned on the people that their priest had seen a vision. Gradually, the crowd melted away, and the stricken Zacharias headed for home.

The impression that had been made by all of this excitement soon faded away. The rabbis probably wrote the whole thing off as hysteria. Zacharias, after all, was merely a rustic priest, and he was old. Why take much notice of him?

The sweet perfume of the frankincense that clung to him heralded Zecharias's arrival home, but he was smitten with dumbness. We can picture his scribbling on a writing tablet the joyful news, tidings that were much more significant than the fact that he could no longer talk.

Elizabeth totally secluded herself. Her body would need its rest, and her soul needed quiet to prepare her for the awesome task of raising the one who would be the herald of the coming Messiah.

So time passed. The sudden flurry of excitement in the temple and among the people died away. The priest, far from cultivating the limelight, retired to his country home. The world went on its way, people went on with their own affairs, and time stood still—or so it seemed. But in heaven God's great clock was ready to chime again.

B. The birth of Jesus announced (1:26–55)
    1. The annunciation (1:26–38)
        a. The angel's descent (1:26–29)

Six months went by, and Gabriel was sent back to earth "unto a city of Galilee, named Nazareth" (1:26).

Galilee! The very word was one of scorn to the aristocrats in the capital. The whole region was overrun by Gentiles whose very accent grated on the ears of the sophisticated Judeans. The fact that Herod had raised pagan temples and held pagan sports activities in Galilee increased their scorn.

As for Nazareth, that only added to the Jews' contempt (John 1:45–46). The situation of the town was pleasant enough—about seventy miles northeast of Jerusalem, about halfway between the capital and Tyre. The road crossed the green plain of Jezreel and then climbed the mountains to Nazareth. Roman soldiers marched along that road. Greek merchants, Jewish priests and Levites, troops of entertainers, and people from all parts of the great Gentile world passed by. The population was probably some fifteen thousand. The final straw in the city's odium was its reputation for corruption. "Can there any good thing come out of Nazareth?" was Nathanael's question (John 1:46). Nathanael came from nearby Cana, so he was in a position to know all about Nazareth.

To this unprepossessing town came Gabriel, fresh from the glories of heaven, to find "a man whose name was Joseph, of the house of David" (1:27) and Mary, a virgin espoused to him. She, too, was of the royal Davidic line. Both of them were insignificant and poor despite their royal lineage. She is also expressly declared to have been a virgin. The word used is *parthenos,* the word for a virgin.

She was betrothed to Joseph, the contract being as solemn and as binding as a marriage contract itself.

The angel found Mary in a humble peasant home. He came from a world where walls were made of jasper and gates were made of pearl. The virgin's home probably had little furniture and was separated from domesticated animals by only a pole and a curtain. It was heated by a small turf fire. Such sparseness must have astonished the visitor from glory—but such were the homes of peasants in those days.

The angel spoke: "Hail, thou that art highly favoured, the Lord is with thee" (1:28). Mary was arrested and alarmed. Her character, she learned, had been under heaven's closest scrutiny, just as centuries before Job's had been.

Ever since Eve, God had been looking for a woman upon whom He could bestow His favor and trust, one upon whom He could bestow the highest of honors, the honor of becoming the virgin mother of God's incarnate Son. City after city, century after century, woman after woman, God was looking for someone sweet enough, strong enough, and spiritual enough to give birth to the Christ. The search was over! The woman had been found!

The words *highly favored* might as readily have come from Paul's pen as Luke's. They can be rendered "graced of God" or "endued with grace." The day of grace had come. From now on, everything was to be of grace. Mary needed grace to be a fitting vessel for the high honor that was to be hers. In that, she was no different than us.

b. The angel's disclosure (1:30–38a)

Again the angel used the word *favor* ("grace"). "Thou hast found favour with God." The whole story of the coming into this world of the Son of God is of grace from beginning to end. And sovereignty! Again and again God asserts His will in this matter: "Thou *shalt* conceive . . . and *shalt* call his name JESUS. He *shall* be great, and *shall* be called the Son of the Highest: and the Lord God *shall* give unto him the throne of his father David; and he *shall* reign over the house of Jacob for ever; and of his kingdom there *shall* be no end" (1:31–33). The first three sovereign assertions relate to the Lord's first coming; the remaining three assertions have to do with His coming again.

The prophecy of the angel moves majestically from one statement to another. As surely as the second person of the Godhead entered into the world by way of the virgin's womb, and as surely as His human name was Jesus ("Jehovah saves"), and as surely as His name and greatness are known in all of the world, and as surely as He is now worshiped as "the most High" (the name is found seven times in Luke's gospel—1:32, 35, 76; 2:14; 6:35; 8:28; 19:38), so surely will He sit upon David's throne, ruling over both Jews and Gentiles alike. Both segments of this angelic prophecy were to have a literal fulfillment. The prophecy focuses on the literal nation now known as Israel.

When Gabriel appeared to Zacharias, the old priest's question was rooted in unbelief. Mary had a question too, but hers was rooted in faith and total acceptance of the prophecy. But she had a problem. How could she bring forth a son when she was unmarried? Perhaps, however, she had no sooner asked the question than the glimmering of understanding crept into her soul. Centuries ago, the prophet Isaiah had foretold that a virgin would conceive and bare a son. And that one's name would be significant too: Immanuel, "God with us" (Isa. 7:14). So that was it! But the practical question of *how* still remained to be answered.

There was a *plan* (1:35). "The Holy Ghost shall come upon thee, and the power of the Highest shall overshadow thee: therefore also that holy thing which shall be born of thee shall be called the Son of God." The Holy Spirit draws a veil over the actual details of the conception as He does over the actual details of the Crucifixion. As for the conception, it would be a miracle. Jesus would have a human mother but no human father. That would be no problem at all to God, who invented the genetic code and knows all of its details and how it works.

The expression "that holy thing" is arresting. Human life is, in itself, a wonderful thing—body, soul and spirit, mind, emotion, and will. The psalmist had written a song about it many years before Mary was born (Ps. 139:14). The human-divine nature of Christ is an even more wonderful thing—it is a holy thing.

There was the *proof* (1:36). Gabriel told Mary that her cousin Elizabeth was six months pregnant—which in itself was a wonderful thing, too, given her great age and lifelong barrenness. If God could make a dead womb spring to life, He could certainly make a virgin's womb spring to life. What was the difference to a God who had Himself conceived the whole wonderful process of conception and birth?

Moreover, there was the *power* (1:37). "For with God nothing shall be impossible," Gabriel said. He knew! He stood in the presence of God. He saw the awesome wisdom, love, and power of God exerted in countless ways. The God who can create a hundred billion galaxies, the God who can pack all of the details needed to create a lion or a lamb in the "code of life," can do whatever

He wills. Mary gave in at once! She presented her body to be a living sacrifice, holy and acceptable unto God for this great work of bringing this Son into this world.

Mary might well have had some concerns. She would have to face the wagging tongues of her neighbors, the outrage of her family, and the incredulity of her betrothed. And what about the local rabbi and the other authorities? To have a child out of wedlock in those days was a serious matter indeed.

c. The angel's departure (1:38b)

As for Gabriel, we picture his ascending Jacob's ladder (Gen. 28:12) with a light heart. He had been instantly believed. God's plans for planet Earth had taken a giant step forward.

2. The adjustment (1:39–45)
a. The counsel Mary required (1:39–40)

Mary was suddenly alone. The house must have been strangely still. Outside, the world went on with its customary noise—a mule driver urging on his stubborn beasts, a boy arguing with his friend, some women laughing on their way to the well. In a moment or two, Mary would have to rejoin that everyday world. What should she do? Should she hide her condition or make it known?

Mark the march of the polysyndeton as Luke gets on with his tale: "*And* Mary arose in those days, *and* went into the hill country with haste, into a city of Judah; *and* entered into the house of Zacharias, *and* saluted Elisabeth." And . . . and . . . and. The *ands* are designed to separate each statement from its neighbor so that due weight can be given to each statement individually. It emphasizes the deliberate nature of each of Mary's actions.

Mary was acting on the angel's hint; she must go and see Elizabeth and Zacharias. Soon, her condition would be common gossip. She needed—right now—a sympathetic ear.

This move included a psychological aspect. Under Jewish law, Mary should have been arraigned before a priest and accused of breaking God's moral law. The Law required that, whether married or betrothed, the offender should be stoned to death (Deut. 22:24). The home of an ordained priest would have been just about the last place Mary would have gone if she had anything to hide.

b. The confirmation Mary received (1:41–45)

There was the *instant sign.* Mary arrived at her relative's home and was soon closeted with Elizabeth, and a miracle happened: "And it came to pass, that, when Elisabeth heard the salutation of Mary, the babe leaped in her womb . . ." (1:41a). The developing child was six months old. It had a life of its own. (This should settle the abortion issue for a believer.) Other instances in the Bible also show cognizance in an, as yet, undelivered child (Gen. 25:19–26). The thrill of joy that stirred Elizabeth's soul when she learned that the Messiah had been miraculously conceived communicated itself to the unborn child in her own womb. The child responded at once and leaped within her.

Then, too, there was the *inspiring Spirit.* Elizabeth broke into song. Filled with the Holy Spirit, she called Mary "blessed." She was not blessed "above" all women, as Rome teaches, but blessed "among" women (1:42). She was carrying in her womb the promised and long awaited "seed of the woman" (Gen. 3:15). Every devout Hebrew woman doubtless wondered, when she was about to give birth to a man-child, if perhaps *her* son would be *His* Son, the Christ of God. Eve evidently cherished such a hope because when her firstborn child arrived she exclaimed, "I have gotten a man from the LORD" even Jehovah *('ish 'eth Jehovah)* (Gen. 4:1–12). She soon learned her mistake. Countless millions of mothers later, Mary could have echoed Eve's exclamation.

Elizabeth continued. She blessed the glorious child in whose presence she stood (1:42). She marveled that Mary had come to her (1:43). As great as Elizabeth's own developing child was to be, the child whom Mary was carrying was far greater. Mary was to be the mother of her Lord, and she was overwhelmed.

She testified, too, to the fact that her own unborn child had recognized the truth and had responded as best it could (1:44).

But Elizabeth was not yet through: "Blessed is she that believed: for there shall be a performance of those things which were told her from the Lord" (1:45). The word for "blessed" here means "happy." Mary would have her share of sorrow, not the least of which was the seeming stigma of being with child out of wedlock. But great happiness was hers as well.

Thus, Elizabeth gave voice to the first hymn of the New Testament.

3. The anthem (1:46–55)

As Elizabeth's voice died away, Mary began to sing. First, there was a *personal* note: "My soul doth magnify the Lord, and my spirit hath rejoiced in God my Saviour" (1:46–47). So much for the so-called "immaculate conception of the blessed virgin Mary." Mary owned herself to be in need of a Savior (1:47). She referred to her "low estate." Her strained circumstances found her—a descendent of David, Israel's greatest king, though she was—among the ranks of the poor.

The fortunes of the house of David had reached their lowest ebb; an Idumean sat on David's throne, and the last of David's illustrious line was a village carpenter and a peasant girl. Lowly she was indeed, but all generations henceforth would call her blessed—not because of any goodness in her but because the One whose name is holy had wrought the miracle in her.

Next, there was a *practical* note (1:50–53). This godly young Jewish woman was a child of fallen Adam, just like everyone else. She fled from the terrifying holiness of God to the tender mercy of God.

Thoughts of God's mercy stirred her to rhapsodize God's majesty (1:50). She spoke of the strength of God's arm (1:51). She was going to need His strength to face the dangers that would threaten her once her condition was known. "He hath scattered the proud in the imagination of their hearts" (1:51), she sang. "He hath put down the mighty from their seats, and exalted them of low degree" (1:52). The imbalance between rich and poor would be addressed (1:53). God's heart goes out to the poor. The Lord Jesus Himself would know the pinch of poverty (9:58).

Moreover there was a *prophetical* note (1:54–55) to all of this: "He hath helped ['laid hold of for help,' or 'taken by the hand'] his servant Israel, in remembrance of his mercy" (1:54); "as he spake to our fathers, to Abraham, and to his seed for ever" (1:55). The nation of Israel had fallen on hard times. The majority of Jews lived in the Diaspora. The homeland had been invaded repeatedly, and now cruel Herod sat on David's throne. For four centuries, God had been silent. Now He was about to speak and act as never before. The divine treaty that God had signed with Israel was unconditional, never to be revoked despite Israel's constant apostasies (Gen. 12:1–3; 15:9–21; 17:1–27). Two women, an old one and a young one, blended their voices, and Zacharias sat there dumb! Probably never in all of the nine long months did his dumbness afflict him more.

Section 2: The Advent (1:56–3:22)
   A.   The comings (1:56–2:52)
      1.   The coming of John (1:56–80)
         a.   The departure of Mary (1:56)

Mary stayed in the quiet of Elizabeth's home right down to the time for her cousin's child to be born. Then she resolutely, and probably reluctantly, went back home. It was time to tell her family and Joseph. Possibly she carried with her a certificate signed by Zacharias giving his priestly endorsement of her story.

      b.   The deliverance of Elizabeth (1:57–66)

Meanwhile, Elizabeth's boy was born, and all of her neighbors and friends came to celebrate.

Eight days passed, and the important day of the child's circumcision, and when he was to be named, arrived. The consensus was that the child should be called Zacharias after his father (1:58–59), but Elizabeth disputed the decision. "No! Not Zacharias, but John," she said (1:60). An argument ensued. Zacharias could not speak because his lips were sealed.

The whole matter was referred to Zacharias. After all, although he could not speak, he could still write. He wrote, "His name is John" (1:62–63). Immediately, Zacharias's tongue was loosed, and he gave thanks to God. "Immediately" Luke says (1:64), using one of his medical words, *parachrēma*. It occurs thirteen times in the New Testament in connection with disease or healing (e.g., Acts 3:7). The old priest's last word had been one of doubt; his first word now was one of delight. Then he had wanted a sign; now he wanted to sing.

News of this remarkable event spread abroad, "and fear came on all that dwelt round about them: and all these sayings were noised abroad throughout all the hill country of Judaea. And all they that heard them laid them up in their hearts, saying, What manner of child shall this be! And the hand of the Lord was with him" (1:65–66). God had broken His long silence! There could be no doubt about that.

"The hand of the Lord was with him!" Or, as we would say, they held hands. If a couple is going to hold hands, one thing is necessary—closeness! It is very difficult to hold hands if two or three people manage to get in between. If John and the Lord were going to hold hands, nobody and nothing must come between.

c. The declaration of Zacharias (1:67–79)
(1) Words about Jesus (1:67–69)

Suddenly filled with the Spirit, this obscure priest took his place among the prophets. His long enforced silence had thrown Zacharias in upon himself, to meditate no doubt on some of the great passages of Scripture that he had known since boyhood but that now came home to him with new depths of meaning.

For three months, he had been Mary's host. No doubt his writing tablet had been busy with questions. Elizabeth was soon to give birth to the Messenger; Mary would soon give birth to the Messiah. Now, his tongue untied, he recorded his musings: "Blessed be the Lord God of Israel; for he hath visited and redeemed his people" (1:68). The name Immanuel would come to mind: "God with us!" At last! God was coming to visit His people and coming as a redeemer and a ruler. Zacharias, like so many of the Old Testament prophets, telescoped together the two advents of Christ.

(2) Words about Jewry (1:70–75)

First, he had a word to say about *Scripture*. He thought about the Old Testament prophecies, great prophecies "that we should be saved from our enemies, and from the hand of all that hate us" (1:71). In Zacharias's day, the Jews were crushed under the iron heel of Rome. In the end times, the Antichrist will have the Jews by the throat. Zacharias saw an end to all of that kind of thing.

He also had something to say about Old Testament promises: "To perform the mercy promised to our fathers, and to remember his holy covenant; the oath which he sware to our father Abraham" (1:72–73). The Abrahamic covenant was personal, spiritual, and territorial. And it was wholly unconditional (Gen. 12:1–3; 15:1–21; 17:1–21).

Then, too, Zacharias had something to say about *service*. The nation of Israel was to be God's servant. It had failed miserably. Far from upholding God's standards of holiness, it had gone "awhoring" after the pagan gods of the heathen (Ezek. 23:30). Zacharias prayed that "he would grant unto us, that we being delivered out of the hand of our enemies might serve him without fear" (1:74).

More! He had something to say about *sanctification* (1:75). Only a sanctified people, reflecting God's holiness and righteousness, could bring about the high and holy aspirations that the law demanded. Holiness has to do with maintaining a right relationship with God; righteousness has to do with maintaining a right relationship toward man. How thrilling it was for the old man to gaze into the cradle where lay the child who would call the nation back to God.

(3) Words about John (1:76–79)

We can see the priest as he stooped down to the cradle to raise the precious bundle in his arms. He spoke directly to the infant: "And thou, child, shalt be called the prophet of the Highest" (1:76a). A prophet! Not a priest! Israel had too many priests. Although John had been born into the tribe of Levi and the family of Aaron, his destiny lay elsewhere than the priesthood. It had already been written in heaven that he would be a prophet—"and more than a prophet" (Matt. 11:9).

In practical terms, John would be the herald of the Messiah as Isaiah predicted (Isa. 40:3–5). There was a desperate need for such a forerunner. The Old Testament sin of idolatry had been exorcised, but, like the demon in the Lord's story, it had come back, bringing other spirits different from and worse than himself (Luke 11:24–26). The nation was now plagued by the cold, dead formalism of the Pharisees, the contemptuous skepticism of the Sadducees, the frozen traditionalism of the rabbis, the compromise of the Herodians, and the fiery radicalism of the Zealots.

d. The development of John (1:80)

John had to cut through all of this distraction to reach the conscience of the nation. His work would be "to give knowledge of salvation unto his people by the remission of their sins" (1:77). He was to alert Israel to the kind of Messiah who was coming—"to give light . . . to guide our feet into the way of peace" (1:79).

Before leaving this theme of the coming of John, Luke pauses to give us one fleeting glance at the kind of life John would live: "And the child grew, and waxed strong in spirit, and was in the deserts till the day of his showing unto Israel" (1:80).

The old man fell silent. John grew up, doubtless taking advantage of the rabbinical school in his neighborhood. Doubtless, too, he became increasingly impatient with the worldliness, carnality, hypocrisy, and formalism of the religious establishment.

It is likely that he was a trained priest. And then, about the time of his ordination, he disappeared. He fled to the wilderness to receive his spiritual gifts in meditation, fasting, and prayer, waiting for the day of his showing to Israel. He mastered his Bible, brought his body into subjection, thought about the Jesus of whom his parents had spoken, a man now, who was six months younger than he. Gradually, one rousing word took shape in his soul—*Repent!* With this battle cry on his lips, he launched his one-man crusade. "Repent!"

2. The coming of Jesus (2:1–52)
    a. The birth (2:1–20)
        (1) The powers of this world (2:1–7)

Jesus was born amid a world movement of international dimensions. One word from a pagan emperor in Rome, and, throughout his vast domains, people began to move. Caesar Augustus had called for the collection of a new tax (2:1–2).

It was the supreme good fortune of Caius Octavius to be Julius Caesar's favored grandnephew. Octavius took the name "Caesar" by adoption and "Augustus" for good measure. The murder of Julius Caesar gave him the chance that he had sought to step forcibly onto center stage. The suicide of his greatest rival, Mark Anthony, cleared the way to supreme power. So Caesar Augustus he became, a god, no less, with his throne above the stars like Lucifer and his feet planted firmly on planet Earth.

What would he have said, we wonder, had he been told that in a despised provincial town in an obscure corner of his realm had been born One who was God indeed, God overall, blessed for evermore?

The tax to which Luke referred was imposed "when Cyrenius was governor of Syria" (2:2). Cyrenius was a man of humble birth, a soldier of fortune who rose to a position of great power. His Cilician victories won him a Roman triumph. His death was marked by a state funeral.

The tax that Caesar Augustus imposed required that every person go to the city where he was born to be registered. Joseph and Mary, married now, and the Babe who was soon to be born, had to return to Bethlehem, the ancestral home of David, Israel's greatest king. Like it or not, Joseph and Mary set out on their journey, which must have been tiring and uncomfortable for Mary. That she should be left behind in her condition was unthinkable.

The hand of God was in the whole business. The journey put Mary in Bethlehem in time for the birth of her child—just where the prophet Micah had declared some six or seven hundred years earlier that Christ would be born (Mic. 5:2).

The journey took at least three days. The travelers arrived at Jerusalem and continued the five or six more miles south to Bethlehem. When they arrived there, the place was packed. Joseph pushed his way inside the inn to beg and plead for a room for by now the birth of Jesus was imminent. The inn itself had a long history. It was known as Chimham's Inn (2 Sam. 19:38–40; Jer. 41:17) and was built by that loyal servant of David after he became a member of David's inner circle. (Jeremiah had spent a night there when he was being abducted and taken to Egypt many years earlier.)

"No room!" That was the innkeeper's last word. "We are full. You can see that for yourself. There's not one room vacant." Then, in a moment of compunction, he said, "But there's the cattle shed. Maybe you could make do there."

"No room!" That was not true. There was the innkeeper's own room, but he never once considered that. No indeed! Let these peasants with the Nazareth accent make do with the shed. The "cattle shed" of such an Eastern inn was often a cave, which seems to have been the case here.

So in a rough, cold cave attached to an ancient inn, the Son of God entered into human life. Oxen shook their shaggy heads, and camels looked around with disdain. The floor was unspeakably foul. Bats flew in and out. No hot water, sanitation, or midwife was available. In the nearby inn, paying guests called for food and drink and sang songs or sought their beds.

The awesome Child was born at last. Joseph knocked some boards together to make a manger and lined it with straw, and the wondrous Child slept, wrapped in swaddling clothes. The word Luke used for "swaddling" is one of his medical terms. It means "bandages," so even in the midst of newborn life is a hint of death.

(2) The princes of that world (2:8–14)

The offhand manner of the innkeeper is now contrasted with the enthusiasm of the heavenly herald and his accompanying hosts. Their first encounter was with a group of shepherds whom they found in a field where they were watching over some sheep.[2] The shepherds, confronted with the angel of the Lord, were terrified. Perhaps as was customary, they were talking to their sheep in loud crooning voices using the special language peculiar to them on such occasions. The

---

2. For proofs that the traditional date for this appearance was December 25, see Frederic Godet, *Commentary on Luke* (1887; repr., Grand Rapids: Kregel, 1981); and Alfred Edershheim, *Life and Times of Jesus the Messiah*, vol. 1 (1884; repr., Peabody, Mass.: Hendrickson, 1993).

temple sacrifices created a constant demand for sheep. The location might have been near where David had been shepherding his father's flock when he was summoned to be anointed by Samuel as Israel's next king (1 Sam. 16:11–12).

Suddenly, the field was ablaze with light (2:9). Luke describes the light as "the glory of the Lord," which suggests that they were bathed in the Shekinah glory, the light of another world, the light that heralded the divine presence (Exod. 24:16; 1 Kings 8:10). The shepherds were filled with fear. The angels were used to that. The herald angel sought to calm their troubled breasts: "Fear not," he said, "for, behold, I being you good tidings of great joy, which shall be to all people. For unto you is born this day in the city of David a Saviour, which is Christ the Lord. And this shall be a sign unto you; Ye shall find the babe wrapped in swaddling clothes, lying in a manger" (2:10–12). A sign indeed! Who would expect the newborn son of a king to be so wrapped and laid to rest?

Salvation! A Savior! A sign! Tidings of great joy indeed! Tidings for all of the people of the world! Just what the world needs! It has had soldiers and sovereigns enough. It needs a Savior! It needs Jesus Christ the Lord.

And a sign! When the wise men came, they were guided by a *star*. The humble shepherds were directed to a *stable*. Signs had been given often enough in olden times—seas turned to blood, the sun standing still, the shadow on the sundial halting and moving backward contrary to nature—such signs as had been seen before would be doubly appropriate now. But no! A Babe, wrapped in swaddling clothes, lying in a manger! Who but God would have thought of such a sign?

Then, suddenly, "there was with the angel a multitude of the heavenly host praising God, and saying, Glory to God in the highest, and on earth peace, good will toward men" (2:13–14). Thus, God announced an amnesty and made an offer of peace to a lost world.

Peace! What does the world know of peace? The Romans, for all of their much-trumpeted *Pax Romana* ("Roman Peace"), constantly had to fight to impose it. It lasted as long as it did because of the thoroughness and ruthlessness with which the Romans waged war. And what about Napoleon's cynical dictum? "If you want peace, prepare for war!" The peace that Christ came to give was, first and foremost, peace with God (Rom. 5:1–2).

(3) The people of their world (2:15–20)

Then, abruptly, it was all over. The anthem ceased, the angels vanished, the stars gleamed brightly in the cold night sky.

"Let us go to Bethlehem!" the shepherds said. And leaving their flocks to fend for themselves, they made a beeline for Bethlehem. "They came with haste," Luke says (2:16). And they found that it was true! There was the man, the woman, the Child, the manger, and the swaddling clothes. Amazing! And all of this was in the crude and pungent stable adjacent to a wayside inn.

Then out from the stable and into the streets! No one seems to have bothered to rouse the innkeeper and his guests. They had no room for the Lord of glory in their inn. Why should they be aroused? Let them sleep! Let them find out for themselves what wonders they had missed.

Wherever the shepherds went, they told their tale. People wondered, Luke says. But how many went? Was a steady stream of people heading for the inn? It seems not, although surely some people came. In any case, Mary "kept all these things, and pondered them in her heart" (2:19). She kept all of these things to herself and turned them over and over in her mind, determined to remember each detail. Many years later, she doubtless shared them with the beloved Dr. Luke.

Meanwhile, the shepherds came back to their sheep. They at least were overjoyed. The last we see of them, they were "glorifying and praising God for all the things that they had heard and seen" (2:20). They were the first evangelists of the gospel age.

> b. The Babe (2:21–38)
> (1) The presentation of Jesus in the temple (2:21–24)

Our Lord's first experience on this planet was one of pain. "When eight days were accomplished for the circumcising of the child, his name was called JESUS, which was so named of the angel before he was conceived in the womb" (2:21).

The rite of circumcision was the covenant sign between Abraham, his seed, and God. It symbolized the cutting off of the flesh as useless as a means of producing a sinless life. The Lord's circumcision identified Him with the ruined race that He had come to save. On the natural level, it identified Him as a member of the Jewish nation (Gen. 17:14) and a member of the Abrahamic covenant.

The rite took place on the eighth day. On this same occasion, Jesus was given His human name. Both Mary and Joseph had been told that "Jesus" was God's own choice of a name for the Child (Matt. 1:18–21; Luke 1:31).

The Mosaic Law required other duties and ceremonies in connection with the birth of a child. The firstborn child had to be redeemed at the price of five sanctuary shekels (Num. 18:16). The earliest date for this particular function was thirty-one days after birth. (Luke, incidentally, refers to the Law five times in telling this part of his story—2:22, 23, 24, 27, 39.) His intent was to make clear that Jesus was born under the Law. He, the Lord Himself, however, did not need to be redeemed. He was immaculately conceived, sinlessly born, and wholly free from sin. He had come to fulfill all of the demands of the Law, so He was circumcised and ceremonially "redeemed" to identify Himself with us.

"When the days of her [Mary's] purification according to the law of Moses were accomplished, they brought him to Jerusalem, to present him to the Lord" (2:22) as required by law (Exod. 13:2; Num. 18:15).

They came also "to offer a sacrifice according to that which is said in the law of the Lord, a pair of turtledoves, or two young pigeons" (2:24). This sacrifice was required according to Leviticus 12:2, 6. Rabbinic law fixed the date for this offering at forty-one days after the birth of a son. The Law called for the sacrifice of a lamb, but, in the case of the poor, the requirement was reduced to a pair of doves or pigeons.

Thus, Mary took her place as one who was ceremonially unclean and in need of cleansing by the shed blood of a substitute. One of the doves was offered as a sin offering, the other as a burnt offering. The sin offering symbolically transferred all of the sinner's guilt to the substitute. The burnt offering symbolically transferred all of the virtue of the substitute to the sinner.

(2) The proclamations about Jesus in the temple (2:25–38)
(a) The words of the prophet Simeon (2:25–35)

Our attention is drawn to a man named Simeon, a godly man who was waiting for "the consolation of Israel" (2:25). This verse tells us that the Holy Spirit was upon him. Simeon had been given inner assurance that he would not die until he had actually seen the Lord's Christ (2:26).

Some scholars have suggested that Simeon was the son of the famous rabbi Hillel and the father of Paul's tutor Gamaliel. This Simeon became president of the Sanhedrin in A.D. 13. The Mishna, however, which tells of the great rabbis and their achievements, ignores Simeon—perhaps because of his belief in Christ. In any case, he was looking forward to "the consolation of Israel." The phrase was used among the Jews as a formula of blessing. The name Simeon means "hearing." The Bible says that "faith cometh by hearing, and hearing by the word of God" (Rom. 10:17). This suggests that Simeon spent much of his time pouring over the prophetic page.

The Old Testament Jews revered the Scriptures; nevertheless, the Old Testament was full of unattainable precepts, unfulfilled promises, and unexplained procedures. The apostle Paul later described his own inability to keep the law (Rom. 7). And to what purpose were all of the endless sacrifices and ceremonies of Old Testament religion? And what about the multitude of prophecies that remained unfulfilled?

Old Simeon understood that these seeming deficiencies could be resolved only in the person of Christ (Dan. 9:24–26). Christ was the answer to his incomplete Bible. The Spirit of God made clear to him that he would see Him when He came. He would not die until then. We can imagine how eagerly he scanned the faces of young and old after that (2:27).

Then one day, however, it happened. He saw a young man and a young woman, both of peasant stock, or so it seemed. They were Galileans by the sound of their voices, poor by their looks. They carried a Babe. They were coming into the temple to present Him to God. The Holy Spirit urged him: *That's Him!* He stepped forward boldly. Of course! A Babe! All doubts were swept aside. This was the One of whom all of the prophets had written! He held out his arms. Probably he spoke. Then he took Him in his arms (2:28).

The old man gazed into the face of a Babe, the face of God manifest in flesh. Instantly, he was ready to die! "Lord, now lettest thou thy servant depart in peace, according to thy word: for mine eyes have seen thy salvation, which thou hast prepared before the face of all people; a light to lighten the Gentiles, and the glory of thy people Israel" (2:29–32). Death was no longer a devourer but a deliverer. By one man sin had entered the world and death by sin. With this small Babe salvation had arrived. Satan's vast realm reeled. Wait until this Babe became a man!

A truth from Isaiah 42:6 flashed into Simeon's mind. This salvation was not just for Jews; it was for Gentiles as well. Here indeed was "a light to lighten the Gentiles" in all of their pagan darkness. The word he used was *apokalupsis*—"revelation, an unveiling," a manifestation no less. The word comes into its own in the first word of the book of Revelation, which is often called "the Apocalypse."

The old seer gazed into the face of a Babe and at the same time looked into the face of God manifest in flesh. He gazed and gazed. At last, he gave the Babe back to Mary. He had a word for her: "Behold, this child is set for the fall and rising again of many in Israel; and for a sign which shall be spoken against; (Yea, a sword shall pierce through thy own soul also,) that the thoughts of many hearts may be revealed" (2:34–35). Alas! Israel would reject this heaven-sent Savior.

Then the light would blaze across the Gentile world, and an amazing age of grace would come. Then, after centuries of sorrow, this rejected Christ would become at last "the glory of thy people Israel." He foresaw that this sign would be "spoken against" (2:34). And so it has been. The name of Jesus has been bitterly execrated by Jews and Gentiles alike. To this day, many people actually use it as a curse word.

This Child, moreover, was "set" (destined) for "the fall" of many in Israel. He would be a stumbling block to many. The nation would stumble over Him. He was not the kind of Messiah they wanted. He was a meek Messiah; they wanted a militant Messiah. So they hounded Him to the cross and, as a people, have pursued Him with bitter unbelief for centuries. It will take the coming of the Antichrist to bring the nation to its senses at last and lead to a wholesale national turning to Christ (Rev. 1:7).

As for Mary, a sword would pierce her soul also (2:35). That sword pierced her at Calvary. Out of pity, Jesus on the tree gave her into the keeping of John, who led her away from the scene.

(b) The words of the prophetess Anna (2:36–38)

Luke turns our attention next to a remarkable widow named Anna. She was a member of the tribe of Asher, an incidental example of the fact that many members of the scattered tribes still preserved their tribal identity. Anna seems to have been married in her teens, as was common enough in those days and in those lands. Then came seven years of marriage and early widowhood. At that point, she gave herself over to God. She would live for Him and wait for His Son from heaven. This she did for the next eighty-four years. She made God's home her home. She found for herself a niche somewhere near the temple courts where she served God with fasting and prayers day and night (2:37).

One day, as she came into the temple, she caught sight of old Simeon. Doubtless they knew each other well. When she saw him with a Babe in his arms, she quickly put two and two together, especially when she saw the light of glory in his face. She knew in an instant that his quest was over—and hers was about to begin. She began her new ministry by giving thanks unto God (2:38). Then she took up her post in the temple court and bore witness to all who would listen to the Good News (2:38): The Messiah had come! As yet, He was but newly born, but He was here! He would grow up! It would take time but He was here! She spoke of Him out of a thankful heart "to all them that looked for redemption in

Israel" (2:38). A threefold cord of testimony was thus woven: first the shepherds, then old Simeon, and finally Anna (Eccl. 4:12; 2 Cor. 13:1).

> c. The Boy (2:39–52)
>> (1) Where He lived (2:39–40)
>>> (a) The place (2:39)

Nazareth! That was the place that God had chosen from before the foundation of the world. It was a busy place, a border city with an unsavory reputation. Jesus was not raised in a cloister but in an earthly village where fallen man could be studied in the raw. "When they [Joseph and Mary] had performed all things according to the law of the Lord, they returned into Galilee, to their own city Nazareth." That was the place.

>>> (b) The plan (2:40)

The Holy Child was to grow up in that place. Luke says, "And the child grew, and waxed strong in spirit, filled with wisdom: and the grace of God was upon him." There was a godlike quality about Him from the start.

There never was such a Boy. Adam was never a boy, and Cain, the first child ever to be born, was born in sin and shapen in iniquity. Jesus went through all of the stages of growing up. He lived in a home that He shared with a bevy of brothers and sisters, all of whom manifested at times the Adamic nature. But He had no such nature. He was filled with the Spirit. He was always happy, always helpful, always holy. He was a familiar sight around the village, doing always those things that pleased His Father. The weak and sickly found a friend in Him for as was the Man, so was the Boy, known and liked by everyone for "the grace of God was upon him."

>> (2) What He loved (2:41–50)
>>> (a) His Father's building (2:41–47)

Luke now has a delightful story to tell, a story that gives us one glimpse of the Lord Jesus between His birth and His baptism. He was twelve, the age in Jewish culture when a boy begins to assume the responsibilities of a man. He was ready for His first Passover.

His education had been thorough enough, first at His mother's knee and then in the local rabbinical school. The weekly Sabbath observance would have been His joy. The Scripture written on the doorposts (Deut. 11:20) of the house had a word for Him every time He left home and whenever He came home. He soon knew His Bible by heart, and, given His flawless memory and His brilliant mind, He doubtless knew it in both Hebrew and Greek. He came to know all of the people who crowd the Old Testament page, all of the precepts of the ritual law, and all of the principles of such books as Proverbs and Ecclesiastes. He knew and understood the full significance of all of the prophecies and promises that God had given to the Hebrew people.

From the age of five until He was ten, His only textbook was the Bible. From ten to fifteen, He was exposed to the Mishna, the traditions of the elders, what came to be known as "the oral law" supposedly given to Moses at Sinai. His keen mind would soon sort out the good from the bad in all of that. Not until He was fifteen would He enter an academy and be taught the endless harangues of the rabbis.

So with a full heart Jesus joined the pilgrims marching to Zion to keep the feast. To date this particular event, Luke mentions in passing the names of some of the great people of the time. The depraved Tiberius was on the throne in Rome. It was his fifteenth year. Pontius Pilate was governor with his seat in the Roman city of Caesarea. Herod Antipas was ruler of Galilee. The infamous Annas was the Rome-appointed high priest. Our history books tell us what a collection of rogues and ruffians they were! Their dark shadows lay across the little land where Jesus would soon exercise His ministry and be put to death. Those men had another eighteen years to get their house in order. Meanwhile, we see the Lord heading joyfully to Jerusalem in the company of crowds of pilgrims singing "the songs of degrees" (Pss. 120–134).

As the Lord entered Jerusalem, His thoughts must have been mixed indeed. Here was a city that Abraham had visited thousands of years earlier, a city where David had reigned, a city that murdered the prophets and that one day would crucify Him. And crowning Mount Moriah and dominating everything was the temple. Tens of thousands of people could find room within its courts. The Lord's eyes would constantly be drawn to it. He called it "my Father's house," although it was, in fact, being built by the Herods.

The crowds kept Passover, and then Joseph and Mary prepared to head for home. Jesus stayed behind. They went a day's journey "supposing" Him to be in the company (2:43–44). If Joseph and Mary took the direct route, their first halting place would have been Shechem. That was when Mary and Joseph discovered their loss. They were frantic. A hasty roll call of relatives and friends confirmed the disaster: Jesus was gone.

Back they went, beating the countryside for some scrap of news. Back to their lodgings. All around the markets and bazaars, not once thinking of the temple— surely the obvious place for them to look for such a one as He. Finally, they went to the temple, and there He was sitting amid the doctors, both hearing them and asking them questions and astounding everyone who was present with His understanding and His answers to their questions.

In Jesus' day, two schools dominated rabbinic thought, and they seemed to delight in contradicting one another. Hillel was the more liberal of the two, but he was a philosopher with little regard for the people—"this people who know not the law" was his sneer. His rival, Shammai, had a smaller following and was intensely national and exclusive and frowned on any dealings with Gentiles. Between them, these two schools held Israel in bondage. Jesus, however, knew full well who He was and why He was there. He was not intimidated by those learned men. Nor was He forward, precocious, or impolite. He already knew His Bible thoroughly and doubtless could see through their legalistic traditions. He amazed them.

(b) His Father's business (2:48–50)

His mother and Joseph were just as astonished. Their Son was a prodigy! Prodigy? No, He was perfect, as Adam had been before the Fall. Jesus' faculties, however, were untouched, untainted, and untrammeled by the blighting hand of sin. Moreover, He was God. They knew this fact. It is astonishing that they had forgotten it. They had gotten used to His being so gifted and so good. They took Him for granted. His brilliance and His behavior became commonplace for them. In the end, they forgot His deity, clothed as it was in such perfect humanity.

Mary spoke first. She was disappointed at what she considered to be His thoughtless behavior, a disappointment sharpened by the nightmare of the past three days and honed still further by the fact that He had never done anything like it before. "Son, why hast thou thus dealt with us?" she asked. "Behold, thy father and I have sought thee sorrowing" (2:48).

The Lord corrected her at once. There must be no misunderstanding here. He answered her "why" with a question of His own: "How is it that ye sought me? wist ye not that I must be about my Father's business?" (2:49). In the first place, Joseph was not His father. He was by now fully aware of exactly who He was.

Surely, too, they should have come directly to His Father's house. As for this "Father's business," it was certainly not that of a carpenter but the work of the cross.

Henceforth, His path led slowly but surely to a cruel cross on a hill outside a city wall. Both Mary and Joseph failed to understand Him. The whole incident undercuts Rome's exaltation of Mary to the rank of coredemptrix, quasi-deity, and "Queen of Heaven."

(3) What He learned (2:51–52)

The Bible says that Jesus learned obedience (Heb. 5:8). Luke says, "And he went down with them, and came to Nazareth, and was subject unto them: but his mother kept all these sayings in her heart." He was now in His thirteenth year, just entering what would be to us the teenage years of life, years that are so often filled with rebellion and disobedience. Not Jesus! Fully aware now that He was the Son of God, He was "subject unto them"—the village carpenter and a local peasant girl. As far as we know, He would remain in that humble home, working at the bench, for another eighteen years.

He developed a magnificent physique. He grew in stature. He advanced "in favour with God," living ever beneath His Father's smile. Complete communion occurred among Himself, His Father, and the indwelling Holy Spirit. And He advanced in favor with His fellowmen. He was well-liked by everyone: the members of His family, His relatives, neighbors, friends, those who did business with Him, those who worshiped with Him. One and all liked Him, and some people loved Him. Luke leaves it at that.

   B. The commencement (3:1–22)
      1. John the Baptist's teaching (3:1–20)
         a. His sudden arrival (3:1–6)

A new day had dawned. The "silent years" were nearly over. God was about to speak again, first through a prophet and then through His Son. Because of this fact and because it was so important, Luke carefully dates the event.

Caesar Augustus was dead, and his stepson, Tiberius, had replaced him on the throne of the Roman Empire. He had been coregent for two years. He had a standing army of 350,000 men and a capitol city of some two million people, half of them slaves and thousands more on relief, always clamoring for bread and circuses. Tiberius hated Jews. His first procurator of Judea swapped the high priests time and again until he found one, Caiaphas, who would be a pliable tool.

Herod was dead, and Luke notes two of his heirs. Herod Antipas ruled over Galilee and Perea, where both John the Baptist and Jesus labored, but he was dominated by Herodias, his brother Philip's wife, whom he had stolen. Philip, his half brother, was the best of a bad lot. He eventually built the city of Caesarea Philippi near the mountain where the Transfiguration took place.

Lysanias's image is blurred. He seems to have been related to Ptolemy, king of Chalsis, whom Antony had assassinated in 36 B.C. Herod the Great likely had annexed the kingdom and brought it under the dominion of Rome.

First one way and then another, Luke paints a vivid picture of the total dismemberment of the Jewish Promised Land.

Pontius Pilate, whom Luke also mentioned in dating the commencement of John's ministry, is well known. He was appointed procurator of Judea in A.D. 25. The Jews hated him, and he seemed to delight in antagonizing them. He was eventually deposed and sent to Rome. According to Eusebius, he committed suicide in A.D. 36.

As for Annas and his son-in-law Caiaphas, they were wolves in sheep's clothing. That unsavory pair bore the ultimate responsibility for the crucifixion of Christ.

So Luke amasses all of this weight of historical evidence to document the sudden appearance of John with his rousing cry: "Repent!"—an emperor, a governor, three tetrarchs, and two high priests—all to introduce the man who was, by all outward appearances, just a backwoods, desert preacher. But what a man! And what a preacher! And what a message!

"The word of God," Luke says, "came unto John . . . in the wilderness" (3:2b). John the Baptist grew up as a child of the desert, moving from place to place but never too far from the river. John, once the call came, did not stand in the temple courts although, having been born into the priesthood, he might well have done so. No! He would not go to the crowds; he would make them come to him.

One word summarized all that he said: *Repent!* Prince or plowman, priest or publican, soldier or scribe, Pharisee or Sadducee, harlot or housewife, rabbi or robber, rich or poor, bond or free, Judean or Galilean—the message was the same: "Repent!"

And all of this had long since been foretold (Isa. 40:3; Mal. 3:1). Valleys were to be filled, crooked paths were to be straightened, and rough places were to be smoothed. Great mountains of pride were to be humbled, deep valleys of degradation and depression were to be dealt with. Crooked people were to be transformed, and rough, violent people were to be tamed. "Repent!"

b. His spectacular appeal (3:7–18)

To begin with, there were those who came to his crusade (3:7–9). After all, there was something novel about it all—a trip to the desert, trooping in from all parts of the country, coming to see one dressed like Elijah and with a bluntness of speech that quickened the very conscience. The trickle of visitors grew to a flood, people coming to hear this new prophet of God, coming all of the way from Dan to Beersheba.

And John was ready for them. Long ago, he had washed his hands of the Jerusalem religious establishment. He called the crowds who came to hear him "a generation of vipers" (3:7). He told the common people to "bring forth . . . fruits worthy of repentance" (3:8). Their favorite conceit was that they were children of Abraham (3:8). Abraham's seed indeed! Why, God could raise up children of Abraham from the very stones that littered the ground. John demolished their conceit that they became children of God by virtue of their being born into a special family.

John's preaching was laced with practical exhortation, demands for a belief that behaved, and warnings that the King was coming and that the kingdom was at hand! Was the nation ready? If not, the ax was already lying at the root of the tree (3:9). If they rejected the ministry of the messenger and of the Messiah, judgment would follow. We now know that the menacing ax did fall and that God's displeasure has pursued the Jews for the past two thousand years.

The people were *convicted at his crusades* (3:10–11). John preached to one and all—the common people were to share what they had with their poor neighbors (3:10). Tax collectors were not to extort money over and above that allowed by the law (3:12). He told soldiers on active service ("men under arms"), likely troops in the pay of Herod Antipas, that they were to refrain from violence and false-hood and to be content with their pay (3:14). Usually, men on active service supplemented their wages by plundering a conquered people and by holding prisoners of war as hostages for ransom. John's preaching was so refreshingly different from the traditions of the rabbis!

So John's voice rang out, and its echoes filled the Promised Land. Some people were *confused by his crusade* (3:15–18). Moreover, the authorities were afraid of his influence with the multitudes, who believed him to be a prophet. Although he performed no miracles, his voice had an Elijah-like ring and his message had an unmistakable authority. Some people even speculated that he might be the very Messiah Himself, but John soon put a stop to those tales (3:15).

Yes! He baptized with water. It was the seal of repentance that he required of his converts. And they came by the thousands—except the religious leaders, who agreed among themselves that John was an imposter and a menace.

But there was more to it than mere baptism in water. That was all well and good for a ministry of repentance. But he was there to announce the coming of One who would baptize with the Holy Spirit and with fire (3:16). Between John and Jesus was a great gulf. John was a voice; Jesus was the Word. John had come in the spirit and power of Elijah; Jesus would come in the spirit and power of Jehovah. John's baptism related to repentance; Jesus' baptism related to regeneration (John 3:3–7).

Had the nation responded to the ministry of John and the messiahship of Jesus, then the baptism of the Holy Spirit would have been for Israel. As it was, that side of things was postponed for some two thousand years, and the Gentiles came into the blessing that the Jews had spurned. The baptism that John foretold took place on the Day of Pentecost when a small nucleus of believers were baptized by the Holy Spirit into the church, the mystical body of Christ (Acts 1:4–8; 1 Cor. 12:12–27; especially v. 13). John, of course, like all of the Old Testament prophets, knew nothing of the mystical body of Christ. All he discerned was that if Israel missed the baptism of the Spirit, they would be faced with a baptism of fire—judgment. He elaborated on that point.

c. His subsequent arrest (3:19–20)

Sooner or later, John's preaching would make him dangerous enemies. He had already denounced the wickedness of the religious rulers of Israel; now he incurred the wrath of Herod Antipas.

John had denounced Herod for stealing his brother's wife. Herod Antipas was sly. The diplomatic skill of his father, Herod the Great, which had enabled that shrewd man to con both Antony and Augustus, was diluted in Antipas to mere cunning.

Herodias was a woman of great beauty and ambition. The hot blood of the Maccabees ran in her veins, and in Antipas she saw an opportunity to gain excitement and power. The fact that he was a kinsman made no difference. The Herods thought nothing of incestuous marriage. John denounced the whole wicked business. Luke does not go into the sordid details or the complications that Antipas faced when he divorced his wife, the daughter of Aretas, king of Petra. Nor does Luke detail the long list of Antipas's sins. He simply states that Herod "added yet this above all, that he shut up John in prison" (3:20), which must have pleased the Jewish religious leaders.

The fortress of Machaerus guarded the southeast frontier of Antipas's realm. The most dreaded feature of Machaerus was its dungeon deep down in the bowels of the earth, hemmed in by heat and darkness. There John languished for some ten long months. The confinement must have been especially galling to a man who was made for the wide-open spaces of the desert. In the fortress itself, Herod and his stolen, murderous wife enjoyed a giddy round of drunken pleasure.

2. John the Baptist's testimony (3:21–22)

Luke pauses and backs up to record what must have been the greatest moment of John's life, something that the preacher recalled many times. It was not the day he denounced Herod Antipas for stealing his brother's wife, a daring deed that earned him the undying hatred of Herodias. No, nothing like that! It was the day he baptized Jesus. He would never forget it. It had been a busy day. The line of repentant sinners who were coming to be baptized had been long. Finally, all of them had been immersed. But what was this? There was one more. It was Jesus. Reluctantly, and then obediently, John had baptized his Lord. It was the peak moment in John's ministry. From now on, he would send his disciples and converts to Jesus. And how could he ever forget the attending sights and sounds?

Jesus was praying even as John prepared to plunge Him beneath Jordan's rushing wave. The heaven was thrown open! The Holy Spirit descended from on high, in visible form, the form of a dove. A voice rang out from heaven: "Thou art my beloved Son; in thee I am well pleased" (3:22).

It had taken Jesus thirty years to reach this point. The divine visitor and the divine voice set their seal of approval on every single moment of His life, from the moment He stepped out of eternity into time until the moment He emerged from the river. Every thought, every word, and every deed was immaculate!

In his dark prison, day after day, John waited. He must have been tormented by his thoughts. What had gone wrong? Why was he in prison? What kind of a Messiah had he announced anyway? Why was He not mobilizing the nation? Why did He not smite Herod and Herodias and set him free? Surely he was not going to die in this hole. He later learned to see things in a very different light (7:18–24).

But even before that, he would recall the praying Christ, the descending dove, and the Father's voice. There really could be no doubt; Jesus was the Son of God.

Luke adds a footnote: "And Jesus himself began to be about thirty years of age." Joseph was thirty when Pharaoh elevated him to the seat of power in Egypt. David was thirty when he came to the throne. The Levites took up their duties at thirty (Num. 4:3, 23). Among the Jews, the scribes graduated and commenced work at thirty. Thirty is the prime of life.

Section 3: The Ancestry (3:23–38)

Luke's genealogy of Jesus is not the same as that of Matthew. Matthew's design was to link onto the lists of names in Chronicles (the last book in the Jewish Bible) and thereby to establish the claim of Jesus to the throne of David. Matthew gives the Lord's ancestry through *Joseph,* who apparently adopted Jesus; Luke gives the Lord's ancestry through *Mary.* Matthew goes back as far as David, the founder of the Hebrew royal family, and then leaps back to Abraham, the founder of the Hebrew racial family. Luke takes his ancestry of Jesus right back to Adam, founder of the human racial family. Matthew traces the line through Solomon, the son of David and Bathsheba; Luke likewise traces the line through David, but he follows a much more hidden and secret line through Nathan (another son born to David and Bathsheba) to Mary (1 Chron. 3:5; 14:4; 2 Sam. 5:14).

Luke is very careful. He says that Jesus was "supposed" to be the son of Joseph (3:23). He was nothing of the kind. He was the long-awaited "seed of the woman" (Gen. 3:14–15: the first prophecy of Scripture). Joseph, the husband of Mary, seems to have had his adoption of Jesus formally registered in the temple archives. When Joseph married Mary, the regal line through Solomon and the natural line through Nathan were united.

Throughout the history of the kings of Judah, we see Satan seeking to corrupt and destroy the royal seed. He seduced Solomon into hundreds of pagan marriages and turned him into an idolatrous and foolish old man. His oppressions eventually brought about a massive revolt by the ten northern tribes against the Davidic throne. Jehoshaphat, a good king, played the fool by marrying his son to the evil Athaliah, the infamous daughter of Ahab and Jezebel. Athaliah almost succeeded in wiping out the royal line of David. Manasseh's long and evil reign plunged Judah into excesses of wickedness from which it never recovered. Jehoiachin (1 Kings 24:6; also called Jeconiah and Coniah) so infuriated God that Jeremiah was told to pronounce a curse on him to the effect that no descendant of his should ever sit on the throne of David (1 Chron. 3:16; Jer. 22:24–28).

It was all in vain. While Satan was so zealously seeking the overthrow of the royal line to Christ, via Solomon, all the time God had another line (almost totally ignored) via Nathan, winding its way down the bypaths of history to Mary! And Satan was completely foiled.

In summary, Luke's ancestry of Christ reaches back in three stages. There was the *royal* line (3:24–31), which embraces the secret years (3:24–27a) and the silent years (3:27b–31). This ancestral path takes the reader back to David. The historian switches now to the *religious* line (3:32–34a), going back and back from David to Abraham. We are back now among people we know, important people in the Hebrew theocracy—Abraham, Jesse, Boaz (who married Ruth the Moabitess), Salmon (who married Rahab the harlot)—and on back to Judah, Jacob, Isaac, and Abraham.

Back we go along the line of *sacred* history. There were names there when the big blusterer Saul was king, when Samuel spoke, and when the judges ruled. The sacred secret line was always there, preserved by God. Now Joshua was conquering Canaan. Now Moses was there in Sinai. Back and back we go, the Spirit of God recording all of the necessary names. Now, as we continue to climb the ladder of history a rung at a time, we see Abraham in pagan Ur receiving his vision of a better land on high. The world's noisy events fill the world with din. The Holy Spirit ignores them. Only one family matters. The Spirit of God keeps our attention riveted on that family—father and son—until the entire roll call is complete.

Finally, there is the *racial* line (3:34b–38). The Holy Spirit takes us to a time before the Flood, from Abraham back to Noah, and then back to a time before the Fall. The Holy Spirit does not pause. The bell keeps tolling: Methuselah, Enoch, Abel, Cain, Adam—and God calls a halt. Adam! He calls him "the son of God" (3:38). So the list, for all of its backward trend, takes us from one whom we know as "the son of God" to One whom we know as God, the Son.

God takes us to the First Adam and then to the Second Adam—from the first man to the second Man—and He employs seventy-five names in doing so. A unique way indeed to record the coming and going of sixty centuries of time! But, then, God always has had a tender love for people, especially His own, and He likes to write their names into His Book.

Section 4: The Adversary (4:1–13)

The time, the place, and the circumstances of the Lord's temptation were all chosen by the Holy Spirit. The Lord returned from His baptism and His anointing filled with the Spirit. Immediately, He was "led by the Spirit into the wilderness." The Devil could not have relished the encounter that he was about to have with Christ. Man, born in sin and shapen in iniquity, had been a pushover all of those years. But Jesus was God, and the Devil knew Him to be God. And although Jesus was to be tempted as a man, Satan had never met a man like this Man, a Man anointed of God, filled with the Spirit, and absolutely without sin or any desire to sin.

The Devil—once the anointed cherub and now the roaring lion, the god of this world, the prince of the power of the air, and the fallen angel of light—is undoubtedly a great force. And yet, when all is said and done, he remains only a creature. Jesus knew all about him. He did not underestimate him, but He was filled with the Holy Spirit. Satan has never been a match for the Spirit of God.

The site chosen for the Temptation was a wilderness. The traditional setting is the mountainous, barren, uninhabited region that ascends toward Jerusalem from Jericho. Off to the right not far from Jericho rises a precipitous limestone peak named Quarantania. The site is one of utter desolation. The rock peaks are penetrated by caves. The area is actually a continuation of the fearful wilderness of Judea, where John the Baptist had made his abode.

The temptation of the Lord Jesus continued throughout the forty-day period of the Lord's fast. He was tempted in all points as we are (Heb. 4:15). This running battle came to a head on the last day, and that part of the battle was undoubtedly more fierce than anything Jesus had encountered before.

In the first place, the Lord's physical surroundings were depressing. Then, too, He had reached the end of His fast and, as Luke puts it, "he afterward hungered" (4:2). The fast had lasted for almost six weeks, about the limit of human endurance, the time when the pangs of quickened hunger clamored for food, just before a person starves to death. So the Lord was weakened to the extreme. This was the time Satan chose to make his attack.

The first temptation was along the line of *the will of God.* "If thou be the Son of God, command this stone that it be made bread" Satan said (4:3). We can almost hear the Devil's voice: "Look at You! You are *famished,* You are down to skin and bones, and You are hungry, starving in fact. Listen to me, and You can have instant *sustenance.* Now then, You claim to be God, then behave like it. Turn this stone to bread."

It was a temptation for Him to use His power to gratify an obvious personal physical need. It would have been as easy for Him to turn a stone into bread as it was for Him to turn water into wine (John 2:9). But Jesus knew that He was in the center of God's will. He had been led by the Holy Spirit into the wilderness. He had been *led* into this long fast, and He had no word from God to break it. If He did not act at once, He would die. So the temptation leaped upon Him in His desperate need—and, as swiftly, it was foiled; the lie was exposed. Jesus answered him, "It is written, That man shall not live by bread alone, but by every word of God" (4:4). That was it! His life was not run by circumstances no matter how demanding; it was run by the Word of God. He would terminate His fast when God said to end it. He dismissed out of hand the implication that God might let Him starve to death. He had not come into this world to die of starvation in a desert. And He refused to take matters into His own hand. The history of King Saul would warn Him against doing any such thing (1 Sam. 13:5–15).

The second temptation was along the line of *the worship* of God (4:5–8). This time, the Devil took Jesus to a high mountain and gave Him a panoramic vision of all of the kingdoms of the world. It took but a mere moment for Satan to display his wares (4:5–6). He said, "All this power will I give thee, and the glory of them: for that is delivered unto me; and to whomsoever I will I give it. If thou therefore wilt worship me, all shall be thine" (4:6–7).

Again we can detect the Devil's voice: "Look at You!" Satan might well have said, "You not only are famished but also have *failed.* Here You are, thirty years of age, and You are still known as 'the carpenter's son.' Now here's my offer. Do as I say, and You shall have instant *sovereignty.* Your great talents deserve a world arena. Worship me—and I'll set You on the throne of the world (4:7). You can have the crown without the cross. The world needs a king like You! Tiberius and his like will never amount to much. But You! Think how You could improve the world if all of its potential and people were Yours to command!"

Back came the answer: "Get thee behind me, Satan: for it is written, Thou shalt worship the Lord thy God, and him only shalt thou serve" (4:8). The Lord did not dispute Satan's claim to dispose of the kingdoms of this world as he willed. It was a right that he had wrested from Adam (Heb. 2:5–9). Jesus had come to get back those kingdoms but not by bowing to the Devil. God's mighty "sword of the Spirit" (Eph. 6:17) was the Lord's sole means of defense. Well did Satan know the power of that sword!

The *third temptation* was along the line of *the Word of God* (4:9–12). Twice the Spirit's mighty sword had flashed before the Devil's eyes. Now he tries his hand at quoting it himself. Satan transported Jesus to the pinnacle of the temple. "Cast thyself down," he said, "for it is written, He shall give his angels charge over thee, to keep thee: And in their hands they shall bear thee up, lest at any time thou dash thy foot against a stone" (4:9–11).

Again we read between the lines. "Look at You!" we can hear the tempter say. "You are *forgotten*. True, there was a flurry of interest in You at the time of Your birth, but that was a long time ago. Most of those people are dead. And You are forgotten by all. You are a nobody. Even Your own brothers don't really know You. Is Your name known in the Sanhedrin? Is there anyone in Athens or Rome to speak for You? You are at the prime of life, and time has passed You by. Who trumpets Your name—John the Baptist? He'll be dead before long, as You very well know, then You will be forgotten indeed. As for the Jewish establishment, they'll kill You if they get half a chance. I'll see to that. But if You go on being forgotten, who will care? However, do as I say, and You can have instant *success*. You want to quote the Bible? Very well, let me remind You of Psalm 91. There! Now You have a verse of Scripture to do something spectacular. Do as I say, and an hour from now You'll be the talk of Jerusalem."

The pinnacle of the temple was part of the temple court, either Solomon's Porch, which was located on the eastern side of the temple platform and which looked down into the Kedron gorge, or the Royal Porch on the south side of the temple platform and which overlooked a frightful abyss. It was from some such dizzy height that Satan wanted the Lord to cast Himself down, doubtless hoping that He would jump to His death.

The Lord, of course, was familiar with Psalm 91. He knew that Satan had torn the text from its context, a favorite trick of Satan. The Devil found it convenient to end his quote at verse 12. But the next verse said, "Thou shalt tread upon the lion and adder: the young lion and the dragon shalt thou trample under feet." Also, Satan conveniently left out the words "he shall give his angels charge over thee, to keep thee *in all thy ways*" (v. 11), that is, God's ways.

The Lord had His Bible ready. He replied, "It is said, Thou shalt not tempt the Lord thy God." So Satan's three attempts were all defeated by the Lord's knowledge of His Bible. All three quotations were from the book of Deuteronomy (6:13, 16; 8:3; 10:20). Satan left, utterly defeated.

PART 3

Events Relating to the Savior's Career

Luke 4:14–21:38

Section 1: The Work in Galilee: His Anointing in Focus (4:14–9:50)
 A. The work is commenced (4:14–5:17)
  1. He comes to be the Savior (4:14–15)

T he Lord had one supreme purpose in mind when He came to earth—He
 came to be our Savior. Once He began on His mission, He had immediate
success: "And Jesus returned," Luke says (i.e., from His temptation), "in the power
of the Spirit into Galilee: and there went out a fame of him through all the region
round about" (4:14).

Galilee! Of all places! Why not Jerusalem, the nation's capital? Because Jesus
knew what Jerusalem was like. The rabbis there were wedded to hair-splitting
wrangles over the law. Almost to a man, the Jerusalem religious establishment
would reject Him. He had time enough to go there. So He went back to the little
corner of the world where He had been born. And how the local tongues wagged!
He had become famous, and it was the talk of every town.

  2. He claims to be the Savior (4:16–5:17)
   a. The Scripture itself attests the claim (4:16–30)

Then He arrived back in His boyhood village of Nazareth! He knew every
house and shop and knew everyone by name. He knew who baked the best bread,
who shortchanged his customers, who bullied his wife, and who helped the poor.

His custom was to attend the synagogue on the Sabbath (4:16). Doubtless, on
this Sabbath the place was packed. He had taken His place in the synagogue
every Sabbath for thirty years. And, in later years, He had read the Scriptures and
made observations about them. As usual, the seats of honor were filled by the
village worthies, the rulers of the synagogue, and the local rabbi.

The usual prayers were said and liturgies performed, and then the time came for
the Scriptures to be read. Someone handed the Lord the book of Isaiah, and He
expertly found the place. We find the relevant passage in Isaiah 61:1–2 in our
Bible. It was a well-known passage: "The Spirit of the Lord is upon me, because he
hath anointed me to preach the gospel to the poor; he hath sent me to heal the
brokenhearted, to preach deliverance to the captives, and recovering of sight to
the blind, to set at liberty them that are bruised, to preach the acceptable year of the
Lord" (4:18–19). Many of the people present knew that Scripture by heart. They

expected Him to complete the sentence—"and the day of vengeance of our God." Instead, He closed the book and returned it to the custodian. Then He sat down.

Every eye was fixed on Him. The whole countryside was amazed by His miracles—the kind of miracles and the kind of ministry foretold by Isaiah, as just quoted. The nation at large, while delighted with His miracles, was really looking for Him to pour out the vengeance of God on the Romans. What would He say about that? Nothing! The day for that kind of thing had not yet come; it has still not come.

Just the same, His words exploded like a bomb when He ended the silence and began speaking. First, He (the village *carpenter*) announced that He was the *Christ,* the Anointed One, the One of whom Isaiah had written these words (4:21).

The people in the synagogue could find no fault. His grace and power were evident to everyone (4:22). But a reaction was already building. The village carpenter—the very Christ? Impossible! They waited. Surely some monumental miracle would now endorse this claim. But no miracle came.

He was speaking again: "Ye will surely say unto me this proverb, Physician, heal thyself: whatsoever we have heard done in Capernaum, do also here in thy country" (4:23). Now Jesus had a proverb of His own to quote: "No prophet is accepted in his own country" (4:24). He followed this blunt observation with two illustrations.

In the days of Elijah, there were many widows, He said (4:25–26). Yet when the great famine blanketed the land, the famine that lasted three and a half years, the prophet was sent to none of them. On the contrary, he was sent to a widow who lived in Sarepta, a city of Sidon—Jezebel's country, no less.

Later, in the days of Elisha, there were many lepers in Israel. The prophet cleansed none of them. On the contrary, he cleansed Naaman the Syrian (4:27).

In Old Testament times, prophets normally surfaced in times of apostasy when the land was under divine displeasure. Under such conditions, God often turned to the Gentiles to give them those glimpses of His grace and glory, which Israel miserably failed to give. At this very early stage in His public ministry, the Lord revealed that He loved Gentiles just as much as He loved Jews.

The people in the synagogue became angry. Instead of miracles, He gave them a lecture and a most unpalatable one at that. The synagogue erupted and they "rose up, and thrust him out of the city, and led him unto the brow of the hill whereon their city [Nazareth] was built," determined to fling Him headlong to His death (4:29).

The city of Nazareth was spread out along the eastern face of a mountain. One of its features is a perpendicular wall of rock some forty or fifty feet high—just the spot for them to carry out their murderous design.

But it was not to be. He had not come into the world to be flung thus to His death. Then He performed what came close to being a miracle. Suddenly, perhaps something of His glory blazed out. In any case, their hands no longer held Him. Their wrath no longer impelled them. Perhaps their eyes were "holden" and they could no longer see Him (24:16). He simply walked away from them—as far as we know never to return (4:30).

b. The Savior Himself attests the claim (4:31–5:15)
(1) He commands the demons (4:31–37)

Now Luke turns a corner in his narrative and records some miracles (4:3–15:15). Having left Nazareth, the Lord moved to Capernaum, a lakeside town about sixteen miles away. It was a thriving city on the north shore of the Sea of Galilee. The region of Galilee itself was crowded, containing some 240 towns and villages. The busy town of Capernaum, with its mixture of peoples and its lines of communication to the outside world, now became the Lord's base of operations (4:31).

The Lord then commenced a series of teaching sessions on succeeding Sabbath days in the local synagogue. The people were astonished at both His doctrine and the authenticating power with which He taught them (4:32). All of their lives they had listened to the traditions and trivialities of the local rabbis and to their dissertations that were focused more on the growing Talmud than on the Torah and the Word of God. The Lord's teaching was based solidly on the Book.

Then, one Sabbath day, a man showed up in the synagogue possessed by an unclean spirit (4:33). The same confusion of personalities is to be observed in this man as can be observed in other demoniacs. The man interrupted the service with a demonic scream. "Let us alone!" he cried (4:34). The word is an exclamation: "Ah!" or "Let be!" It was a cry of terror. The foul fiend that possessed the wretched man saw the yawning mouth of the Abyss before him. Like other demons, he irreverently addressed the Lord as "Jesus." The Lord insists that He be addressed as "Master" or as "Lord" (John 13:13). Thereafter, the demon addressed Him as "Jesus of Nazareth" and as the Holy One of God.

"Hold thy peace!" Jesus said; literally, "Be muzzled." The same word is used by Paul when he wrote, "Thou shalt not muzzle the mouth of the ox that treadeth out the corn" (1 Cor. 9:9). To this day, evil spirits cannot confess that Christ has come in the flesh (1 John 4:1–3). With one final spiteful convulsion, the demon left his victim and departed, obeying the Lord's command that he come out of the man (4:35). The people were astounded, and His fame was spread abroad (4:36–37), including in Nazareth, no doubt.

(2) He cures the sick (4:38–44)

Demons fled from Him. Now Luke shows that disease, too, was under His control (4:38–41). The Lord left the synagogue and headed for Simon Peter's house. They found Peter's mother-in-law in the grip of a great fever. What Jesus did was extraordinary. He did not treat the fever as though it were a medical ailment needing treatment. He spoke to it and rebuked it! And it left her (4:38–39). Did Jesus speak to the virus or to the bacteria? Had Satan caused this fever as he caused poor Job's boils (Job 2:1–7)? We do not know. We do know that the cure was instantaneous. The woman stood to her feet and bustled off to the kitchen to minister to the family with a meal.

Sunset! The Sabbath was over! People flocked to the house bringing with them the sick and the possessed, and Jesus healed them all (4:40–41). Luke emphasizes the variety and number of those who came: "All they that had any sick . . . with divers diseases . . . he laid his hands on every one of them, and healed them." It was the same with the people who were demon possessed: "And the devils also came out of many." As Christ confronted them, they cried out, testifying, "Thou art Christ the Son of God" (4:41). "Crying out" is the way Luke puts it. The word that Luke used is *screaming*. And, as always, the Lord silenced them.

Early the next morning, the Lord slipped away to a desert site to be alone with God and to renew His energies. The crowd, however, soon discovered where He was and "stayed" Him. The word used means "held Him fast." The same word is used to describe the Holy Spirit's restraining ministry during this age (2 Thess. 2:6–7). The Lord, however, was not to be deterred from His purpose by the clamor of the crowd. "I must preach the kingdom of God to other cities also," He said, "for therefore am I sent" (4:43).

"I must preach," He said. His miracles had their place, but they were not the really important things; they were only temporary and transient at best (Luke 10:17–20). What mattered most was the preaching. So the Lord disengaged Himself from the crowd and continued on His way, preaching in the synagogues of Galilee (4:44).

(3) He controls the fish (5:1–11)

Luke now takes us to the lakeshore. The people thronged Him, and the situation was inconvenient to say the least. The Lord noticed a couple of empty boats drawn up by the shore, one of which belonged to Simon Peter (5:1–3). Peter willingly let the Lord borrow his boat and pushed it out a little from the land. The Lord sat down and began to teach the people from this unconventional platform.

The acoustical properties of this area are remarkable. The still water acts as a sounding board, a loudspeaker. It picks up a speaker's voice and throws it up the beach and the hillside so that everyone can hear what is being said even when it is spoken in a conversational tone of voice. The Lord did not have to raise His voice to be heard by one and all.

We can picture Peter, pleased and proud that the great preacher Himself should be sitting there in his boat, His voice ringing out to one and all. Peter's companions were nearby, busily mending their nets with their hands while listening to Jesus with all of their ears (5:2).

Once He was through teaching, Jesus set about paying Peter for the use of his boat because the Lord is no man's debtor. "Launch out into the deep," Jesus said, "and let down your nets" (5:4). Peter argued. He and his friends had been hard at it all night long. No fish were there. Still, just to make his point, he let down a single net (5:5), and, to Peter's blank astonishment, they instantly had more fish in that net than they could handle.

Note an interesting progression here: (1) "Thrust out a little from the land"; (2) "Launch out into the deep"; and (3) "Let down your nets." That is often the way the Lord works things out in our lives.

Peter thought that he knew more about fishing than Jesus did. "Let down the nets? Nonsense, there's nothing there to catch. We ought to know; we've fished over this corner of the lake all night. Still, just to humor You, Lord, I'll let down a net." Peter's experienced hand felt the astounding response at once. Suddenly, the net, wholly inadequate for the task, was full to overflowing. Peter still knew it all. He summoned his partners, who by now had launched the other boat, and they drew alongside. Peter was still quite sure that he could handle things. He pulled on the net—and it broke. Still confident of his ability to handle things, Peter headed for the shore with this spectacular catch on board at last. Then the ship began to sink! That was the end of his self-will. He fell at Jesus' knees, saying, "Depart from me; for I am a sinful man, O Lord" (5:8). The Lord had said nothing at all about sin!

Peter was about to have his life changed forever. "Fear not!" Jesus said, "from henceforth thou shalt catch men" (5:10). On the Day of Pentecost, Peter would cast out the great gospel net and bring in a catch of three thousand men (Acts 2:41). In the house of Cornelius, he would lower his line and catch one notable man (Acts 10:23), plus his family and friends.

The astounding catch of fish that morning astonished everyone present. The Lord's words to Peter about henceforth catching men included his partners, James and John, the sons of Zebedee. From then on, all three men were to live by faith, trusting the Lord for their physical needs (the Lord had just demonstrated His ability to do that). Perhaps that very thought crossed their minds as they pulled the boats ashore and abandoned the record catch. From then on, too, their ministry was to be spiritual. Perhaps the Lord's teaching that day had prepared their souls for that truth. One way or another, "they forsook all, and followed him" (5:11).

(4) He cleanses the leper (5:12–15)

The next miracle Luke describes is a mighty one indeed—the cleansing of a leper (5:12–15). It took place "in a certain city," probably one of the cities in which most of His mighty works were done—Chorazin, perhaps, or Bethsaida.

Nine cases of leprosy are recorded in Scripture (Exod. 4:6; Num. 12:10; 2 Kings 5:1, 27; 7:3, 15:5; 2 Chron. 26:20; Matt. 8:2; 26:6; Luke 17:12). The Lord Jesus *healed* the sick, but He *cleansed* the leper. The Jews regarded leprosy as "the stroke of God." Everything about leprosy was ghastly and repulsive. It is a classic picture of sin: what leprosy does to the body, sin does to the soul. Interestingly, the first leper mentioned in the Bible was Moses and the second was his sister Miriam. In Bible times, it was incurable apart from a miracle. The Law demanded total segregation and quarantine of the leper. Outstanding lepers were Naaman, King Uzziah, and Gehazi.

Luke does not tell how this leper was able to get close to Jesus. According to the Law, a leper was required to stand afar off, cover his lip, and cry "Unclean!" if anyone came his way. Maybe his leper's cry cleared a space for him. Luke's introduction of the man into the narrative is striking: "And, behold a man." There is no verb. The man suddenly appeared like an apparition. The next moment, he was on his face at Jesus' feet. His was a terrible case. Dr. Luke notes that he was "full of leprosy."

"Lord," he said, "If thou wilt, thou canst make me clean." Jesus responded at once. He did something most wonderfully kind; He touched him. The people in a wide circle around Him, wanting to see everything but afraid that somehow they might inadvertently touch the man, must have gasped with astonishment. He touched him!

"I will!" Jesus said. "Be thou clean!" Just like that—with what the Holy Spirit calls "the word of his power" (Heb. 1:3). One word from Him—and it's done! Just as it was on the morn of creation when "God said, Light be!" and light was (Gen. 1:3)! The Lord had just preached in the Nazareth synagogue about the cleansing of the leper Naaman, and it had made them angry. We wonder what they must have thought of this miracle.

Then the Lord charged the man to tell no one but rather to present himself to the priest and to offer the sacrifice required under the Mosaic Law pertaining to the cleansing of a leper "for a testimony unto them"—the priests, that is. No one had ever performed this ritual, which is described in Leviticus 13, since, possibly, the cleansing of Miriam in the days of Moses.

At the heart of the elaborate procedure, two birds were taken. One of the birds was slain—the sinner can live only because Christ has died in his stead. The living bird was dipped in the blood of the slain bird. The leper also was sprinkled seven times with the blood to identify him with both the substitute and the shed blood. The living bird was then released to fly toward heaven, bearing with it the shed blood of the other bird. The blood on the ascending living bird bore witness to heaven that the leper was cleansed. The blood on the leper himself bore witness to the fact that he personally appropriated the blood that secured his cleansing. The whole ritual, of which this ceremony was but a part, depicts how sinners find in Christ a perfect Savior. He died for us and shed His precious blood to atone for our sin. After His death, burial, and resurrection, He ascended on high to bring the blood of atonement into heaven itself. Meanwhile, the sinner sprinkled with the blood is declared cleansed and fit to be brought into the fellowship of the people of God.

Luke, of course, does not go into all of this explanation. He does, however, record that the Lord's fame spread far and wide and that great crowds came to hear Him and to be healed by Him (5:15).

c. The Spirit Himself attests the claim (5:16–17)

The Holy Spirit bears a twofold witness to Christ. He says that Jesus "withdrew himself into the wilderness, and prayed" (5:16). We can see for ourselves how busy the Lord was and how the people hindered Him when He tried to get away. Every new miracle fed the flames of public enthusiasm and brought more crowds. All of this public applause, however, was to be offset by growing criticism, hostility, and opposition.

He needed to pray because although He was God, overall, blessed for evermore, He was also Man with human needs. He needed time to be alone with His Father in heaven. Besides, a critically important meeting was coming up, and He had to be prepared for it spiritually. Luke now takes us to that meeting.

"And it came to pass on a certain day, as he was teaching, that there were Pharisees and doctors of the law sitting by, which were come out of every town of Galilee, and Judaea, and Jerusalem: and the power of the Lord was present to heal them" (5:17). Note the polysyndeton (the constant repetition of the word *and*), which draws our attention to not only the occasion itself but also the people who were "sitting by." It was a somewhat intimidating gathering, a group not brought together by chance but by choice. And note that it was focused on "a certain day."

The rulers in Jerusalem had already been in conflict with the Lord. John's gospel shows an early developing hostility toward Him. The time had come for them to confront this country preacher on His own ground. Members of the religious elite arrived from all parts of the country. Especially visible were the Pharisees, who took the lead throughout the Gospels in opposing Christ. Their very presence and the presence of learned doctors of the Law from the capital itself would, it was hoped, intimidate this man from Nazareth. Nazareth! "Can there any good thing come out of Nazareth?" (John 1:46).

This meeting was going to be a turning point for the nation. The Holy Spirit would abundantly confirm the ministry of Christ, but the presence of critical professionals from all over the country might well have intimidated a lesser man than Jesus. The Galileans had not thought to challenge the teaching and miracles of the Lord. They were simply thrilled and awed. Within the hour, however, we see them accusing Him of blasphemy. All it took to cow *them* was the presence of a dozen or so learned, powerful men from other parts of the country, especially from sophisticated Jerusalem. Never before had they thought it a breach of the Law for Jesus to heal on the Sabbath. Now they did (6:7). It had never occurred to them to criticize His kindness to publicans and sinners. Now they did (5:30). The presence of hostile observers, the scribes and the Pharisees, tilted the scales.

The Lord instantly recognized the threat that these visitors were to Him, but that did not intimidate Him. "The power of the Lord was present to heal," the

Holy Spirit says (5:17). The Galileans went away awed by Him. The scribes and Pharisees murmured against Him. Whatever initial impression the Lord made upon them (5:26) was soon dispelled by the Lord's choice of a publican to be one of His disciples (5:27), by His disregard of their religious taboos (6:1–2), and by His deliberate healing of a cripple on the Sabbath (6:6).

The Lord saw through their momentary awe of Him. It would soon turn to mounting hostility. The Lord's love for these potential enemies remained unchanged. He knew them through and through, even their thoughts (6:8). He knew all about them, and He not only loved them but also died for them.

> B.   The work is criticized (5:18–6:11)
>   1. The silent criticism (5:18–26)

Luke gives us three specific examples of the kind of criticism the Lord had to face. First, He faced silent criticism. The setting of this incident is probably still Simon Peter's residence, which apparently was the Lord's home while He was in Capernaum.

The story begins with a man "taken with a palsy" (5:18), that is with paralysis. The man could do nothing to help himself. In this, he was a type of the sinner just as was the leper. This man's condition was such that he could not come to Christ by himself; others had to bring him. Happily, he had friends who were determined to bring him to Jesus and surely not against his own will.

Unhappily, however, the crowd was in the way. It often is—especially our own particular crowd. The crowd is often obstructionist, selfish, and hard to get past. The crowd now came between this man and Christ. The man's friends, however, were determined, crowd or no crowd, to bring their helpless friend to Jesus. Where there's a will, there's a way. They went up onto the flat roof of the house to force their way in to where Jesus was.

Peter's house seems to have been one of the better class homes, one with a covered gallery around the courtyard. Jesus was probably standing beneath that gallery. The scribes and Pharisees would be sitting in the guest room with Jesus at the entrance. The whole place was packed. The atmosphere was bristling with muted suspicion, prejudice, and hostility emanating from the outsiders. So far, they had been unable to find anything to criticize. Probably everyone was glad of the diversion when the friends of the paralytic began to dig holes in the tiles on the roof. Then came a truly astonishing sight—the sick man being lowered on four long ropes into the crowded room below (5:19)!

Then the bomb exploded. Jesus looked at the paralyzed man, saw his faith, saw the faith of his friends, and said, "Thy sins are forgiven thee" (5:20). The people present were astounded; the visitors pricked up their ears. The man himself was evidently greatly conscious of sin in his life, so the Lord's words were as a balm to his soul. The critics in the guest room, however, could hardly believe it— this young preacher from Nazareth had spoken blasphemy! Waiting for more, they held their tongues, but their thoughts were transparent enough, especially to Jesus.

They thought, *What a copout! Here these fellows had brought this paralytic for healing, and He simply changed the subject. Any preacher could say, "Your sins are forgiven"—if he didn't mind being charged with the capital offence of blasphemy. Well, He might have been able to fool these ignorant Galileans with such a slick trick, but He doesn't fool us.*

Nor did they fool Him because "Jesus perceived [read] their thoughts" (5:22). They were thinking, "Who is this which speaketh blasphemies? Who can forgive sins, but God alone?" (5:21). The Lord continued, "Whether is easier, to say, Thy sins be forgiven thee; or to say, Rise up and walk?" (5:23).

Naturally, they thought it much easier to pretend to forgive a man's sins than to heal his obvious paralysis. Jesus then turned to the man even as He spoke to His critics: "But that ye may know that the Son of man hath power upon earth to forgive sins . . . I say unto thee, Arise, and take up thy couch, and go into thine house" (5:24).

The response was instantaneous. The man rose to his feet, took up his bedroll, and headed for home, glorifying God.

Everyone was amazed, even the hostile guests. They likewise glorified God. Moreover, they were filled with fear. "We have seen strange things [paradoxes] to day," they said. But they were on their guard now. He had beaten them this time, but they would keep an eye on Him from henceforth. Sooner or later, they would get Him.

2. The spoken criticism (5:27–6:5)

Luke now brings together several examples of the more outspoken criticisms that were being circulated about the Lord.

One source of hostility lay in the fact that the Lord ignored *their religious prejudices* (5:27–32). The Lord's enemies did not have to wait long to find something to criticize. Soon after the incident in Simon's house, the Lord approached a publican (tax collector) who was conducting his business near the lake at Capernaum on the road leading from Damascus to the Mediterranean. His tax office was likely one of considerable importance. The publicans were usually renegade Jews whom their countrymen detested. They were not only collaborators with Rome but also crooked. Their profession was riddled with graft, extortion, and fraud. They were excommunicated from normal Jewish religious activities.

Doubtless, Matthew (or Levi, as he is often called) had often heard Jesus preach and had seen some of His miracles. Probably, too, he knew the Zebedee boys and their partners. News that they had lately become full-time disciples of Jesus might have stirred buried longings in Matthew's soul. Perhaps he had already had some talks with Jesus.

Then, suddenly, Jesus showed up at his office. We are told that Jesus "saw" this publican. The word that Luke used is *theaomai,* which means "to look with attention." Our word *theater* comes from the same word. It carries the idea of gazing with a purpose. The publican looked up from his desk, and his eyes met the Master's eyes. Jesus spoke just two words: "Follow me!" And Matthew's life would never be the same again (5:27). His response was immediate. He pushed back from his desk, walked out of his office—and fell in step with Jesus.

Then Matthew did a wise and wonderful thing. He made a great feast and invited all of his old friends to come and meet his new Friend. A great number of publicans "and others" showed up for the party. The word translated "others" here is *allos,* "others of the same kind," others who were ostracized by society.

The scribes and Pharisees were scandalized by the Lord's utter disregard for "political correctness" and their rigidly enforced religious taboos. The local scribes and Pharisees, nervous enough under the cynical stares of their more sophisticated Judean colleagues, were embarrassed and humiliated by this whole affair. They held Jesus in considerable awe, however, so instead of challenging Him, they picked on His disciples (5:30). They said, "Why do ye eat and drink with publicans and sinners?"

Jesus came at once to the rescue of His tongue-tied disciples. He answered the critics: "People who are not sick do not need a doctor, it is those who are ill who need a physician." He made the application: "I came not to call the righteous, but sinners to repentance" (5:32).

The Lord's critics changed their tactics. He had effectively silenced them regarding their religious prejudices; now He ignored *their religious practices* (5:33–39). They initiated the controversy when they attacked Him along the line of fasting and praying: "Why do the disciples of John fast often, and make prayers, and likewise the disciples of the Pharisees; but thine eat and drink?" (5:33). John the Baptist practiced the sternest asceticism and self-denial. The Lord did the opposite. He even had fellowship with publicans and sinners!

Again, the Lord was ready for them, "Can you expect the members of a bridal party to fast at the wedding when the bridegroom himself is present? Of course not!" But when the bridegroom goes away, then fasting might well be appropriate. He Himself was the Bridegroom, and He was present on earth. It was no time for fasting. When He was gone, however, it would be a different story.

The Lord now took the offensive (5:35). He had two illustrations ready. First, He took His critics into *the workshop*. Nobody patches an old garment with a piece of new cloth. The tough new cloth only makes the tear in the old, worn-out garment worse. He had not come to patch up Judaism by darning some new religious ideas on to that old threadbare system. The worn and faded Judaism, so beloved by the rabbis, was beyond repair. His plan was to give people a new garment altogether. His own teaching—so rooted in God's Word and so new, vital, and refreshing—could never be tacked on to rabbinical ramblings.

Interestingly and significantly, when the Lord died, Old Testament Judaism died with Him. God reached down from heaven and tore the temple veil in two (Matt. 27:51), signifying that Judaism was null and void.

Next, the Lord took His critics into *the wineshop*. "No man," He said, "putteth new wine into old bottles [wineskins]; else the new wine will burst the bottles, and be spilled, and the bottles shall perish" (5:37). In Bible times, goatskins were commonly used for holding wine. In time, they became seamed and cracked.

Again, the new wine was the Lord's teaching, so full of life and power. This new wine could not be poured into the old, shrunken, and cracked Judaism. The church, something brand-new, was being prepared to receive it (5:38).

The scribes and Pharisees, the rabbis, the Levites, and the doctors of the Law were practically incapable of receiving the revolutionary teaching of Jesus. When one of their best representatives came to see Jesus, the Lord told him bluntly that he needed to be born again (John 3:3).

The religious institutions consisted of the temple, the Sanhedrin, and the synagogue. They were too far gone for reform. The members of the establishment were steeped in dead ritual, hairsplitting controversies, and endless man-made rules and regulations. The Lord had no intention of pouring the new wine into their old wineskins of legalism, prejudice, and exclusivism.

For good measure, the Lord added, "No man also having drunk old wine straightway desireth new: for he saith, The old is better" (5:39). These additional words of Jesus, preserved here by Luke, underline the pathetic slowness and reluctance of those who were under the influence of the rabbis and their traditions to accept the new vibrant teachings of Jesus. The Lord likened these people to people attending a banquet. Having drunk deeply of the old, mellow wine, they are offered new, sweet wine. But they have a taste for the old and resist changing to the new. Paul, who was Luke's mentor, had been reared in the old Judaism, and in his unconverted days he reacted for some time against what Christ had to offer.

Next, Luke shows us how the Lord ignored *their religious pretenses* (6:1–5). Criticism arose because the Lord's disciples, while going through a cornfield, broke off ears of corn and ate them. The Pharisees pounced on this as a violation of the Sabbath. The Lord had been criticized before because of alleged Sabbath violations (John 5:9, 16). This was the first time, however, that Jesus allowed His disciples to do in His presence something contrary to Jewish Sabbath regulations.

The rabbis had tinkered with the simple Sabbath requirement (Exod. 20:8–11) to the extent that Sabbath keeping had become, for many people, a burden. For instance, "a Sabbath day's journey" was said to be about a thousand yards, but a man could circumvent this rabbinical rule. He could deposit at the thousand-yard boundary food for two meals before the Sabbath. He could then make this spot his dwelling, which would enable him to go another thousand yards.

And what constituted work? The rabbis defined a "burden" as "the weight of a dried fig." To pick up anything heavier than that was work. If a person were in one place and his hand, filled with fruit, was stretched in another, he must drop the fruit if overtaken in that position by the Sabbath! The rabbis forbade a woman to look in a mirror on the Sabbath because she might notice a gray hair and pluck it out, and that would be work! And so on, page after page—endless, mind-boggling pettiness, burden heaped upon burden.

The rabbis accused the Lord's disciples of having broken the Sabbath. By plucking an ear or two of corn, they were guilty of reaping; by rolling the cob between their hands to remove the husk, they were guilty of sifting; by rubbing the grains together, they were guilty of threshing; bruising the cobs was grinding; and throwing them up in the air was winnowing. So just by plucking a corncob or a stalk of wheat, they had violated the Sabbath.

The Lord brushed aside the accusation. Instead of answering the charges involved according to their book of rules, He gave them a Scripture lesson. "What did David do when he was hungry?" He demanded. He went into the tabernacle and ate the showbread on the table. Moreover, he gave some of it to his friends—fully aware that the showbread was consecrated and intended for the priests alone (6:2–4). The Lord assumed that His critics had read their Bibles. Had David sinned? Of course not! A man's life was more important than a ritual.

But then the Lord exploded a bombshell. "The Son of man," He said, "is Lord also of the sabbath." Given the Pharisees' veneration of the Sabbath, that statement bordered on blasphemy. Who did this carpenter from Nazareth think He was? Lord of the Sabbath indeed—able to do with it anything He pleased! Well, Lord of the Sabbath He proved to be because within a few short years, the Jewish Sabbath would be replaced by the Christian Sunday for countless thousands of people (Acts 20:7; 1 Cor. 16:1–2).

3. The subversive criticism (6:6–11)

The tide of opposition had not yet burst its banks, but it was rising rapidly. Again, the Sabbath was the center of the controversy.

First, there was *the man*. The poor fellow had a withered hand. The scribes and Pharisees eyed first the man and then *the Master*. This was a perfect setting for a snare. Which would win—caution or compassion? Well, "Jesus knew their thoughts" (6:8), as well as if they had put them into spoken words. The word the Lord used, coupled with the imperfect tense, meant that He knew all along, just as if they had spoken them aloud. Then came the miracle. "Stand up!" Jesus said to the man. If this was a setup, so be it! The Lord intended to make His response as public as possible. "Come and stand here in the midst," Jesus said to the man.

We must not forget that Jesus loved the scribes and Pharisees as much as He loved the man with the withered hand. He reached out to both. They had withered hearts that were as shriveled as the hand of the cripple. He put the man on display where everyone could see and hear.

"One question!" Jesus said to His foes, "Is it permissible on the Sabbath to do good? Is it lawful to do evil? Is it lawful to save a life or to destroy it?"

They were instantly on their guard. The rabbis had accepted the proposition that the Sabbath could be violated lawfully if it came to the matter of saving a person's life. But this led to endless debate. The rabbis forbade all applications of external medicine. Help could be summoned if someone had swallowed a piece of sharp-edged material. A splinter could be removed from an eye. Although the condition of the man in the synagogue was crippling, it was not life threatening. By using him as a test case, the Lord put the legalists on the defensive. Surely, even their narrow rules left room for doing good on the Sabbath. And surely it would be a good work to heal this poor man, Sabbath or not! *Not* to heal him would be tantamount to doing evil. The scribes and Pharisees remained silent, but inwardly they boiled.

The Lord's glance swept around the synagogue. Then He deliberately performed *the miracle* (6:10–11) and said to the man, "Stretch forth thy hand" (6:10). He did so. Instantly, his hand was made whole. It was an exhibition of power divine.

The place exploded. "They were filled with madness," Luke says (6:11). The word used suggests senseless rage. Nor did it stop there. They "communed one with another what they might do to Jesus" (6:11). From this time, the thought of His death was never far from their minds—nor from His.

C. The work is climaxed (6:12–9:50)
    1. A dependent Savior (6:12–16)

A fixed law of Jesus was never to act in independence of *His Father.* The original sin in the Garden of Eden was the sin of acting in independence of God. Luke begins this section by showing us the dependence of the Lord upon His Father: "And it came to pass . . . that he went out into a mountain to pray, and continued all night in prayer to God" (6:12). He was about to make a momentous decision, one that would affect the future of the world, but first He must spend time talking it over with God. Luke emphasizes here the essential humanity of the Lord Jesus. Consequently, he emphasizes the Lord's habits of prayer. All too often we make decisions and blunder into distressing situations simply because we fail to pray earnestly enough about them. Jesus never made that mistake.

The Lord not only was dependent on the faithfulness of His Father but also was about to become dependent on the faithfulness of *His friends.* No wonder He felt the need for a full night of prayer. "And when it was day, he called unto him his disciples: and of them he chose twelve, whom also he named apostles" (6:13). He had numerous followers at this time, but He needed a dozen men to be set apart for intensive training, men to whom He could entrust His ministry when He was gone. The decisions He was about to make called for great spiritual discernment. The character, capacity, and commitment of each disciple had to be weighed.

Most of the Master's men are little more than mere names to us, but the Lord knew them through and through—doubting Thomas, devoted John, diligent

Matthew, devious Judas, dependable Andrew, daring Peter, discerning Nathaniel. It is likely that Luke had met them all, except for Judas, and that he knew about their homes and families, where they lived, what they did, and where they went. The same restraint, however, was upon him, as it was on the other Evangelists, to be sparing of details. The focus is always on the Master, not His men or His miracles. Luke lists them all but mostly without comment (6:14–16).

The Bible includes four such listings of the apostles (Matt. 10:2–4; Mark 3:16–19; Luke 6:14–16; Acts 1:13). All of the lists arrange the apostles in three groups of four, and all of them head each of the three groups with the same apostle. The first group is headed by Peter, the second by Philip, and the third by James, the son of Alphaeus. Moreover, the men in each group are always the same, although sometimes the order varies within the group. An apostle from one group is never listed in another group. The leading apostle in each group likely supervised the others in his group. If so, then Peter took care of Andrew, James, and John; Philip was responsible for Bartholomew, Matthew, and Thomas; and James, the son of Alphaeus, was leader over Simon Zelotes and the two men named Judas. Of the three companies, the first group stood closest in proximity to Jesus.

With the exception of Judas Iscariot, all of the apostles were Galileans. The first five men were neighbors, all hailing from Bethsaida on the Lake of Galilee. Two of the apostles (Philip and Andrew) had Greek names. Galilee abounded in Gentiles, which was one reason the sophisticated Judeans and the people of Jerusalem sneered at "Galilee of the Gentiles." Both Matthew's and Luke's listings suggest that the apostles were paired. Indeed, the Lord did sometimes send them out in pairs. Doubtless, the Lord's nightlong prayer vigil was occupied in discussing with His Father just who should be linked with whom.

Thus, when the Lord talked to His Father about Peter, He also talked about Andrew, Peter's brother, who had brought blustery, bombastic Peter to Jesus. The Lord instantly recognized both the strengths and the weaknesses of Andrew's brother and gave him a surname—Cephas (Peter). The two made an ideal pair.

Then there was another natural pair of brothers, both among the very first of the Lord's disciples—James and John, the sons of Zebedee. Their mother was a sister of Mary, the Lord's mother, so this pair of apostles were the Lord's natural cousins. They were a fiery pair. The Lord nicknamed them "Boanerges—sons of thunder." James was the first apostle to be martyred. John outlived them all. With Peter, this pair formed an informal "inner circle" whom Jesus chose on three occasions for special revelations of His greatness, glory, and grief.

The next pair also seemed to fit naturally together—Philip and Bartholomew. The name Bartholomew *(Bar-Tolmai)* means "son of Tolmai." It was a surname—his other name was Nathanael, or, to use his full name, Nathanael Bartholomew. The Lord seems to have been on particularly friendly terms with Philip. He sought him out especially and invited him to become a disciple. Philip had an inquiring mind. He, in turn, brought his friend Nathanael to Jesus. Nathanael was both skeptical and guileless. He dismissed his doubts instantly, however, when he met the Lord and owned Him to be both the Son of God and the King of Israel. They were another ideal couple.

The next pair, Matthew and Thomas, probably called for longer pondering and prayer. Matthew's talents were obvious. He was an energetic, educated businessman. He made friends easily among his own class. Public opinion would not move him much because before coming to Christ he had been a detested tax collector, a political and social renegade. Perhaps that is why he was paired with Thomas, a cautious man who was plagued by doubts. Yet, he was both brave and resolute, a man who could be trusted to do his duty and who truly loved the Lord.

Four more men still had to be paired. We know little about three of them, so we can only guess why Christ coupled them as He did. We can be sure, however, that He made no mistakes. He associated James, the son of Alphaeus, with Simon Zelotes. Some have identified this James with Cleopas, in which case he would have been "James the Less," son of Cleopas and Mary, and thus another cousin of Jesus. Simon Zelotes (sometimes called Simon the Canaanite) was indeed a brand plucked from the burning. The Zealots were a band of fanatics, willing to embrace any deed of violence as long as it contributed to Jewish national independence. He had much to unlearn when he espoused the cause of Christ. Possibly, something in the character of James the Less had a mellowing effect on Simon. Doubtless, too, James needed something of the fiery messianic zeal of Simon.

That left the Lord with two men named Judas. How He must have agonized before His Father about Judas Iscariot. He knew all about him, of course. He was the only Judean in the group. He came from Kerioth near the northern border of Judea. Jesus knew what covetousness and treachery lurked in this man's heart. The Lord was able to purify the others of the alloy of selfishness, worldliness, and materialism, but not Judas. He deliberately put Judas in a place of trust as the treasurer. It did not help; nothing helped.

And who was this other Judas whom the Lord put alongside Iscariot? He is sometimes called "the brother of James," also "Lebbaeus and Thaddaeus." Lebbaeus comes from a Hebrew word for the heart (Thaddaeus has a similar meaning). The two words suggest that something about this man was especially loving, devoted, and tender about this man. If anyone could love Judas Iscariot, Judas called Lebbaeus Thaddaeus could. But it must have been a burden just the same. After the treachery of Judas Iscariot, the very name *Judas* must have been indeed a heavy cross to carry.

>   2. A dynamic Savior (6:17–9:17)
>   a. Dynamic in His words (6:17–49)
>   (1) What the multitudes sought (6:17–19)

Jesus was a dynamic person if ever there was one. He was vibrant, attractive, as bold as a lion, and as gentle as a lamb. He was gloriously different in character, conduct, and conversation from the religious stereotypes with whom the common people were all too familiar! They watched Him eagerly, heard Him gladly, hailed Him joyfully.

So down He came from the mount, possibly the upper slopes of the Horns of Hattin, where He had been all night. He arrived at the level space between the two peaks. Before Him were His disciples and a vast crowd from all Judea, Jerusalem, and the seacoast of Tyre and Sidon. Multitudes also had flocked in, Matthew says, from Galilee, Decapolis, and Transjordan. Mark adds that some people came from Idumea. In that vast congregation were Jews, Romans, Greeks, Phoenicians, and Arabs. Jesus knew and loved them all. But particularly His eye fell on "the company of his disciples" and even more attentively on the dozen men whom He had decided to make apostles, His special "sent ones." These men He called to Him and, in company with them, continued toward the waiting crowds.

The multitudes "came to hear him," Luke says, "and to be healed of their diseases" (6:17). Among those needy people were some who were "vexed with unclean spirits" (6:18a). Others came with hungry hearts, aware of deep longings in their empty souls.

"And they were healed," Luke says. People sought to touch Him "for there went virtue out of him, and healed them all" (6:18b–19). The word for "virtue" is *dunamis,* which suggests inherent, invincible power. The word gives us our English words *dynamo* and *dynamite*. Here we have a dynamic Savior indeed, and "He healed them all!" That is what impressed Dr. Luke as he looked over his notes. What stories were carried home that day to distant parts!

(2) What the Master said (6:20–49)
(a) Unusual beatitudes (6:20–23)

We recognize here at once words spoken by Jesus in the Sermon on the Mount (Matt. 5–7). But there are enough differences to decide that these sermons are not the same. The Lord must have often repeated Himself as He traveled here and there. The discourse here was addressed to the Lord's disciples, particularly to the Twelve. The words doubtless had a foreign ring about them. He called "blessed" the very kind of people we commiserate! They were addressed to His new apostles.

There were those, for instance, who were *disadvantaged*—the poor (6:20). The word for "blessed" is *happy*. It can be rendered "happy, happy!" The poor—happy? "Yours is the kingdom of God," Jesus explained. The poor have always been more open to the gospel than have the rich. The Lord knew what it was like to be poor. The rich young ruler's wealth got in his way (Matt. 19:16–22). The wealth of the rich fool blinded him to death's stealthy approach to foreclose on his spiritual bankruptcy (Luke 12:16–21). The rich man in hell found that his wealth bore witness against him (Luke 16:19–31).

Then there were those who were *distressed*—"Blessed are ye that hunger now: for ye shall be filled" (6:21)—anticipating the contrast between current miseries and millennial blessings. But even under current circumstances in a world ruled by Satan, where hunger is endemic and famines approach apocalyptic proportions, there is a benefit to being hungry. For one thing, a hungry person often has a greater appetite for the gospel than does a man whose physical needs are glutted. Jesus knew what it was like to be hungry, right down to the very doors of death in the forty-day fast that was the prelude to His public ministry (Matt. 4:1–4). Indeed, He began His work by being hungry and ended it by being thirsty (John 19:28–30).

Then, too, there were those who were *detested*: "Blessed are ye, when men shall hate you, and when they shall separate you from their company, and shall reproach you, and cast out your name as evil, for the Son of man's sake" (6:22). These unusual beatitudes are not directed to the lost multitudes but to the Lord's disciples, especially to His newly called apostles. They were fully expecting the momentary establishment of the millennial kingdom. The Lord had to disillusion them. Poverty, privation, and persecution lay ahead for these men. "Your reward is great in heaven," Jesus said. The Lord's teaching here strikes at the very roots of the so-called "prosperity gospel" that is so popular in our materialistic, Laodicean age.

The Lord now looked ahead to the crowning day that is coming. "Rejoice ye in that day, and leap for joy: for, behold, your reward is great in heaven: for in the like manner did their fathers unto the prophets" (6:23). The person who cannot see beyond this current age, and this present life, to the life that is to come is blind indeed.

When poor Uncle Tom was so cruelly treated and so fearfully threatened by the cruel Simon Legree, he had recourse to his heavenly home. Simon Legree threatened to truss him up and roast him over a slow fire. The godly old man simply looked away to heaven and acknowledged that Simon could do many cruel things, but there would be eternity after that.

(b) Unusual barriers (6:24–26)

The beatitudes are followed by woes—and again the targets of these woes sound strangely discordant in the ears of so many affluent, successful, and worldly believers today.

The Old Testament blessing and the future millennial blessing embrace material prosperity, good health, long life, and the praise of men: "The blessing of the LORD, it maketh rich, and he addeth no sorrow with it" (Prov. 10:22). Job, for instance, was hailed and extolled as long as he was prosperous, healthy, and blessed with a large and loving family. Once he was stripped of these things, however, even his friends attacked him.

The Lord's woes are aimed at things that people covet but that are, in reality, an encumbrance to spiritual life. The first woe is directed at those who are *prosperous* in this life: "But woe unto you that are rich! for ye have received your consolation" (6:24). The word for "consolation" here can be translated "comfort" (John 14:16, 26). Often, rich people derive their sense of well-being from their wealth rather than from God's Word. In the Lord's parable of the sower (Matt. 13:1–9), both "the cares of this world" (worry) and "the deceitfulness of riches" (wealth) militate against the soul's well-being.

The second woe is directed against those who are *pleased* with this life: "Woe unto you that laugh now! for ye shall mourn and weep" (6:25b). The Lord has lived down here. He knows what it can be like. He was "a man of sorrows," and He was "acquainted with grief" (Isa. 53:3). Much of our laughter is shallow and short-lived. We never read of Jesus' laughing. As He saw life (as the One who was here to deal with the appalling horror of sin), it was far too serious for lightness and levity. His heart was broken over the sins and sorrows of the lost people of Adam's ruined race.

Every graveyard, every orphan, every widow, every leper, every demoniac, every broken home, and every act of injustice broke His heart. He saw soldiers with their weapons and engines of war, Pharisees robed in hypocrisy, and Sadducees stupidly denying the great verities of the faith. He saw a temple corrupted by vested interests and commercial enterprises. He could look into human homes and hearts.

Jesus knew from of old the history of this planet. He knew all about the Fall and the consequent curse. He knew about the wars and famines, the plagues and persecutions, the earthquakes, and the other perils of life down here. He knew the destructive deceiving power of false religion and its terrible history, so full of wickedness and woe. Above all, He knew the horrors of a lost eternity and the dreadful doom of the damned. No wonder Jesus wept—for a lost loved one (John 11:33, 35), for a lost city (Luke 19:41–44), and for a lost world (Luke 22:41–45). And oh! what weeping it was (Heb. 5:7). Jesus found little down here at which to laugh. Sin (as the prophet Hosea makes clear) breaks not only God's laws but also His heart.

And always before Him was the shadow of an accursed cross on a skull-shaped hill outside a city wall. No wonder Paul warned his friends at Ephesus against "foolish . . . jesting, which [is] not convenient" (i.e., not fitting) (Eph. 5:4).

The third woe is directed against those who are *popular* in this life: "Woe unto you, when all men shall speak well of you! for so did their fathers to the false prophets" (6:26). We can be sure that if all men praise us, we have not touched the raw places in their consciences. We have not denounced their favorite sins. We are in danger of endorsing their sins by our silence. Note the contrast of John the Baptist's lifestyle and lack of popularity.

(c) Unusual behavior (6:27–49)

Next, the Lord addressed the matter of a believer's behavior. He begins with the kind of behavior that we should exhibit *toward our foes*. The driving force behind our Lord's behavior in all places at all times under all circumstances was love. What was true of Him should be true of us. He said, "I say unto you which hear, Love your enemies, do good to them which hate you, bless them that curse you, and pray for them which despitefully use you" (6:27–28).

That was Jesus' way. He loved Judas as much as He loved John, Pilate as much as He loved Peter, and Annas as much as He loved Andrew. He loved the man who plowed His back with that terrible scourge. He died for the man who crowned Him with thorns and prayed for those who nailed Him to the tree.

And for our part, how should we react toward those who smite us and those who steal from us? "Unto him that smiteth thee on the one cheek offer also the other; and him that taketh away thy cloak [mantle] forbid not to take thy coat also" (6:29). Both Jesus and Paul rebuked those who struck them contrary to the law (John 18:22–23; Acts 23:3), but in neither case did they strike back. This reaction is in marked contrast to the principle behind the Mosaic Law, which called for an eye for an eye, a tooth for a tooth, and a blow for a blow (see Exod. 21:23–25).

The Lord next spoke of the kind of behavior that we should exhibit *toward our fellows* (6:30–40). The Lord's great expectation from His disciples was simple but revolutionary: "Give to every man that asketh of thee; and of him that taketh away thy goods ask them not again" (6:30). Love looks with compassion on beggar and burglar alike. Our material possessions are temporal. Their real value lies in our using them for the glory of God—or in losing them in the same spirit. Our supreme example is Jesus Himself. Can we imagine His turning a cold shoulder to a man in need or pursuing to the full extent of the law someone who had stolen from Him—Judas, for instance?

Next, Luke records one of the most famous of the Lord's sayings: "As ye would that men should do to you, do ye also to them likewise" (6:31). We call this the "Golden Rule." It is the law of love reduced to its simplest terms; even a child can understand it. If it were universally practiced, it would usher in the Millennium and turn this planet into a paradise. It would end all wars; banish all poverty; dissolve all courts of law; revolutionize all halls of learning; cure all sicknesses; end all immorality, drunkenness, gambling, and drug addiction; dissolve all crime syndicates and street gangs; and end all unfairness, inequality, and injustice. The only problem is to practice it, which requires a new heart, one that is regenerated and indwelt by the Holy Spirit.

The Lord's demands here are revolutionary indeed. He is calling for behavior that is far beyond the normal (6:32–38). He points out that even sinners respond to gracious, good, and generous overtures extended to them. There is no particular virtue in being kind to those who are kind to us; even sinners can do that.

Then comes another of the Lord's now-famous sayings, although this one is often quoted out of context: "Judge not, and ye shall not be judged" (6:37a). The Lord does not forbid us to use common sense and discernment in our lives down here. We must judge and condemn many teachings and philosophies. The Lord here calls on us to avoid that censorious spirit that attacks the motives of others. The Pharisees were given to that kind of thing. They were forever judging the

Lord because He refused to be penned in by their religious rules. On the contrary, we must be generous to our foes: "Condemn not, and ye shall not be condemned: forgive, and ye shall be forgiven" (6:37b). And we must be generous with our funds: "Give, and it shall be given unto you; good measure, pressed down, and shaken together, and running over, shall men give into your bosom. For with the same measure that ye mete [measure] withal it shall be measured to you again" (6:38). The person who has a generous spirit makes many friends, warms hearts, and is liked by one and all. How the Lord hates stinginess!

The Lord rounded out this series of statements regarding our behavior toward our fellows with a down-to-earth analogy: "Can the blind lead the blind? shall they not both fall into the ditch? The disciple is not above his master: but every one that is perfect shall be as his master" (6:39–40). Evidently, the Lord had the Pharisees in mind here. They thought that they had a monopoly on divine truth, whereas they were, in fact, blind. They had mean little souls and could not lift their disciples into a victorious living of which they themselves were ignorant.

By contrast, those who followed Him would avoid the peril of the ditch because He taught truth with authority from on high. He was a Master worth following. One wonders how the Lord's new apostles responded to all of these teachings. They had never heard teaching like this!

But there was more. Next, the Lord dealt with the kind of behavior that we should exhibit *toward our faults* (6:41–45). There was, first, the matter of *criticism* (6:42–45). There was the person who saw a small splinter of wood in his brother's eye. He failed to see that he had a whole plank of wood in his own eye! Ignorant of his own problem, he offered to pull the splinter from his brother's eye when he, himself, was nearly blinded by the plank in his own eye! Jesus called this person a hypocrite (6:42). How swift we are to see even the smallest blemishes in other people while being blind to the glaring and obvious faults that we ourselves exhibit. The Lord here employed irony to emphasize His abhorrence of hypocrisy. The parable comes as close to sarcasm as anything we find in Scripture. Elijah employed similar sarcasm in his contest with the Baal cult on Mount Carmel (1 Kings 18:26–27).

Then, too, there was the matter of *corruption:* "A good tree bringeth not forth corrupt fruit; neither doth a corrupt tree bring forth good fruit. For every tree is known by his own fruit" (6:43–44). The application was obvious. A good man brings forth that which is good; an evil man brings forth evil from his evil heart. "Of the abundance of the heart his mouth speaketh" (6:45). We do what we do because we are what we are. The Lord, while expounding these obvious contrasts, put an unerring finger on the crux of the matter. It is usually easy to tell what a person is like by listening to what he says. He will always, sooner or later, irrevocably betray himself. He will declare himself to be regenerate or unregenerate, spiritual or carnal, godly or worldly, clever or ignorant, wise or foolish, or good or bad.

Finally, the Lord spoke of the kind of behavior we should exhibit *toward our faith* (6:46–49). Few people can stand long in the glare of this sermon. Its bright light dazzles us. We stand exposed before the all-seeing eye of God. The Lord here gives us a threefold look at our faith.

First, there is *the test of a confessed faith:* "And why call ye me, Lord, Lord, and do not the things which I say?" (6:46). We must have a belief that behaves.

The British form of government is unusual. It is known as a constitutional monarchy. In the old days, kings wielded considerable power, but with the passing of time Parliament cut increasingly into "the divine right of kings" to wield absolute power until now all that remains is a monarchy that has virtually no political power. The British have a sovereign who sits in splendor on the throne, but all decisions are made by Parliament. The reigning monarch's function is reduced to signing into law decrees voted into being by the people. In a constitutional monarchy, a king sits upon a throne and a representative government makes all of the decisions.

Many Christians try to set up just such a constitutional monarchy in their hearts. They are quite willing to own Jesus as King—as long as they can run their own affairs and make all of the decisions. They say, "Lord, Lord," but then they proceed to please themselves. The Lord will have none of it.

Next, there is *the triumph of a correct faith:* "Whosoever cometh to me, and heareth my sayings, and doeth them, I will show you to whom he is like: He is like a man which built an house, and digged deep, and laid the foundation on a rock." The Lord used the word *vehemently* to describe the onslaught of wind and wave. It is one of Luke's medical words. It is the usual word for a rupture. Tests do come. They come to put the foundation to the test and to expose it for what sort it is.

Finally, there is *the tragedy of a counterfeit faith:* "But he that heareth, and doeth not, is like a man that without a foundation built an house upon the earth" (6:49). The storm came. The house collapsed.

In both cases, there was a readiness to hear. The difference lay in what they did in response to what they heard. The person who listens to the Lord and is content with simply giving intellectual assent to the truth is on dangerous ground.

He is building for eternity on shifting sand. The person who takes the Lord's words to heart and acts upon them, however, is on the solid rock. Happy is he!

So there it is. Two men—both are builders, and both are willing to hear Christ. One is sincere, but the other isn't. The test comes. One falls; the other remains unshaken. Which am I?

The focus returns to Christ—dynamic in His words but also:

b. Dynamic in His works (7:1–17)

Luke now shows us the Lord Jesus triumphant over all. First, *distance could not hinder Him* (7:1–10). Our attention is drawn to *the setting:* "When he had ended all his sayings in the audience of the people, he entered into Capernaum" (7:1). That township was where Jesus now made His home. The Lord performed many of His miracles in Capernaum. There He healed a nobleman's son, a demoniac in the synagogue, Peter's mother-in-law, a paralytic, and a woman with a constant hemorrhage. There He also raised the daughter of Jairus. There He healed numerous others.

Capernaum lay in one of the lake's small bays. It was in the path of sudden storms that lashed the bay. From Capernaum, one could see up and down the twelve-mile length of the lake as well as across the half-dozen miles to the other side—where the feeding of the five thousand took place. Just two miles away, the Jordan flowed into the lake. Snow-capped Hermon was in full view to the north. A Roman garrison and an important customshouse were located in the town. Near the shore was a synagogue. Jesus once described that town as being "exalted up to heaven." There Peter lived, and there Matthew became a disciple.

And there lived *the soldier* (7:2–8). In the Gospels and the book of Acts, we meet a number of centurions, all of them honorably mentioned. The pagan world was filled with the wreckage of its moral institutions. The Roman army was one of the few such institutions left in which some of the old virtues still survived. This particular centurion was born a heathen but had strong leanings toward Judaism. Many thoughtful Gentiles were completely disillusioned with the shallowness, immorality, and spiritual bankruptcy of pagan religions. Such people, like this centurion, felt attracted to the high moral and religious standards of the Jewish faith. They balked, however, at having to submit to the Jewish initiation rite of circumcision and held out against the Jewish dietary laws. And, often enough, the exclusiveness, bigotry, and hypocrisy of the Jews were further deterrents to Gentiles considering whether to become proselytes.

The centurion had a slave of whom he was very fond but who was seriously ill. The centurion decided to appeal to Jesus, but because he was a Gentile, he decided he needed a mediator. He appealed to the local Jewish elders. They were willing to take up his case because this Gentile not only loved the Jewish people but also had actually built the local Jews a synagogue. The elders came to Jesus and urged Him to act on this soldier's behalf.

Thus, Luke brings in the Savior (7:6). "Jesus went with them," he says. He was not far from the centurion's house when the centurion sent a message to Jesus. "I'm not worthy You should enter my house," he said. "Nor do I think myself fit to come to You. I am a soldier, under authority and entrusted with authority. I order my soldiers to go here and there and they do what I say. Such is the power of my word. I believe You have only to speak a word of command and all will be well."

What a remarkable statement! The elders of the synagogue said, "He is worthy." The centurion said, "I am not worthy." He had evidently been having second thoughts about sending the delegation to plead his cause. They would plead his merits, and that would never do. "I am not worthy," he said. No one can approach God on the ground of personal merits.

"Say the word and my servant shall be healed!" Jesus did not have to be physically present to perform a miracle. Distance was no obstacle to Him.

Which brings us to *the Savior.* "When Jesus heard these things, he marvelled." He turned around and said, "I say unto you, I have not found so great faith, no, not in Israel" (7:9). Thus, we have three estimates of this Gentile Roman soldier. The Jewish authorities said, "He is worthy." The centurion said, "I am not worthy." Jesus said, "I have not found so great faith."

Then comes *the sequel:* "And they that were sent, returning to the house, found the servant whole that had been sick" (7:10). The word for "whole" here is another of Luke's medical words. It means "to be in good health." The man, moments before, had been down at death's door. Now he was the picture of good health. A remarkable cure indeed! Paul later declared that "neither height, nor depth can separate us from the love of God which is in Christ Jesus our Lord (Rom. 8:38–39).

So, then, distance could not hinder Him. Luke now shows that *death could not thwart Him* (7:11–17). Jesus raised the dead on three different occasions. He raised a young girl of twelve who had only just died as He approached where she lived. He raised the young man of whom Luke tells us here, a man on his way to the tomb. And He raised Lazarus, a man dead and buried for several days and whose body was already in the process of decomposition. Jesus broke up every funeral He attended.

First, Luke notes *the Lord's coming* (7:11–12). "And it came to pass the day after, that he went into a city called Nain." It was about two dozen miles from Capernaum, a long day's walk. It would likely be late afternoon when Jesus and His followers arrived at Nain. The road came from the northeast by way of Endor. The cemetery was about a ten-minute walk to the east of the town. It was the longest walk the poor widow had ever taken. Nain was only a short distance from Endor. To the west stood the hills beyond which lay the Lord's boyhood home of Nazareth. To the south was Shunem and the famous Plain of Jezreel. Every direction was full of history.

Luke next mentions the crowd, some from Capernaum, others possibly from points along the way. As they approached the gate of the city, they met a funeral procession coming out of Nain. The widow had rent her upper garment as custom required. The youthful corpse had been washed, anointed, and wrapped in a shroud. The widow had secured the services of a couple of flute players and an official mourner as custom decreed. "Alas for the lion! Alas for the hero!" They wailed the words aloud. The body itself was in an open coffin, probably with the face covered. Neighbors and friends in bare feet took turns carrying the bier, making frequent stops so that as many people as possible could share in the task. Lamentations arose at each stop. Behind the coffin walked the relatives and friends.

The two processions met. One was led by the angel of death, the other by the Lord of life. The two groups met at the gate. One procession would have to give way. Custom decreed that the funeral procession be given right of way and that the others join in the journey to the grave.

Luke now tells us of *the Lord's compassion* (7:13–15). When the Lord saw the widow, His heart went out to her. "Weep not!" He said. To tell a widow on the way to the graveyard to bury her only son and support would have been cheap and flippant coming from anyone else. But one word from Him and distance would be abolished again. The vast gulf that divides the living from the dead would be spanned.

Then He made His move: "He came and touched the bier: and they that bare him stood still." Then He spoke to the dead man. "Young man, I say unto thee, Arise!" Immediately, the dead man sat up and began to speak. Then Jesus handed over the young man to his mother. On the three occasions when the Lord raised the dead, He talked to the dead as though they could hear. To Jairus's daughter

He said, "Damsel, I say unto thee, Arise!" To this young man He said, "Young man, I say unto thee, Arise!" To Lazarus He said, "Lazarus, come forth!"

Not far from Nain was the ancient village of Endor. In the days of King Saul, a witch lived there. She was supposed to be able to talk with the dead—something that the law of God forbade (Exod. 22:18; Deut. 18:9–12). As his last and fatal battle approached, Saul was in despair. The prophet Samuel was dead, and God no longer spoke to Saul. Saul desperately needed advice. Finding the door of heaven closed to him, Saul went to Endor and knocked on the door of hell. He demanded that the witch do something that she could not do—commune with the dead. People who tamper with spiritism imagine that they are talking with departed loved ones; in fact, they are in communication with evil spirits (1 Sam. 28:6–25).

Possibly the Lord had this incident in mind when He came past Endor on His way to Nain. He was going to do what no witch or medium can do—speak to a dead man. He spoke to him as though he were right there.

News of this mighty miracle spread far and wide. The people from Capernaum must have thought it well worthwhile to have walked all of that way to see such a miracle! It was the experience of a lifetime. Those who saw it probably were still talking about it when Luke came doing research for his book. He records for us the reaction at the time: "And there came a fear on all: and they glorified God, saying, That a great prophet is risen up among us; and, That God hath visited his people" (7:16). Theirs was far too small a view of Jesus; He was much more than a prophet.

Finally, there is a word about Judea: "And this rumour [report] of him went forth throughout all Judea, and throughout all the region round about" (7:17). News of it even reached the capital.

c. Dynamic in His ways (7:18–35)
    (1) Perfecting John's faith (7:18–23)

Meanwhile, John the Baptist was still languishing in Herod's prison for his daring denunciation of Herod Antipas for having stolen his brother's wife. John was incarcerated in the virtually impregnable fortress of Machaerus. The castle towered over town and countryside. It was surrounded by massive walls and flanked by towering bastions. Within was Herod's luxurious palace. Its dungeon was deep, and in that terrible prison lay John the Baptist.

A year and a half had passed since John had presented Jesus to Israel as the promised Messiah. But nothing had changed. The Romans still held the country.

Corruption in court and temple remained unchanged. The Herods still triumphed. The hypocritical scribes and Pharisees still sought the chief seats in the synagogue, and the Sadducees still spread their unbelief.

John was discouraged. Perhaps he had made a mistake. Perhaps Jesus was not the Messiah. John somehow doubtless kept informed about the Lord's ministry, movements, and miracles. That was all well and good, but when was He going to make a move to seize the throne (7:18)? John sent a couple of his own loyal disciples to put the question to Him as bluntly as possible—"Are you the One that is to come? Or are we to look for someone else?"

The delegation arrived at an opportune time. "In that same hour he cured many of their infirmities and plagues, and of evil spirits; and unto many that were blind he gave sight" (7:21). The key word is *many!* The people came in droves, bringing their "infirmities" (chronic diseases) and their "plagues" (acute scourges)—Luke uses precise medical terms—and one and all, then and there, openly and unquestionably, He healed them. People who were possessed by evil spirits joined the parade. The word for "evil" used to describe the demons carries the idea of malignant evil that causes pain and sorrow. When used as a noun, it is used of Satan, the Evil One.

Evil spirits seem to have infested Palestine in the days of Jesus. It is as though Satan marshaled all of his forces against Christ. The same kind of feverish demon activity is to be the hallmark of the end times (1 Tim. 4:1; 2 Thess. 2:3–10). It is becoming an increasing characteristic of our day. The demons were no match for Jesus. They fled at His command. John's disciples were awed at this extraordinary demonstration of divine power.

That was the answer John's disciples were to carry back to the troubled forerunner. "Go your way, and tell John what things ye have seen and heard; how that the blind see, the lame walk, the lepers are cleansed, the deaf hear, the dead are raised, to the poor the gospel is preached. And blessed is he, whosoever shall not be offended in me" (7:22–23). Who but God incarnate could do what Jesus did?

The Lord did not explain why, with all power at His command, He did not instantly free His faithful ambassador. But surely John understood. The kingdom that Jesus had come to establish had both spiritual and temporal dimensions. The Lord turned John's thoughts away from the political and imperial aspects of the kingdom, the aspects most commonly emphasized in the messianic and millennial prophecies of the Old Testament (Isa. 9:6; 11:6; 35:1). The nature of people had to be changed before the nations of the world could be changed.

The Lord was showing His mighty power to heal bodies. It would call for similar power to change hearts. His kingdom, when it came, would be a righteous kingdom based on love, joy, and peace—all of which John knew. As for the imprisonment of John, the Lord urged His dear friend and forerunner not to stumble over that circumstance. He was a prisoner of war! It was a vivid demonstration of the need for repentance that John had so fearlessly preached. He would understand it better by and by.

The Lord was not impressed by the crowds that followed Him. A popularity that rested on miracles was a poor enough thing. The Lord knew that John was soon to be murdered by Herod. But then He Himself was soon to be murdered by Caiaphas and his crowd.

All of which gave the Lord a chance to hammer home some of His own observations about John to the milling crowds (7:24–35). "What went ye out into the wilderness for to see? A reed shaken with the wind?" (7:24). Vast crowds had flocked into the wilderness to hear John preach. What had drawn them was John's sterling character, his boldness in preaching God's Word, and his fearless denunciation of the establishment. It was no feeble reed shaken in the wind, bowing this way and that before this burst of applause and that angry chorus of rage that drew them from their comfortable homes to the inhospitable wilderness.

Nor was he dressed in soft raiment. "Behold," Jesus said, "they which are gorgeously apparelled, and live delicately, are in king's courts" (7:25). John could easily have chosen that kind of life. He had been born into the priestly clan and could have chosen the soft and secure life of a priest. With his drive and determination, he could have become the High Priest and lived in the episcopal palace in Jerusalem. Instead, true to the circumstances of his birth, he chose the lonely, rigorous life of a desert ascetic. Israel, he decided, had priests enough and to spare. What Israel needed was not another priest after the order of Aaron but another prophet after the order of Elijah. Doubtless, some people urged him to work from within the religious establishment, but John had no intention of letting the world pour him into its mold.

(2) Praising John's faithfulness (7:24–35)

The Lord continued His eulogy of His brave and beloved John. He talked about his *calling* (7:26–28). "What did you go out to see?" Jesus demanded for the third time. "A prophet? Yea, I say unto you, and much more than a prophet. This is he, of whom it is written, Behold, I send my messenger before thy face, which shall prepare thy way before thee" (7:26–27). This statement was a quotation from the last of the Old Testament prophets, speaking just before God closed the Old Testament canon with a four hundred-year silence (Mal. 3:1)

The Lord pointed to John's *career* (7:27). More than a prophet! A herald. Multitudes had owned John as prophet, submitting to his baptism. John ranked higher than Moses and Samuel, higher than Elijah and Elisha, and higher than all of the major prophets and the dozen minor prophets. He was greater than the prophets noted for their manuscripts. Greater than those who predicted things and those who proclaimed things! Greater than those who brought revival and those who brought ruin. John was greater than them all. Jesus said so.

Jesus added, "Among those that are born of women there is not a greater prophet than John the Baptist: but he that is least in the kingdom of God is greater than he" (7:28). John stood alone, head and shoulders above everyone else, a prophet without parallel. Praise indeed.

But then comes the astonishing *climax:* "But he that is least in the kingdom of God is greater than he" (7:28). John demanded repentance; Jesus demanded rebirth (John 3:3). Among those who are "born of God," the difference is not one of degree but of kind. The least person who is born again, born of the Spirit, is greater than the greatest unregenerate person alive. The lion is the king of beasts, the greatest in the animal kingdom. But the weakest child born of Adam's race is greater than a lion because he belongs to a different and higher kingdom, a greater and nobler order of creation.

"And all the people that heard him, and the publicans, justified God, being baptized with the baptism of John" (7:29). Such was John's career. That is, they owned God to be right about their sin, their need for repentance, and their need to submit to John's baptism as the token of their repentance. Just the same, it was the common people who accepted God's verdict and who thus vindicated John. The Lord mentions the publicans who repented—the lowest of the low in the thinking of the Jews. Luke mentions John's *critics:* "But the Pharisees and lawyers rejected the counsel of God against themselves, being not baptized of him" (7:30). The Jewish religious authorities turned a deaf ear to John's message. They scorned his baptism and rejected the notion that they, too, needed to repent of their sins. They certainly had no intention of making an exhibition of themselves by being baptized in the river Jordan.

"Whereunto then shall I liken the men of this generation? and to what are they like? They are like unto children sitting in the marketplace, and calling one to another, and saying, We have piped unto you, and ye have not danced; we have mourned to you, and ye have not wept" (7:31–32). The reference is to children quarrelling over their games. One group suggested that they play at weddings. No response. The first group then suggested that they play at funerals. No response! The people of the Lord's generation were like that—uncooperative, out of tune with both John and Jesus, "For John the Baptist came neither eating bread nor drinking wine; and ye say, He hath a devil. The Son of man is come eating and drinking; and ye say, Behold a gluttonous man, and a winebibber, a friend of publicans and sinners!" (7:33–34). They rejected John. They rejected Jesus. "But wisdom is justified of all her children" (7:35). The religious leaders stood exposed by their rejection of both the Baptist and the Christ. It would have been the part of wisdom to take sides with either one or the other. By their refusal to do so, they showed of what sort they were—wedded to their folly. Wisdom's children stood in clear contrast to the Christ-rejecting religious elite who were wedded to their folly.

>   d. Dynamic in His walk (7:36–8:3)
>   (1) Accepting the hospitality of Simon (7:36–50)

The next story is a study in contrasts. There was a sinful woman on one hand and a scornful Pharisee on the other. Only Luke tells this story. We do not know from which of the two people he gleaned this incident. The name Simon is common in the New Testament; we can pick out nine of them, two of whom were apostles. The scene is set in Capernaum.

No group of men was more consistently hostile to Christ than the Pharisees. Luke mentions them twenty-eight times and always as being hostile to Jesus. The woman in this instance was daring in the first place to enter the house of a Pharisee. No people were more proud, exclusive, and self-righteous than the Pharisees. They looked with scorn and contempt on the type of woman who now appeared.

The Lord assuredly knew that He was on hostile ground in Simon's house. But the same love for lost people that brought Him down from high heaven above to this hostile world was the love that took Him into Simon's inhospitable house. The Lord held His peace, but He noted the fact that Simon made no attempt to extend to Him the common courtesies that an Oriental host generally offered guests. Once in the house, the Lord was seated for supper. On such occasions, the various ones present reclined on couches arranged around the table. Each one rested his left elbow on the table with his feet pointed away toward the wall.

Into this private apartment and this hostile environment, the woman came.

She is described as "a woman in the city, which was a sinner" (7:37). She brought with her an alabaster flask of ointment and stood at His feet behind Him weeping. She washed His feet with her tears. She wiped His feet with her hair and kissed His feet and anointed them with ointment (7:37–38). Evidently, this gesture was not an impulsive gesture; it was planned. She had come prepared. As a woman from "across the tracks," she would know what to expect from Simon—bitter scorn from a biting tongue. But she came anyway.

She came because Jesus was there. The likelihood is that she had already met Jesus and that He had forgiven her all of her sins. It was a full heart of love for "the Friend of sinners" that made her dare to enter Simon's hostile house. She had never met a man like Jesus, "holy, harmless, undefiled, separate from sinners" (Heb. 7:26). Other men had looked at her with lust; Jesus looked at her with love, pure and good.

When she arrived at Simon's house and saw the door open, she seized her opportunity and made straight for Jesus' feet. Tears ran down her cheeks and splashed upon His feet. She shook down her hair and dabbed at His feet to dry them. She kissed them and continued kissing them. Then suddenly, mindful of the flask, she broke the seal and poured out the perfume, and the whole room was filled with fragrance (7:38).

Simon was outraged. He held his tongue, but the Lord read his thoughts: "he spake within himself, saying, This man, if he were a prophet, would have known who and what manner of woman this is that toucheth him: for she is a sinner" (7:39). He seems to have derived a sardonic satisfaction from it. It exposed Jesus as a fraud, or so it seemed to him. He had plenty of friends who would be pleased with him for exposing this would-be prophet (7:39).

Little did the man know that the Lord was about to expose *him*. "Jesus answering said unto him," Luke says. The man had said nothing, but Jesus read his thoughts. "I have somewhat to say unto thee."

"Master, say on," Simon said.

Then the Lord told him a story of two debtors. Both people owed money to the same creditor, but one of them owed ten times more than the other one. Both people were bankrupt, and both of them were forgiven their debts. "Which of them will love him most?" Jesus asked.

"I suppose," said Simon cautiously, "that he, to whom he forgave most." The answer was correct though grudgingly given. Simon and the woman were the bankrupts. Simon, for all of his self-righteousness, was just as hopelessly in sin's debt as the woman he despised (7:40–43).

Then the Lord exposed the man as a hypocrite indeed. "Seest thou this woman?" Jesus asked. The expression *this woman* rang out again and again, three times in three verses (7:44–46). The Lord faced her, speaking to Simon over his shoulder. "Seest thou this woman?" Simon had seen nothing else since the moment she burst into the room. The Lord did not attack Simon along the line of his sin, simply along the line of his bad manners. Simon had given Jesus no water for His feet, but this woman had washed them with her tears and wiped them with her hair. Simon had not given Him the common courtesy of a kiss of welcome, but this woman had not ceased kissing His feet. Simon had not anointed His head with oil, as was customary with an honored guest, but this woman had anointed His feet with ointment (7:44–46). Thus, the Lord stabbed Simon to the heart.

"This man! This man!" Simon said.

"This woman! This woman!" Jesus replied.

"He would have known!" Simon said.

But Jesus knew both the woman's contrite heart and the Pharisee's miserable soul. The old nursery rhyme summarizes it:

> Simple Simon met a pie man
> going to the Fair.
> Said Simple Simon to the pie man
> "Let me taste your ware."
> Said the pie man to Simple Simon,
> "Show me first your penny."
> Said Simple Simon to the pie man,
> "Sir, I have not any!"

Maybe they were brothers! In any case, sinful Simon was as bankrupt as that "Simple Simon" we met in the nursery rhyme when we were young. The pie man soon took Simple Simon's measure. The Lord already had His host's measure. It is well worth noting, as Scofield says, that when the Lord wanted to justify the woman in the eyes of Simon, He looked at her works but when He wanted to send the woman away in peace, He looked at her faith (7:50).

(2) Accepting the help of some (8:1–3)

First, there was *proclamation* (8:1). This trip seems to have taken the Lord as far south as Nain, and it marked a change in His ministry because He no longer confined Himself to Capernaum. Luke seems to have picked up his narrative with the return journey, which has taken Him to the farthest boundary of Galilee. The Lord had been accompanied by His twelve disciples along with a number of women who gave of their substance to help finance His work.

He went everywhere, Luke says, proclaiming "the glad tidings of the kingdom of God" (8:1). This view is a much broader concept than Matthew's "kingdom of heaven." Matthew wrote primarily for Jewish readers interested in the establishment of God's kingdom on earth. The expression "kingdom of God" includes that concept, but it is much broader. The coming of the Son of God meant that God had stepped back into the arena of human affairs. Help has arrived from on high. The usurper's days are numbered. That is very good news indeed.

A person has to be born into the kingdom of God (John 3:3, 7). The kingdom of heaven as detailed in the "mystery parables" (Matt. 13:1–58) is temporal, contains discordant elements, and will continue to do so until it has fulfilled its role in history. The kingdom of God is spiritual; the kingdom of heaven is imperial. The kingdom of God is eternal; the kingdom of heaven is millennial.

The Lord's method of making known the Good News was by *proclamation*. The Greek word comes from the word for a herald. It does not embrace the idea of teaching. Jesus marched through the towns and villages of His native land with a proclamation. God has not invited us to come and discuss His glad tidings; we are simply to accept them and proclaim them.

Then there was *provision* (8:2–3). Here He was, the Lord of glory, the Creator and Sustainer of the universe, the One who had the means to spread a banquet in the wilderness, to command stones to be turned into bread, or to change water into wine. He was the incarnate Son of God, yet He was totally dependent for His livelihood on the freewill offerings of His friends. Jesus was poor. For years, He had been a village carpenter. Now He had given up even that occupation. Moreover, He had a dozen men who looked to Him for all of their needs. He, in turn, looked to His Father in heaven. And to complete the circle of the astonishing, His was a Father to whom such women as the ones Luke mentions here turned. These women became His "mothers" and His "sisters." All of the women to whom Luke specifically refers had desperate needs of their own. They were women who had been "healed of evil spirits and infirmities."

Three of the women are named: "Mary called Magdalene, out of whom went seven devils, and Joanna the wife of Chuza Herod's steward, and Susanna . . ." (8:3). Of these three, we know Mary Magdalene best. She seems to have come from Magdala, a village on the western shore of the Sea of Galilee. That village was noted for its dye works, woolen goods, and trade in the pigeons and doves needed for the sacrificial offerings as required under the Mosaic Law. Magdala, moreover, was also known for its moral corruption. Mary grew up in that place and fell prey to evil spirits. Her case was hopeless—until Jesus came and set her free. She became the Lord's devoted follower.

All we know of Joanna is that she was the wife of a court official—some scholars think that he was the man whose son Jesus had healed with a word at Cana (John 4:46–54). In any case, Chuza was connected with Herod Antipas. Some people have suggested that it was Joanna who quickened Herod's interest in Jesus.

As for Susanna, all we know about her is her name. It means "lily." Jesus said that a lily is arrayed in splendor far beyond the glorious raiments that Solomon wore.

Luke says that there were "many others" in addition to these three women. In the crowning day, when the books are opened and the names are read aloud, these women will receive their reward, as will all of those who have followed in their path.

> e. Dynamic in His wisdom (8:4–21)
> > (1) Understanding the hearts of men (8:4–18)

The Lord now unfolds two parables. The first one was *a parable about fruit bearing* (8:4–15). The ever-expanding nature of the Lord's ministry at this time caused Him no illusions. The two parables recorded here are rooted in the increased popular attention that was coming His way. He knew that it was superficial.

The first parable is the well-known one about the sower, the seed, and the soil. The same parable with variations occurs elsewhere. The version that Luke recorded here was given as the Lord was making His way toward Capernaum near the end of His tour. The use of parables marks a new phase in the Lord's teaching ministry. He increasingly resorted to parables as much to conceal truth as to reveal it. Opposition to His preaching was on the rise. The "Galilean revival" had ended. When the Lord left Capernaum to carry His message farther afield, the enthusiasm was at its peak. The Lord was too wise, however, to think that it could last—hence, this parable, which emphasizes the factors that hinder the germination, growth, and fruitfulness of the Word once it is sown, and also the factors that expose the human heart for what it is.

The crowds were flocking from the cities all over the land. The disciples doubtless thought that things were on the move at last, but Jesus knew better. The time had come to sift the crowds.

"A sower," He said, "went out to sow his seed" (8:5). It was a common enough sight to see a sower, a bag of seed looped around his neck, tossing the seed here and there. No sower, however optimistic, could expect *every* seed to bring forth fruit. Some seed fell by the wayside and was trodden down and devoured by the birds. Some seed fell on a rock, showed initial promise, but soon withered away for lack of moisture and depth. Some seed fell among thorns, which choked it. Some seed, however, fell on good ground, sprang to life, and bare fruit an hundredfold.

There it was, the wayside, hardened by the constant tramp of hoof and paw and foot, of no use at all for sowing seed. There, too, were the outcroppings of rock, indicating a rock shelf beneath a shallow layer of soil, soil so thin that it could not be plowed, so thin that rain falling on it would dry up or drain away. Other soil was infested with thorns of various sorts and sizes. To the sower's joy, still other ground comprised deep, rich, productive, fertile soil.

To ensure that everyone got the point, Jesus raised His voice: "He that hath ears to hear, let him hear" (8:8). Only the Lord used this expression, and He used it on seven different occasions (Matt. 11:15; 13:9, 43; Mark 4:12; 7:16; Luke 8:8; 14:35) while down here and eight times after His resurrection (Rev. 2:7, 11, 17, 29; 3:6, 13, 22; 13:9). The first use of the expression warns us against careless hearing of the Word of God. The final use warns against worshiping the Antichrist. The one instance shows where unbelief begins; the other instance shows where it ends.

The Lord then turned away from the careless crowds and addressed His disciples, who asked Him the meaning of the parable (8:9). They were puzzled. The Lord gave them an expanded commentary. There was, first of all, the problem soil. There was no problem with the seed because, as Jesus said, "The seed is the word of God" (8:11), primarily a reference to His own teaching, teaching that was saturated with Old Testament quotations and allusions. The seed was good seed, bursting with life awaiting germination by faith (Heb. 4:2).

The *problem* was all with the soil (the roadside soil, the rocky soil, and the ruined soil) just as the *potential* was all in the receptive soil.

We note the *demonic factor* in the roadside soil. "Those by the way side are they that hear; then cometh the devil, and taketh away the word of their hearts, lest they should believe and be saved" (8:12). There are the disturbances that detract even while the preacher is proclaiming the Word. There is the immediate roar of small talk the moment the benediction is announced. There is the critical dissection of the preacher at home around the kitchen table. Satan is busy snatching away the seed.

We note also the *disappointment factor* in the rocky soil, the factor of unbelief. "They hear, receive the word with joy," Jesus said, "and these have no root, which for a while believe, and in time of temptation fall away" (8:13). Although they show immediate promise, underneath their hearts are of stone, worse than the soil by the roadside. They come forward when the invitation is given. They say the right words, pray an appropriate prayer, start to attend church, and rejoice in their new family of friends. But it is all very disappointing before long. The truth takes no real root in their hearts. Come the first breath of opposition or disagreement, off they go. They *professed* Christ but never *possessed* Christ in their hearts.

The *deterring factor,* so characteristic of the ruined soil, is the presence of thorns and thistles. They are already in place waiting to choke the life from the seed as soon as it is sown. The people depicted here have divided hearts. The Word of God is eagerly received and shows all of the early signs of having genuinely taken root. However, what these people really want are the material benefits of the faith rather than the spiritual blessings. They imagine that becoming a believer will guarantee wealth, health, and a joyride to heaven on flowery beds of ease. When these things fail to materialize, they drift away. The "cares of this world" overwhelm the poor, the "deceitfulness of riches" snare those who have great wealth, and "pleasure" becomes an end in itself for the affluent (8:14). Worry, wealth, and worldliness are all enemies of the gospel. The Lord says of such that they give some place to the Word when they hear it, but then they "go forth," and it is choked. The word that the Lord used describes the bustle of an active life and the coming and going of people who are transacting business. In other words, they profess faith in Christ, but then it is "business as usual." This world remains the predominant factor in the equation of life. They love this world rather than the world to come.

In contrast to the poor ground is the good ground: "they, which in an honest and good heart, having heard the word, keep it, and bring forth fruit with patience" (8:15). The word for "keep" can be rendered "hold fast." The Lord demands a response of some sort to the proclamation of His Word. Honesty and openness will result in God's Word taking permanent root in a human heart. Demonic activity, shallowness, materialism, and ulterior motives are primary causes for hearing God's Word in vain.

Soil can usually be improved. No sower scatters seed on soil that has not been plowed and harrowed. Hard hearts can be softened. False beliefs can be uprooted. God's kindness shows Him how to break up the soil of a human soul.

Let's take one last look at these soils. The first kind of hearer is illustrated by the scribes and Pharisees, who "rejected the counsel of God against themselves" (Luke 7:30). Judas, Herod, and Pilate belong to the same terrible company. The second kind of hearer is illustrated by Demas, who abandoned Paul in his hour of need when the going got tough. The Lord had His share of those who "went back, and walked no more with him" (John 6:66). The third kind of hearer is illustrated by the rich young ruler (Matt. 19:22). The fourth kind of hearer is illustrated by the Lord's own disciples, Nicodemus, Joseph of Arimathea, Cornelius, and the various Marys.

The Lord next gave *a parable about light bearing* (8:16–18). The Lord was still speaking to His own. Parables were not intended to conceal the truth from them. His explanation of the parable of the sower shows how plain and simple even His teaching in parables can be to those who love Him and are willing to heed well what He says.

"No man, when he hath lighted a candle, covereth it with a vessel, or putteth it under a bed," Jesus said, "but setteth it on a candlestick, that they which enter in may see the light" (8:16). The "candle" here was simply a saucer filled with oil in which was placed a wick. "For nothing is secret, that shall not be made manifest; neither any thing hid, that shall not be known and come abroad" (8:17). The Lord lit the lamp. When the disciples paid proper attention to the Lord's teaching, even His parables, everything was made clear unto them. Jesus added a warning: "Take heed therefore how ye hear: for whosoever hath, to him shall be given." Light begets more light. We get more and more light as we respond to the light. The opposite is also true; the light fades from those who handle it carelessly. Error creeps in, and darkness descends (8:17–18).

(2) Understanding the heart of Mary (8:19–21)

About this time, Mary, the Lord's mother, came to see Him, and she brought the boys of the family with her. "Then came to him his mother and his brethren, and could not come at him for the press. And it was told him by certain which said, Thy mother and thy brethren stand without, desiring to see thee." The throngs that surrounded the Lord made it virtually impossible for Mary and her boys to get close to Him. Naturally, they tried sending a message. The sacred ties of family would surely secure the visit they desired.

Mark's gospel fills in many of the details. The Lord's enemies accounted for His extraordinary life by accusing Him of being demon controlled. His natural family decided that something would have to be done. The Lord's brothers did not believe in Him. At first, they were possibly proud of Him as well as being astonished at His miracles and revolutionary teaching. Israel had seen and heard nothing like it. When the establishment turned hostile and consummated its opposition by blasphemy, accusing Him of being hand in glove with Beelzebub, the prince of demons, however, the family became alarmed. They decided that something must be done to protect Him from Himself and, equally to the point, to protect the family from the long arm of the Sanhedrin. They decided to go and see Him. They would persuade Him to come home, or, failing that, they would force Him to come with them.

The Lord saw through it at once. Doubtless, too, He was sorry to see His mother mixed up in this sad affair. So when the news came that His mother and brothers had come to see Him, He ignored them. Or, rather, He used the occasion to make an announcement: "My mother and my brethren are these which hear the word of God, and do it" (8:21). As strong and sacred as human ties of love should be, the ties that unite believers in Christ are greater far. They are forged not by natural birth but by spiritual birth, forged by our hearing of and our response to the Word of God (8:21).

> f. Dynamic in His will (8:22–9:17)
> (1) The stilling of the tempest (8:22–25)

Luke now introduces a series of five pictures that illustrate the Lord's absolute sovereignty over various circumstances. He is indeed a dynamic Savior, the One who can still the storm.

The story begins with the simple suggestion that He and the disciples sail across the Sea of Galilee to the other side. He fell asleep on board the boat. Then came the fearful storm, and soon the boat was awash with water and about to sink (8:22). Satan was behind that howling wind and those heaving waves. What a way to get rid of Jesus once and for all—drown Him! The Sea of Galilee is susceptible to sudden tempests born in the hills and valleys all around the shore. The Lord, of course, was familiar with the treacherous storms that plagued the lake. He knew, too, what Satan was up to. Neither one nor the other bothered Him at all.

So the storm came, and the boat was in jeopardy. But as the old hymn "Master, the Tempest Is Raging" by Mary Baker (music by Horatio Palmer) puts it,

No waters can swallow the ship where lies
The Master of ocean, and earth, and skies.

The Lord slept on much to the disciples' unease. At last, the boat being in imminent danger of sinking, they burst in upon Him with the words, "Master, master, we perish!" (8:24). They had seen Him rise to every occasion, subdue every terror, and solve every problem. Was He up to this challenge? Of course He was! We don't know what they expected Him to do. He stood to His feet and spoke with sharp rebuke to the wind and the tumultuous waves. "And there was a calm" (8:24). The wind ceased. The waves hushed to rest. Calm descended on the lake.

Of particular interest is the word *rebuked*. Except for two occasions (2 Tim. 4:2; Jude 9), use of this word is restricted to the Synoptic Gospels. It is frequently employed in the Lord's dealings with evil spirits, a fact that adds credence to the idea that Satan was the one who stirred up this particular storm. All it took was a word from the Lord, and Satan was stopped in his tracks.

As for the disciples, they were overcome with awe. It dawned on them that between Him and them there was a great gulf.

(2) The saving of the terrorist (8:26–39)

Our attention is directed now to a *maniac* (8:26–29). The man terrorized the neighborhood. Parents dared not let their children out of their sight. Women were confined to the village within call of help. Strongmen venturing beyond the village went in armed bands. But the dynamic Christ was about to change all that.

The Lord and His disciples finished their journey across the lake and "arrived at the country of the Gadarenes, which is over against Galilee" (8:26). Authorities differ as to the exact location of the place. Gerasa (Gersa) meets the requirements. A short walk south of the town is a steep bluff that descends abruptly onto a narrow ledge of shore. A terrified herd running down this cliff and unable to stop would be hurled into the lake. The surrounding countryside, likewise, suits the story because it is riddled with limestone caverns and rock chambers suitable for burying the dead. The demon-possessed man lived in such a place.

Luke describes the plight of this wretched man. He was possessed by demons, wore no clothes, and had his dwelling in the tombs. He lived in the suburbs of hell, demented, and beyond all human help. Moreover, he had been in this condition for a long time. His nakedness was the badge of his condition, beyond all shame. Cut off from all social contact, he lived in the local cemetery, a halfway house on his journey to the grave (8:27).

Moreover, he was hopelessly disoriented—a mark of demon possession as distinct from ordinary insanity. An insane person might imagine himself to be Julius Caesar, a poached egg, or a man from Mars. A demoniac is actually indwelt by alien personalities. We note in the ensuing dialogue the voice of the demoniac and the voice of the demons. At times, it is difficult to discern which of many voices is speaking, seizing and using the poor man's faculties as its own (8:28).

Demons are to be distinguished from fallen angels, some of which are high ranking in Satan's hierarchy (Dan. 10:13–21; Eph. 6:11–12; Col. 2:15). Demons are uniformly described as wicked spirits and are always depicted as vile, fierce, wholly without pity, and driven by a craving to seize and use human bodies. Once they take up residence in a human body, they invade the personality and become exceedingly difficult to expel (Matt. 17:14–21; Acts 19:13–17). They know Christ, however, as this demoniac reveals. "What have I to do with thee, Jesus, thou Son of God most high?" (8:28). One of the Lord's titles was "Son of the Highest" (Luke 1:32). Similarly, the demon-possessed prophetess at Philippi kept saying, "These men (Paul and Silas) are the servants of the most high God" (Acts 16:17).

When Jesus commanded the evil spirits to come out of the man (8:29), they pleaded for Him not to torment them, doubtless expecting Him to cast them at once into the lake of fire. They slandered Christ, who had come not to torment them—their time would come—but to release their poor human captive, whom they tormented mercilessly.

Luke notes, too, that the man was out of all control. He simply snapped the chains and fetters put upon him after ferocious struggles. "What is thy name?" Jesus demanded of the man, perhaps to remind the poor fellow that he had once answered to a name.

Immediately, the demons seized his tongue. "Legion," they replied, "because many devils were entered into him," Luke says (8:30). A legion in the Roman army numbered six thousand men.

The demons spoke again. They pleaded that He would not command them to go out into the deep (8:31). The word used is *abussos*. It occurs here and in Romans 10:7 as well as seven times in the Apocalypse (Rev. 9:1, 2, 11; 11:17; 17:8; 20:1, 3). The demons were in terror of that place. From that dread place Satan will summon the soul of the Antichrist after his death to give him a copy-cat resurrection (Rev. 17:8). Satan himself will be incarcerated in this fearful abyss during the Lord's millennial reign. The demons are all too aware of this prison and go in terror of it.

The demons spoke again. A herd of many swine was feeding on the mountain. Would He allow them to enter into them rather than to go forth unclothed and naked (8:32)? The Lord gave them what they asked. The swine, however, preferred death to demonism. They rushed down the precipice into the lake and were drowned.

There was a sequel to all of this. The swineherders fled and burst into the city with the news. The terror of the countryside would terrorize it no more. However, someone had lost a lot of money, and that person was furious. People from all over trooped out to the place to see for themselves. Sure enough, there was the former demoniac, "sitting at the feet of Jesus, clothed, and in his right mind: and they were afraid" (8:35). It bespeaks a serious state of soul when people are more afraid of goodness than of wickedness. They were not only afraid but also angry. They had lost a lot of money, and, because they were operating an unclean business, the owners could not hope for any kind of compensation. So they asked Jesus to go away, and He did (8:37).

As He was boarding the boat, however, the transformed man begged Jesus to let him remain with Him. But no! The man was to remain where he was as the Lord's ambassador to his fellow countrymen. Four times the word *besought* is found in this story: the demons besought Him not to send them into the Abyss (8:31), they also besought Him to let them enter into the swine (8:32), the people besought Him to go away (8:33), and the healed demoniac besought Him to let him go away with Him (8:38). All of these prayers were granted, except the last one. Jesus refused the request of the cleansed demoniac. "Go home," He said, for that's the proper place to begin living a new life in Christ. "Show how great things God hath done unto thee." And so he did and with remarkable success (Mark 5:20).

(3) The subjection of the tomb (8:40–56)
(a) A distracted father (8:40–42)

The Lord recrossed the lake to find a welcoming crowd awaiting Him. The underlying thought is that the people had a warm welcome ready for Him. Evidently, a considerable fund of popularity for Jesus still existed in Galilee. The rest of this chapter is taken up with a man, a woman, and a child.

The man was Jairus, well known to Jesus we can be sure because he was a ruler of the synagogue. There were various synagogue officials, of which the "minister" ranked lowest. He often acted in the capacity of the village teacher as well. He was usually chosen with great care. Above him were the elders, or rulers, presided over by the chief of the synagogue. These officials were usually chosen only after being thoroughly examined as to their knowledge. They formed the local Sanhedrin. They were chosen as much for their gentleness and humility as anything else, and they often were chosen by the congregation. The chief of the synagogue, although officially only "the first among equals," often virtually ruled the synagogue. He would superintend the order of service and determine who was to be called to read from the Law and the Prophets, who was to conduct the prayers, and who, if anyone, was to deliver the sermon. Jairus was such a ruler. He seems to have been greatly drawn to Jesus.

We are given a glimpse into Jairus's home. He had "one only daughter, about twelve years of age, and she lay a dying" (8:42). One only daughter! We find here the same note of tenderness that we find in Luke's account of the widow of Nain's son and in the story of the demon-possessed boy (Luke 7:12; 9:38). One only daughter!

She was about twelve. Jesus well remembered when He was twelve (2:42). The young girl took ill. The doctors came, shook their heads, and washed their hands of the case; it was hopeless. As they went out of the house, the distracted father thought of Jesus. He would go to Jesus! Where else could he go? He pushed his way through the throng.

The Lord responded at once to the father's urgent plea. How Jairus must have chafed at the hindering crowd, but Jesus Himself was not disturbed. He would get to Jairus's house in God's good time. God is always right on time. His ways are perfect. He orders the sun, moon, and stars in their journeys with mathematical precision so that we can foretell to the very moment when the sun will rise, the phases of the moon, and the appearing of a comet.

(b) A diseased woman (8:43–48)

The distracted Jairus, however, was not so calm. And as if his frustration with the multitude was not enough, now came another distraction. Luke interrupts the narrative of Jairus and his daughter to mention "a woman having an issue of blood twelve years, which had spent all her living upon physicians, neither could be healed of any" (8:43). Luke, a doctor himself, admitted the limitations of the medical profession and probably knew of people who had bankrupted themselves paying doctors' bills to no avail.

Twelve years! Twelve years of joy and delight for Jairus with his little girl. Twelve years of despair, embarrassment, pain, and loneliness for this long-suffering woman. Her condition branded her unclean under the Mosaic Law, and consequently she was excommunicated (Lev. 15:1–33).

"[She] came behind him." Naturally, she would not want to draw attention to herself. She "touched the border of his garment." The "border" of the Lord's garment was one of the four tassels that were always a part of the Jewish mantle. When worn, the garment was so arranged that one of the tassels hung down over the shoulder at the back. There was a certain distinctiveness about them. Their use was regulated by the Levitical code (Num. 15:38–41; Deut. 22:12). The woman in the story decided to steal up behind Jesus and touch the tassel. She would not touch Him; her touch was a contamination. And she would not even touch His garment, just the tassel. The moment she touched that ornament, she was healed! Power flowed from the Master to the woman. New life from Christ coursed through her veins. She was gloriously set free (8:43–44)!

Immediately, Jesus asked, "Who touched me?"

Instinctively, everybody around denied having touched Him. Peter voiced the general feeling. Why, the whole multitude was thronging Him. How could He ask such a question?

But Jesus was not to be put off. "Somebody hath touched me"—not accidentally but deliberately. Inherent power had been released (8:45–46). He was not, of course, exhausted by it, but He knew that a demand had been made upon His power and that it had cost Him something (8:46).

The woman realized that her cover was blown, and she came trembling to Jesus, fell down before Him, and openly admitted before everyone why she had touched Him and how she had been healed instantly (8:47). It was for her own good that she had been made to come forward. Had she not confessed, she would have been haunted by the fear that she had stolen the blessing. Instead, He sent her home with joy bells ringing in her heart. "Daughter, be of good comfort: thy faith hath made thee whole; go in peace" (8:48).

(c) A dead child (8:49–56)

All this while, Jairus had been standing there on tenterhooks. His daughter was *dying*. Why all of this delay? He must have wrung his hands, paced on ahead, and then come back again, unable to stand still and barely able to stand the strain. Then came the crushing news that he had been half expecting. Someone from home came hurrying to him and said, "Thy daughter is dead; trouble not the Master" (8:49).

Not only was his daughter dead but also all of Jairus's hope was dead. All that he could do now was arrange for the funeral.

The Lord heard the sad news and read Jairus's despair. "Fear not," He said, "believe only, and she shall be made whole" (8:50). Death did not trouble Jesus any more than disease. The Lord called upon the man to trust Him absolutely. "Fear not"—a word to still that fear; "believe only"—a word to secure his future. Beautiful words! Wonderful words! Wonderful words of life! How those words must have marched alongside Jairus to the end of his days: Fear not! Believe only! She shall be made whole! Who but God incarnate could speak such words? People often try to encourage someone who is caught up in a great trouble by saying, "Everything is going to be all right!" The value of that remark depends on who is making it. Often it is nothing more than optimism. But when Jesus says it— "Everything is going to be all right"—that settles it because He is God overall, blessed for evermore.

The scene shifts to Jairus's house. The Lord allowed only Peter, James, John, and the child's parents to accompany Him into the death chamber. The ragtag and bobtail of hired mourners, probably summoned earlier to be in attendance the moment death occurred, were firmly shut out. Jesus told them to quit their crying and lamenting. "She is not dead, but sleepeth," Jesus said.

"They laughed him to scorn." Luke used two words, the one signifying loud laughter and the other meaning derisive laughter. They knew perfectly well that she was dead. They had been to too many funerals to have any doubt about that (8:52–53).

The Lord put out the whole group of hired mourners. Then He took the child's hand in His. He spoke to the child in the local Aramaic, *"Talitha cumi,"* "Little lamb, arise!" A touch! Two words! And a grave robbed of its prey! "Her spirit came again," Luke observes. "The damsel arose, and walked," was one of the things that Mark noted in his account of this incident (Mark 5:42). The Lord at once told the parents to feed the child.

Finally, the Lord charged those who were present to keep this whole incident to themselves. Unlike the so-called faith healers of our day, who would undoubtedly exploit such an incident (if they could even produce one), the Lord forbade all publicity. A response based on miracles is shallow at best. Jesus knew the human heart too well to put much stock in miracles. Let this story get out, and more and more crowds would congregate, hoping, like Herod, to see signs and wonders themselves.

(4) The sending of the Twelve (9:1–10)

The Lord had now completed two tours of Galilee. He was accompanied on the first one by four disciples and on the second one by all twelve. More and more disciples were gathering around Him, but at the end of this tour He deliberately separated the Twelve to Himself. This group of a dozen men had traveled everywhere with Him on the Galilean tour that He had just completed. It was time for these chosen ones to go out and represent Him on this third and final Galilean tour. It took place during the third year of the Lord's public ministry. It is estimated that it possibly took the better part of a year because it was to probe into all parts of Galilee. It would seem that on this tour Jesus went His way and the Twelve went theirs as He directed and sent them.

Luke records half a dozen things about this great commission. There was the matter of their *might* (9:1). A dozen Galilean peasants, most of them uneducated, and all of them, except Judas, from despised Galilee! They desperately needed enabling of some sort to march boldly into city after city and command the respect and response of the people. So the Lord endued them with power and authority over demons and disease. The Lord intended to hammer hard and for the very last time on the fast-closing door of Jewish response.

Then there was the matter of their *message:* "And he sent them to preach the kingdom of God, and to heal the sick" (9:2). The disciples were to relieve suffering, but their real mission was to preach the kingdom of God—which, of course, included the need for people to be born again (John 3:3).

There was also the matter of their *money:* "And he said unto them, Take nothing for your journey, neither staves, nor scrip, neither bread, neither money; neither have two coats apiece" (9:3). This was the rule for those people in that place at that period and for that purpose—to prepare the way for the kingdom to come. They were a special group with a special goal. The Lord changed these ground rules after His rejection by the nation of Israel—to which these men were the Lord's ambassadors (Luke 22:35–36). The Lord told His disciples on this occasion that they were to take no scrip—a collecting bag for money. The Lord's disciples were not to be beggars. They were servants of Christ, and He would take care of their needs. Their mission was to a little land where the people were accustomed to extending hospitality to heaven-sent messengers. In the Old Testament, one whole tribe was called to live on the tithes that were to be set aside for that purpose by the other tribes.

Then, too, there was the matter of their *method* (9:4–5). The Lord knew that the people in some places would not receive them. In that case, they must leave after shaking off the dust of that place—a menacing gesture (Exod. 9:8–12). That kind of thing would be quite wrong today in this age of grace. Pentecost changed everything.

Next came the matter of their *move:* "And they departed, and went through the towns, preaching the gospel, and healing every where" (9:6). Thus, tersely, Luke summarizes the mission. There never was such a year in this world's long and tragic history. Luke, who was a Gentile, seems to have taken little interest in this mission. Matthew, a Jew writing for Jews, devotes much more space to it. One thing that did catch Luke's attention was Herod's reaction.

News of what was happening all over the land reached the ears of Herod Antipas. Various opinions were being voiced. Some people said that John the Baptist was back from the dead. Others said that Elijah had come. Still others were more vague; they thought that one or another of the old prophets had risen (9:7–8). The message reminded the people of John the Baptist; the movement made them think of Elijah, whose return to earth was long foretold; and the miracles reminded them of Moses. Jesus was not just a prophet, even one back from the dead. He was the Son of God and the King of Israel (John 1:49).

Herod had his own ideas as he sat in his mountain fortress, haunted in his guilt-ridden soul by the memory of his crime. He listened to every report that his informers brought to him. "John have I beheaded," Herod declared, "but who is this, of whom I hear such things?" Who indeed! Herod grasped at a straw. He could not admit that Christ had come, but he could not deny that *Someone* had come. He was "perplexed" indeed (9:7). One thing he did know: he wanted to see this Man of many miracles. He dared not arrest Jesus; He was still far too popular with the people to risk that. And Herod had no intention of going to see the Man for himself. So he sat in his stronghold, a tormented man, hoping that one day things might fall out such that he would see Him face-to-face. Oh, how he wanted to see a miracle, a real live miracle!

Meanwhile, the Twelve returned to Jesus full of good news and wonderful tales. The Lord decided that they needed a holiday, to go somewhere where they could be away from the crowds. He chose a desert place called Bethsaida Julias, a small town that Herod Philip had renovated and renamed after Julias, the daughter of Caesar Augustus. The place was outside of Herod's jurisdiction.

(5) The spreading of the table (9:11–17)

The holiday was short-lived. Word of His whereabouts reached the people on the other side of the lake, and off they went to demand more—more stories, more sensations, and more signs. The crowds, augmented by Passover pilgrims arriving in Capernaum on their way to Jerusalem to keep the annual feast, were delighted that the great Prophet was in the neighborhood.

Jesus was not disgruntled by the sudden end to His holiday. As soon as the crowds settled down, He took up where the mission tour had ended—teaching truths about the kingdom and healing the ever-present sick.

The day began to wear away. The Twelve urged the Lord to dismiss the crowds; time was getting on. The people would be getting hungry. It was time that they scattered throughout the countryside to get food before the shops closed. Some people would need lodging for the night. And the place where they were was a wilderness in any case. Perhaps still feeling resentment for their interrupted holiday, the disciples said to Jesus, "Send the multitude away" (9:12).

It was not just "a multitude" to Him, however. He saw men and women, boys and girls, individuals to be loved and cared for. Where the disciples saw crowds, Jesus saw people. That is where socialism breaks down. It sees the masses as "the working class," "the underprivileged," "the industrialists," "the capitalists," "the bourgeois," and "the unemployed." But Jesus sees individuals, people whom He loved with an everlasting love. Send them away? Certainly not! Invite them to stay for supper!

The incredulous disciples looked at the crowd—about five thousand men. Their assessment of the demand was that it was impossible! All they had were five small rolls and a couple of fish. It was crystal clear to them that there was not enough to go around to the disciples, much less that hungry multitude. One of the disciples suggested a trip to the market back in the nearest town. But probably the common purse was as empty as the cupboard. We can well imagine the outraged face of Judas at the mere suggestion.

People were already beginning to mill around. "Make them sit down," Jesus said, "by fifties" (9:14). He brought instant order to and eager anticipation from the crowds. The people arranged themselves in one hundred groups of fifty each with room for an orderly distribution of the food when it came. There was to be no disorderly conduct, no pushing and shoving, none of the selfish behavior of a mob (9:14–15).

Then came the miracle. In the hands of Jesus, those few loaves and fish became a banquet. They had bread enough and to spare. Back and forth went the disciples, their baskets full to overflowing, the provisions handed out. Back for more and more. The Lord had taken what was available into His hands. He had looked up to heaven to see His Father's smile and nod. He had blessed the provisions and begun to multiply a meager supply into a bountiful feast. The disciples, when the last hungry boy or the last famished man was filled, trooped back, baskets in hand to the Master, and behold, each one's basket was full (9:17).

> 3. A divine Savior (9:18–45)
>   a. His deity is declared (9:18–27)

Luke's point of view in his gospel is the humanity of Christ. He does not, however, overlook His deity. The incident recorded here takes us to another time and place. The Lord had gone to the cities of Tyre and Sidon on the coast and had returned for a brief tour of Decapolis. Then He had set His face toward the north, to the frontier of the Promised Land. Caesarea Philippi was a beautiful city, some 1,147 feet above the sea, nestled between three valleys. The massive snow-capped peaks of Mount Hermon towered over everything. Not far away, bursting from a cave, were the upper sources of the Jordan River. There, too, was one of the impregnable fortresses that the Herods were so fond of building.

Somewhere in this vicinity we see the Lord at *prayer*—the fourth of seven occasions when Luke shows us the Lord praying. The ebb tide in our Lord's affairs had begun its flow. There would still be smatterings of applause, but the end was in sight. Jesus prayed (9:18a).

Luke turns our attention from the Lord's prayer to the Lord's *person* (9:18b–21). The Lord asked, "Whom say the people that I am?" The answer was immediate—John the Baptist, one of the long-dead prophets. The people had observed the life of the Lord. They saw a man wholly good, free from sin, full of grace and truth, humble and holy, and loving and lowly. They heard a man speak with the ring of authority, with unflinching honesty, and with total integrity. They saw His miracles. They were countless, incontrovertible, incomparable. How could they account for this extraordinary man? In all of history there had never been such a one as Him. He could be described only as some kind of supernatural being—perhaps John the Baptist back from the dead, or one of the prophets (Elijah?) come back to earth. It was the best they could do. It fell far short of the truth.

The Lord put His disciples to the test. They had seen in Him a moment-by-moment, situation-by-situation, full-color, three-dimensional, audiovisual demonstration of God, manifest in the flesh. So whom did they think He was? Peter blurted it out: "The Christ of God," he said (9:20). Probably Peter had pondered the question for years. The truth had taken root in his heart. "Of the abundance of the heart his mouth speaketh" (Luke 6:45). "The Christ of God!" Peter spoke for them all.

The Lord accepted this confession of faith because that was exactly who He was. The Lord at once told them to keep this truth to themselves. This was to be their secret.

Now Luke mentions His *passion* (9:22). Peter's great confession led the way for the Lord to begin a new line of teaching. "The Son of man," He said, "must suffer many things, and be rejected of the elders and chief priests and scribes, and be slain, and be raised the third day" (9:22). Nothing in their wildest imagination could have been farther from their minds. He was the Christ of God; the Anointed One; God's prophet, priest, and king—the Revealer, the Redeemer, the Ruler. The Lord's disciples had surely sensed the growing opposition of the entrenched religious establishment in Judea and Jerusalem. So what? He was the Christ of God. He was invincible. All power was His. What could those petty little men in the Sanhedrin do to stop Him from taking over all of the seats of power? And then, having swept those petty puppets aside, He would sweep Rome aside and take the throne of the world. "Be slain?" Incredible! Impossible! Inconceivable!

Then Luke gives us the Lord's *perspective* (9:23–26). The Lord took the disciples a step further. He took away the immediate prospect that they would sit upon twelve thrones judging the twelve tribes of Israel and offered them a cross instead: "If any man will come after me, let him deny himself, and take up his cross daily, and follow me" (9:23).

A cross for Him. A cross for them! The Lord had a different perspective than they did. He saw everything from heaven's point of view. He saw a world in space invaded and held by Satan and his hosts. The war was already being waged in the unseen world. He would eventually triumph over Satan's principalities and powers, his rulers of this world's darkness, and those wicked spirits of his in high places (Eph. 6:11–13; Col. 2:15), which were now being ranged against Him. But it would take the cross to do it. The disciples were more or less in the dark about these things at that time. The Lord was sounding the alarm as He wended His way down the mount: "For whosoever will save his life shall lose it: but whosoever will lose his life for my sake, the same shall save it" (9:24). Then came the challenge: "For what is a man advantaged, if he gain the whole world, and lose himself, or be cast away" (9:25). We are given here a glimpse of God's balance sheet of our lives.

Someone has well said that the first question we have to answer is "Heaven or hell?" Which world is it to be? Once that question is settled, we are faced with the second question: "Heaven or earth?" Again, which world is it to be? We can picture the face of Judas as the Lord placed these stark choices before the disciples. Astonishment! Disillusionment! Abandonment! We are not told at what point in his discipleship he secretly changed sides. Very likely it was right here. He had not signed up for any such thing as the Lord was now revealing for the first time.

Perhaps, too, the Lord had Judas in mind when He added, "For whosoever shall be ashamed of me and of my words, of him shall the Son of man be ashamed, when he shall come in his own glory, and in his Father's, and of the holy angels" (9:26). Judas was in peril. He was about to sell out to this world. Later, his sense of betrayal would be so bitter that he would sell the Lord for cold cash, for the price of a female slave. But at what cost! He would miss the second coming of Christ, and he would become a castaway, forfeiting everything, even bringing eternal loss upon himself.

In contrast, we have the Lord's *promise.* He said, "But I tell you of a truth, there be some standing here, which shall not taste of death, till they see the kingdom of God" (9:27). This is usually taken to be a reference to the Transfiguration and the experience of the Lord's glory given to Peter, James, and John a week later.

> b. His deity is demonstrated (9:28–45)
> (1) Glory on the mount (9:28–36)

Jesus then took the chosen three aside to give them a vision of Himself that stayed with them to the end of their days (2 Peter 1:18). Mount Hermon has three peaks, two of which stand on the north and the south and are separated by a mere five hundred paces. These twin peaks have an altitude of about nine thousand four hundred feet. Across a narrow valley to the west is another peak about one hundred feet lower than the other two. The Transfiguration is thought to have taken place on one of the slopes. They would be standing amid the snows. A magnificent view was spread before them whichever way they faced. The Promised Land and, indeed, the world lay before the Lord as He stood there on the great mountain barrier that divided the Promised Land from the Gentile lands beyond. The Lord came there with the three disciples to pray (9:29).

As He prayed, it happened! "The fashion of his countenance was altered, and his raiment was white and glistering" (9:29). His face was changed. The word for "altered" is *heteros*. The appearance of His face was different. The word *heteros* stands in contrast with *allos,* which means another of the same kind, whereas *heteros* means another of a different kind. It usually suggests a generic distinction. Matthew says that the Lord's face did "shine as the sun" (Matt. 17:2). Luke says that the Lord's clothing became white and glistering. The word he uses suggests that it flashed like lightning. Commentators differ as to whether this effulgent glory was a revelation of the glory that Jesus had worn like a robe of light from all eternity—a revelation of His glory as Creator, a glory that He set aside when He came to earth—or whether this blazing brightness was a revelation of the splendor of His sinless humanity.

Suddenly, two men appeared from the past. The first was Moses, up from his unmarked grave, dug for him by the angels of God on Nebo's lonely mountain and kept out of Satan's hands (Jude 9) by the archangel Michael. Moses had been kept out of the Promised Land as punishment for his sin in smiting the rock (Num. 20:3–13; Deut. 34:1–7). Now God repealed the ban and brought Moses to the mountain peak of Hermon.

Whereas Moses came up from the grave, Elijah came down from the glory to which he had ascended with an angel escort when his work on earth was done. Moses represents the Law; Elijah represents the prophets. Moses represents all of those who have died in Christ and who will be raised at Christ's coming again; Elijah represents all of those who are caught away living at the coming again of Christ. The sacrifices of the Law had much to say about the death, burial, and resurrection of Christ; the sayings of the prophets likewise had many a testimony to the two comings of Christ. On the Holy Mount, Moses and Elijah spoke with the resplendent Christ of "his decease which he should accomplish at Jerusalem" (9:31). What a conversation it must have been!

His death was no accident; it was an accomplishment. He was in charge throughout the whole appalling affair. The Romans were not in charge. The rabbis were not in charge. The rabble was not in charge. Jesus was in charge. The place itself witnessed the absolute sovereignty of Jesus. The sun was plunged in darkness. The veil of the temple was torn in two. The earth shook. Graves burst open everywhere. He sovereignly dismissed His spirit and died of His own volition before the executioners could finish Him off. His death was indeed an accomplishment and made possible salvation for one and all.

The odd thing is that Peter, James, and John seem to have slept through most of it. They awakened just in time to see the glory of the Lord and His two friends from long, long ago. Then Peter blurted out the first nonsensical thing that came into his head: "It is good for us to be here," he said, "here on holy ground, alone with Jesus, Moses, and Elijah." Still talking nonsense, he continued, "Let us make three tabernacles; one for thee, and one for Moses, and one for Elias" (9:33). Thus, Peter put the Lord on equal ground with the other two. They were mere men after all and not to be equated with the Christ of God. So quickly had he forgotten his own confession of a week earlier (9:20).

God broke in. First came the glory cloud, well known to Moses from the old wilderness days. The Shekinah glory enveloped them, and fear fell upon them. (See Numbers 9:15–23, where this cloud is mentioned ten times in about as many verses.) Peter finally stopped talking.

Out of that mysterious cloud rang the voice of God: "This is my beloved Son: hear him" (9:35; Matt. 3:17). It was God's unqualified endorsement of the Lord's life from His birth to that hour.

The voice died away. The vision was gone. The visitors vanished. The Lord stood there alone. From now on, the opposition would grow, but the lips of Peter, James, and John were sealed about this heavenly vision. As they headed down the mountain, the disciples must have realized that they had been in the company of "the spirits of just men made perfect" and of "Jesus the mediator of the new covenant" and had been given a foretaste of the kind of kingdom the Lord was planning to establish, "a kingdom which cannot be moved" (Heb. 12:23–24, 28).

(2) Grace in the valley (9:37–45)

As they came to the foot of the mountain, "much people met him" (9:37). "Much people" are always in the valley. That is why we must come down from the mount.

The mountaintop experiences of life are thrilling enough, but the real work awaits us in the valley where the hurting people are. Christ's heart went out to them, as it always did. That is why He came down from the mount—and why He would not come down from the cross (Matt. 27:40).

In the valley was a demon-possessed boy, a desperate man, a powerless "church" (the disciples, that is), and a mocking world. Christ's sudden appearance changed it all.

A father was there with an only son, a demon-possessed son. The evil spirit would come "suddenly" on the poor child. The word used for "suddenly" is used a number of times in the New Testament and always in connectional events. It is used, for instance, to describe how suddenly Saul of Tarsus was converted on the Damascus road—something that never ceased to amaze Paul himself (Acts 9:3).

"It teareth him," the father continued. The word that Luke used here is found in the Septuagint to describe an earthquake (1 Sam. 14:15). Moreover, the boy was badly bruised, shattered to pieces by this terrifying demon. And the poor lad foamed at the mouth. The symptoms suggest epilepsy, but here they were produced by demonic activity. "He is mine only child," the father said. The words can be rendered "He is my only begotten son." Every phrase in the description must have torn the heart of God's only begotten Son.

Much to their humiliation, the disciples of the Lord were unable to cast out this fierce evil spirit. They had lost their power. Worse still, some of the scribes were there, doubtless laughing up their sleeves at the discomfort of the disciples.

The Lord's first response was a general statement about the spiritual condition of the nation. The poor father finally finished his recital of his woes and those of his boy. Jesus did not answer him directly. "O faithless and perverse generation," He said, "how long shall I be with you, and suffer you?" The commentary seems to have taken in everyone present. The Lord's heart was broken by the pervading atmosphere of unbelief. Well did He know that before long His days on earth would be done. This "faithless and perverse generation" would turn against Him and reward all of His wisdom, love, and power with howls of rage and rejection in Pilate's judgment hall. The contrast between what He encountered on the summit of the mountain and what He now faced at the foot of the mountain was striking. It drew forth this exclamation. Nevertheless, His grace triumphed.

"Bring the boy to me." Even as the father attempted to obey, the ferocious demon threw the lad to the ground and tore at him. "Dashed him down." is one rendering. Jesus at once rebuked the demon and healed the child. What a red-letter day that would be in the life of this lad! The day his daddy led him to Christ! That is what fathers are for.

The multitude was amazed. Caesarea Philippi, nearby, marked the northern outpost of the Promised Land. Doubtless, the people there had heard about Jesus, but probably few, if any, had seen Him work a miracle. While everyone marveled at the miracle, the Lord turned to His disciples. The miracle probably stirred afresh in their souls their hopes of an immediate inauguration of the kingdom. The Lord sought to quench that fire. "Let these sayings sink down into your ears," He said, "for the Son of man shall be delivered into the hands of men." He knew where it all would end, but the disciples were no better than the common crowd. They "understood not this saying, and it was hid from them, that they perceived it not: and they feared to ask him" (9:43–45).

4. A discerning Savior (9:46–50)

The ebb tide had set in, and the journey was resumed. The Lord led the way south, heading homeward. Before long, a wrangle broke out as to which of them would be the greatest (9:46). Possibly the fact that the Lord had taken only three of them to experience some remarkable happening, and they had been close-mouthed about what had taken place, prompted this new argument. Evidently, the disciples chose to disregard the Lord's words of warning.

Shortly after they got back home to Capernaum, the Lord decided to deal with their disputes. According to Mark's account, they were in a house when Jesus took a child and set the child alongside Him. The Lord set these big burley men in contrast with the young child, prattling about little concerns. Then He said, "Whosoever shall receive this child in my name receiveth me: and whosoever shall receive me receiveth him that sent me: for he that is least among you all, the same shall be great" (9:48).

We are to love, help, and protect children, who are the very symbol of all who are weak, helpless, and dependent. In doing so, we serve Him and, by extension, His Father as well. So much for their boasts as to which of them would wear the brightest crown!

About this same time, another display of the flesh occurred. This time John spoke up and exposed his carnality: "Master, we saw one casting out devils in thy name; and we forbad him, because he followeth not with us" (9:49). That is the very essence of sectarianism. Many of the terrible persecutions that clutter the history of the church are the outgrowth of this spirit. It was the very spirit that moved Cain to murder Abel (Gen. 4:1–8) and that moved Joshua to deny Eldad and Medad the right to prophesy (Num. 11:26–29).

Jesus put an immediate stop to it. "Forbid him not," He said, "for he that is not against us is for us" (9:50). No person, however brilliant, and no church, however revered, has an exclusive hold on truth. Penetrating was Job's opening sarcastic remark after his friends had all had their say. Job was unimpressed. "Ye are the people" he said, not a doubt about that, "and wisdom shall die with you" (Job 12:2).

Section 2: The Way to Golgotha: His Adversaries in Focus (9:51–21:38)
 A. The scholastic approach (9:51–10:42)
  1. The Savior sets His face (9:51)

Luke has been dwelling on *the work in Galilee* and the Lord's *anointing* has been prominent (4:14–9:50). We have followed the Lord's path from the Temptation to the Transfiguration. From now on, every step will be dogged by opposition. As we glance down the chapters ahead, we are amazed by the variety of approaches that the enemy uses to hinder and halt the Lord in His mission on earth.

The first tactic we can call the scholastic approach. It was headed by an attorney. However, Luke gives us some background information first. He records the Lord's inflexible determination to follow a path that would take Him at last to the cross: "And it came to pass, when the time was come that he should be received up, he stedfastly set his face to go to Jerusalem" (9:51). He "crossed the Rubicon," as the Romans would have said. Most likely, the disciples themselves were cheered by this steady march south. Where else could a king be crowned than Jerusalem? The proper question to ask would be where else a rejected king could be crucified.

Jesus knew far better than they did that Jerusalem was the place of all places that posed the most danger for Him, and the place was implacable in its hostility. The religious parties were against Him—Pharisees and Sadducees, priests and scribes, zealots and Herodians. The Roman power that had left Him alone as long as He was roaming around Galilee, Samaria, and Decapolis was not friendly when He showed up in Jerusalem announcing His messianic claims. The Lord did not share the disciples' rose-colored views of Jerusalem.

  2. The Savior sends His followers (9:52–10:24)
   a. The dispensational question (9:52–56)

The Lord's foreknowledge of things to come spurred Him on for one more evangelistic crusade to reach and teach the people. The final rejection, when it came, would be in the face of every possible effort to reach and to save even His bitterest foes. He sent His disciples before Him, "and they went, and entered into a village of the Samaritans, to make ready for him. And they did not receive him, because his face was as though he would go to Jerusalem" (9:52–53).

The Samaritans were a mongrel people, descendants of settlers brought into the area by the Assyrian conqueror Esarhaddon to replace the Hebrews he had deported. The Samaritans adopted a cultic form of Judaism and built a rival temple on Mount Gerizim. The Jews detested them. During the dreadful days of Antiochus Epiphanes, the Samaritans were quick to come to terms with the Syrian despot. They denied all relation to Israel and dedicated their temple to Jupiter. The Maccabees, led by John Hyreanus, eventually took and destroyed the Samaritan temple. It has not been rebuilt.

The Lord seems to have decided to take a shortcut to Jerusalem instead of taking the Perean bypass, so He sent messengers to a nearby Samaritan village to announce His coming and to make suitable arrangements. They were not welcome. As soon as the Samaritans discovered that the Lord was actually on His way to Jerusalem, they slammed the door in His face. The disciples James and John were outraged. "Lord!" they said, "Do you want us to call down fire from on High and blot them out, as Elijah did?" (9:54; see also 2 Kings 1:10).

The Lord rebuked them. "Ye know not what manner of spirit ye are of," He said (9:55). Fresh in the minds of these two disciples was the vision of Elijah that they had seen on the Mount of Transfiguration. They supposed that because Elijah called down fire from heaven they should do the same. "The Son of man is not come to destroy men's lives, but to save them," Jesus added.

The question that James and John asked was a dispensational one. Fire on Samaria? All in good time—not punitive fire but Pentecostal fire, the fire of a different day and age, the blessed fire of a day of grace that was yet to come (Acts 2:1–4; 8:5–25). Meanwhile, the Lord rebuked His overeager friends. The word used for "rebuke" here (9:55) is the same word that He used in rebuking the demon who tormented the poor boy at Caesarea Philippi (9:42). They moved on to another village (9:56). The word that Luke uses for "another" is *heteros*, another of a different kind.

b. The discipleship question (9:57–62)

The next incident teaches us not only the character of our discipleship but also the cost of our discipleship. *Financial* considerations can be a hindrance (9:57–58). A certain man called out to Jesus as He was passing by, "Lord, I will follow thee whithersoever thou goest." Perhaps this man had visions of a soon coming kingdom and positions of prosperity and power to be doled out by the Messiah to His men. If that was the case, the Lord quickly disillusioned him.

"Foxes have holes," Jesus said, "and birds of the air have nests; but the Son of man hath not where to lay his head." In Matthew's account of this incident, the volunteer was a scribe, an educated man of the upper middle class. As a group, the scribes were hostile to Jesus because He totally rejected their false traditions (Matt. 8:19). Evidently, this man was prepared to give up a great deal to be enrolled as a disciple of Jesus. The Lord, however, saw the weak spot in this man's soul. Privation, not promotion, was all that Jesus offered. He was on His way to crucifixion, not coronation.

Then, too, *family considerations* can be a hindrance to discipleship (9:59–60). Looking over the thronging crowds, Jesus picked out a man and gave him a special call. "Follow me," He said.

The man replied, "Suffer me first to go and bury my father." Perhaps this man had been hovering on the brink of a decision for some time. Jesus forced him to declare himself. He had his excuse ready: he had family responsibilities. It is likely that the man's father was not yet dead. But even if the man's father was newly dead, the man was still resisting. The Jews in that hot climate buried their dead within a day. But that was not the end of it; the mourning period dragged on for ten days. By that time, all sense of urgency as to discipleship might well have evaporated. Then would come the reading of the will and all of the involvement in the distribution of the property, arrangements for the widow, maybe, and all of the other activities. All of them were legitimate concerns—but not for a disciple. The Lord was not against treating one's parents with honor; He was against its becoming an excuse.

"Let the dead bury their dead," He declared, "but go thou and preach the kingdom of God" (9:60).

Moreover, *formal considerations* can be a hindrance to discipleship (9:61–62). Luke introduces us to another volunteer. "I will follow thee," he said, "but let me first go bid them farewell, which are at home at my house."

Jesus said, "No man, having put his hand to the plough, and looking back, is fit for the kingdom of God."

It was not just a matter of saying good-bye—even the stern prophet Elijah permitted that (1 Kings 19:19–21). Elijah read Elisha's heart just as Jesus read this man's heart. Elisha had no willingness to dillydally and delay. He was following the plow when the great master, Elijah, called him. Within the day, he had made a fire of his plow and a holocaust of his oxen and was hard on the heels of his new lord. The man here in Luke's story might well have been secretly hoping that his family would talk him out of all of his notions of being a disciple. He was already looking back even while volunteering to go forward. Nobody can plow a straight furrow when he keeps looking back.

The fatal flaw in the last two men leaps out at us. Both of them said, "Me first!" Any man who wants to start his discipleship with such words simply does not qualify. Come the first hard test, and he'd be off, heading for the family or the farm.

c. The diocese question (10:1–24)
    (1) The call (10:1–2)

The Lord's diocese was the nation of Israel. The time had come for the Lord and His disciples to make one last attempt to arouse the nation to its destiny—and then, if that failed, to leave it to its doom.

So the Lord called His disciples and seventy other of His followers and sent them forth in pairs. Their goal? To enter each city on His itinerary and there to reap a harvest. The Lord well knew how vast the harvest field really was and how pitifully few the ones He could call to the work. They should all pray for reinforcements. Were the would-be disciples now numbered among the followers or the fallen?

(2) The commission (10:3–16)

The Lord surveyed the men before Him. First, they must consider *the terms* (10:3–7). They would have no special protection. They would be as sheep surrounded by a pack of wolves (10:3). They would have no special provision. They were not to take along purse, scrip, or shoes. The "purse" was merely a money box, the scrip was a beggar's bag, and the shoes were a spare pair of sandals. They were not to prepare for anticipated needs. They were to ask for no money. They were not to store extra things to take along in case of need. He would take care of all of these things. And they were not to share social pleasantries: "And salute no man by the way" (10:4). This instruction refers to the long and tedious salutations so common in the East. They were not to stop and exchange social niceties with every Tom, Dick, and Harry along the way. They were men on a mission; they had more important things to do than chat with people.

These instructions were for that particular people in that particular place at that particular period and for that particular purpose. Once the nation of Israel became openly hostile toward and adamant in its rejection of Christ and the church was about to replace Israel, these terms were changed (22:35–38)

The Lord told His disciples what to expect. When they entered a home, they were to bless it. If they were warmly welcomed, then their blessing of peace would rest upon that home. They were to stay there and accept the hospitality of its host. His ambassadors must not gad about from house to house. We can be sure that the Lord saw to it that those who thus ministered to His servants were rewarded.

Luke draws our attention next to *the tidings* (10:8–16). The disciples would encounter two kinds of cities. There was the blessed city, the city that would receive the messengers of the Messiah (10:8–9). The disciples could have fellowship with the people of that place. Moreover, they were to minister to not only their spiritual needs but also their physical needs. They were to heal their sick and tell the people that the kingdom was near to them.

Then there was the benighted city, the city that refused to receive the Lord's men. The disciples were to stand in the street and denounce the city: "Even the very dust of your city, which cleaveth on us, we do wipe off against you: notwithstanding be ye sure of this, that the kingdom of God is come nigh unto you" (10:10–11). This was not yet the age of grace. It was the declining period of the Old Testament age—the age of the law and the prophets and the curse of the law still lingered in the land.

The Lord took no such action as we saw against the Samaritan city and rebuked James and John for suggesting that He should do so. The Samaritans were not party to the Abrahamic or Mosaic covenants. But within the boundaries of Israel, when the disciples found themselves faced with a refusal to receive them, the messengers were commanded to convey their Lord's displeasure. Regardless of whether they received Him, the fact remained that the Lord's nearness meant that the kingdom of God had drawn near to them.

The Lord went on to describe three especially culpable cities. The city that refused to receive the Lord's disciples He compared with Sodom: "But I say unto you, that it shall be more tolerable in that day for Sodom than for that city" (10:12). No viler city ever existed than Sodom, a city upon which God poured out fire and brimstone without warning.

He continued, "Woe unto thee, Chorazin! woe unto thee, Bethsaida! for if the mighty works had been done in Tyre and Sidon, which have been done in you, they had a great while ago repented, sitting in sackcloth and ashes. But it shall be more tolerable for Tyre and Sidon at the judgment, than for you" (10:13–14).

Tyre and Sidon were Phoenician cities on the coastland of Canaan, the homes of the vile and merciless religions of Baal, Ashtoreth, and Moloch. Jezebel came from Sidon. Both of those cities were denounced in the Old Testament, and both of them perished. Tyre especially reaped the whirlwind for its deeds.

Chorazin and Bethsaida were sister cities of Capernaum. The Lord pronounced their doom. In doing so, He incidentally announced the principle that God always takes our opportunities and privileges into account along with our less fortunate circumstances. The more light we have, the more searching the judgment. As for Capernaum itself, it had been exalted to heaven and would be thrust down to hell (10:15). Jesus had chosen it as His hometown and had made it His headquarters since He left Nazareth. Peter and Andrew both lived there. A little way along the shore was where Jesus called the pair of them to be His disciples. At Capernaum, He had performed countless miracles. He had taught in the local synagogue many times. Severe would be Capernaum's doom.

(3) The Christ (10:17–24)

Luke records the *return* of the Lord's ambassadors, full of excitement and jubilant at the success of their efforts. Even the demons had fled, made subject to them by the power of the Lord's name (10:17). The Lord was not impressed. He knew Satan only too well, having known him from his creation as Lucifer. He had been there when Satan fell as lightning from heaven (10:18). He knew the limitations of Satan's power. He knew the fear that gripped the soul of Satan, fear that was focused and fixed on Jesus the Lord. Jesus, as Man, had fought him to a standstill in the wilderness. Satan was terrified of Him.

The Lord continued, anticipating and looking beyond Calvary to the church age and even beyond that to the Tribulation, when the world will be held in the grip of the Evil One. He told His followers, "Behold, I give unto you power to tread on serpents and scorpions, and over all the power of the enemy: and nothing shall by any means hurt you" (10:19). This pledge will come to full flower and fruit when the 144,000 specially anointed, armed, and commissioned witnesses will blaze trails all over the empire of the Antichrist, whose wrath against them will beggar description. The great promises of Psalm 91 will be fulfilled in them (Rev. 7:1–8; 14:1–5).

The Lord looked at His rejoicing messengers. "Rejoice not, that the spirits are subject unto you," He said, "but rather rejoice, because your names are written in heaven" (10:20).

We see the *rejoicing* of Jesus as well (10:21–22). Rejoicing in spirit, He turned His thoughts to His Father. "I thank thee, O Father, Lord of heaven and earth, that thou hast hid these things from the wise and prudent, and hast revealed them unto babes: even so, Father; for so it seemed good in thy sight." Despite the many seeming setbacks in the ages ahead, the ultimate victory was sure. There would be many a great and glorious triumph too.

The Lord turned back to His disciples and said, "All things are delivered to me of my Father: and no man knoweth who the Son is, but the Father; and who the Father is, but the Son, and he to whom the Son will reveal him" (10:22). This statement was a direct declaration of His deity. There are no mysteries within the Godhead that Jesus did not fully comprehend and share—for He, Himself, was God.

The Lord then looked at His disciples. In the privacy of the place where they were, Jesus said, "Blessed are the eyes which see the things that ye see: For I tell you, that many prophets and kings have desired to see those things which ye see, and have not seen them; and to hear those things which ye hear, and have not heard them" (10:23–24).

Had it been possible, how eagerly would Moses and Elijah have opted to follow the Lord down from the Mount of Transfiguration, to have seen Him deal with the demon, to have spent time with Him, to have heard His magnificent teaching, to see those things that the disciples saw every day, and to have heard what they heard and so dismally failed to understand. But it was not to be. Back they went to heaven's holy hill to tell what they *had* seen and what they *had* heard—a prophet, and more than a prophet, giving them His perspective on the matter of His decease that He was soon to accomplish at Jerusalem.

How Samuel would have liked to have seen Him! How David would have shouted for joy could he but have seen Him and heard Him! How Isaiah's pen would have been busy indeed if only he could have seen and heard!

And what about those would-be disciples who backed out because the cost was too high? Oh, what they missed—and what *we* miss when we back out for some toy or trinket of time.

3. The Savior silences His foes (10:25–37)
   a. The first question (10:25–28)

The attack soon began. The opposition would increase until, at last, the Lord's enemies had hounded Him to the tree. The first approach was scholastic and was led by "a certain lawyer." His purpose was to "tempt" Him, or to "put Him to the test." "Master," he said, "what shall I do to inherit eternal life?" (10:25). The questioner was an expert in the Law, a man with letters after his name. This man and his kind, however, were jurists rather than theologians. This particular fellow doubtless hoped that Jesus would fail the test. He is the type of person, common enough in scholastic circles, who likes to trap people with subtle arguments.

Jesus threw the man's question back to him: "What is written in the law? how readest thou?" If something has to be *done* to acquire eternal life, then surely the Law is the place to go.

The lawyer glibly tossed two key passages from the Mosaic Law back to Jesus: "Thou shalt love the Lord thy God with all thy heart, and with all thy soul, and with all thy strength, and with all thy mind; and thy neighbour as thyself" (Lev. 19:18; Deut. 6:5).

The Lord gave the man's "do" right back to him: "This do, and thou shalt live," He said (10:28).

There we have the gospel of good works, the theology of the man who says, "I'm doing the best I can." The Lord overlooked the flaw in this clever lawyer's original question—"What shall I *do* to *inherit?*" Usually, an inheritance is received, not earned. In any case, we cannot *do* anything to gain eternal life for the simple reason that we are *incapable* of doing anything good enough for God (Rom. 3:9–20). The two passages that the lawyer quoted prove man's incompetence to produce anything good enough for God. No one but Jesus ever loved God with all of his heart, mind, soul, and strength. No one but Jesus ever loved his neighbor as himself. Nobody has ever done the best he could. People who imagine that works is the way to heaven stand condemned by their own religion.

b. The further question (10:29–37)

By this time, the lawyer was doubtless beginning to wish that he had not tried to trip the Lord. He tried to confuse the issue. "Willing to justify himself" (something most people try to do when they are driven into a corner), the lawyer asked another question: "Who is my neighbour?" Rather than answer the lawyer's pettifogging question, the Lord told him a parable, thereby forcing the man to answer a much more pointed question: "Am *I* a neighbor?"

The story that Jesus told this lawyer (a man whom Jesus loved with all of His heart) is in three parts. It is, first, *a story of ruin.* A man went down from Jerusalem to Jericho. He fell among thieves, who stripped him, wounded him, and left him half dead. It is a picture of fallen man. When a person has turned his back on the city of God for a city accursed (Josh. 6:26), the only way he can go is down. The way down was also dangerous. Perils lurked everywhere, as the traveler soon found out.

It is moreover *a story of rejection*. The poor fallen man had no one to help him, and he certainly could not help himself. He might well have expected help from the two other people who came that way. They, however, acted abominably. They wanted nothing to do with the helpless victim.

Both of the men who showed up at this man's great point of need represented organized religion. The man, who was in such desperate need, realized that he could do nothing for himself. All of the doing must be done by someone else—how about *that*, Mr. Lawyer?

Along came a priest. He was surely the man the wounded wayfarer needed! He looked at him with dawning hope. In vain! The priest "saw him . . . [and] passed by on the other side." So much for the priest, the man who stood for the rituals of the Law. And there were many of them. This shoddy, shallow priest knew all about the sacrifices, all about the feast days and the fast days, and all about circumcision and the Sabbath. A lot of help this priest was! The *rites of religion,* however rooted in truth and tradition, cannot help a lost soul. What good would it have done for Jesus to have told the dying thief that he needed to be baptized?

Then came a Levite, a man who, just like the priest, was consecrated to God. Likely enough, the lawyer who had challenged Jesus was a Levite. The Levites' great duty was to preserve the law of God from any form of dilution or attack and to see that its requirements were kept, its precepts were properly administered, and it was passed on intact to posterity. In short, the Levite was concerned with the *rules of religion.* What good would it have done to tell this poor, broken man to recite the Ten Commandments—or even just the two commandments that the lawyer had recited to Jesus? In any case, the Levite was no help. He crossed the road and took a look at the man. Then he, too, left him to his misery and, like the priest, passed by on the other side. Between them the priest and the Levite demonstrated the failure of God's rules and organized religion to save us.

The Lord now turns the lawyer's attention to the true Savior, one whom the lawyer chose to despise. The Samaritan, despised by the Jews, turned out, after all, to be the one who brought salvation to the fallen man.

It now becomes a story of *redemption*. The Samaritan "came where he was" (10:33). Blessed be God! Just like Jesus! Out of the ivory palaces He came, into a world of sin, right to where we were in all of our helplessness and need. The Samaritan dressed the poor man's wounds, pouring in oil and wine—oil to soothe and wine to cleanse. Then the Samaritan brought the poor man to an inn to be cared for until his return—all of which whispers to us of Christ—the inn representing the church and the two "pence" the interval of time that the gracious Savior expected to be gone.

But the Lord was not through with this lawyer. "Which now of the these three, thinkest thou, was neighbour unto him that fell among the thieves?" He demanded.

Unwilling to speak the words *the Samaritan*, the lawyer said, "He that showed mercy on him." The truth had to be dragged out of him. In the end, the Lord left the lawyer where he was when he first challenged Jesus.

Jesus said to the man who wanted no part in a salvation that came by way of one whom he despised, "Go, and *do* thou likewise." (Note the constant beating of the drum: Do! (10:25), Do! (10:28), Do! (10:37). The Law says, "Do!" The gospel says, "Done!")

4. The Savior sees His friends (10:38–42)

The Holy Spirit pauses here to describe a welcome interlude. The opposition was mounting still; even so, the Lord knew where to find His friends. We are taken to Martha's *house* (10:38).

This event probably took place during the Lord's brief visit to Jerusalem at the Feast of Dedication late in December. In the next spring, at the Feast of Passover, the Lord would be crucified. The scene is set in Bethany in Martha's house. Bethany was on the Mount of Olives near Jerusalem, which stands at 2,500 feet above sea level. The Mount of Olives is slightly higher and stands as a screen between Jerusalem and the Dead Sea, which is about 1,290 feet below sea level. In the course of about twenty-five miles, the land drops nearly 4,000 feet into the subtropical heat of the Jordan Valley. Down on one side was the sterile desert, a breeding ground for prophets. Over on the other side was Jerusalem, ever ready to kill the prophets (13:34). Martha's house was a sweet resting place, a shelter in the time of storm. Jesus seems to have come to Martha's house for a short rest before facing the storm ahead.

Martha had a sister named Mary and a brother named Lazarus. No mention is made of Lazarus at this time. Possibly he was away from home, probably in Jerusalem for the feast. The sisters welcomed the Lord into the home, and at once we get a glimpse of Martha's *hospitality* (10:39–40). As soon as He was settled, Mary found a place at His feet where she could give herself wholly to hearing His words. Martha busied herself making a meal. Before long, she began to resent that Mary was making no attempt to help her. Now, alas for Martha's *haste* (10:41) and impatience! She appeared before the Lord and blurted out,

"Dost thou not care that my sister hath left me to serve alone? bid her therefore that she help me" (10:40). We generally find the Marys of the world holed up in some corner with a book. They are a sore trial to the busy bustlers of this world, the ones who get things done.

The Lord, as always, was equal to the occasion. He gently chided His friend. "You are too anxious," He said. "You are too agitated." Her wonderful gift of service was being spoiled by a wrong spirit. "But one thing is needful," the Lord added. As we would say it nowadays, "A sandwich will do." Then He added, "Mary hath chosen that good part, which shall not be taken away from her" (10:42). Martha had chosen to serve; Mary had chosen to sit. Both had chosen aright. And the Lord loved them both.

The Lord needs dreamers and doers. John was a dreamer; Peter was a doer. The church accommodates both types of people. Each must learn to respect the other. Blessed is the congregation that has plenty of room for both types of people.

    B.   The slanderous approach (11:1–28)
        1. A suggestion that was unprincipled (11:1–14)

The attacks upon Christ, as recorded by Luke, are intermittent at first. Thus, before focusing on the terrible slander of Christ by His foes, Luke tells us a little more about the Lord's teaching. The disciples observed their Lord as He engaged in prayer. They asked Him to teach them how to pray, just as John had taught his disciples. This is the sixth of seven occasions in Luke's gospel when we see the Lord at prayer. The next time will be in Gethsemane. The Lord knew what lay ahead for Him, and He prayed.

The Lord responded to His disciples at once. Actually, He had already given them the prototype in the Sermon on the Mount (Matthew 6:9–13). Here He extracts a few sentences from it.

When we pray we must be occupied with the Father's *person*. We begin with the words *Our Father,* presuming that the person praying is a child of God (John 1:11–13). Prayer is a God-centered activity. It lifts our thoughts and hearts to God Himself.

We are also to be occupied with the Father's *place:* "Our Father which art in heaven." Heaven is a real place; it is God's home. Jesus came from there, and, when His days on earth were done, He went back there. The Lord would have us school our thoughts heavenward to God's dwelling place on high.

Then, too, we are to be occupied with the Father's *purity:* "Hallowed be thy name." God's name is holy and reverend (Ps. 111:9). He exalts His name. He promises to punish those who take that holy name in vain (Exod. 20:7). As a believer approaches God's throne in prayer, he must come with the hallowed name of God upon his lips. He must pay tribute to the holiness of God.

Moreover, in prayer we are to be occupied with the Father's *purposes:* "Thy kingdom come. Thy will be done, as in heaven, so in earth." It has always been God's purpose to establish a glorious, righteous kingdom here on earth. God anointed Adam to have dominion. Adam, however, surrendered his sovereignty to Satan, so we live in a world where sin and death now reign. Then Jesus came, and the kingdom was offered to Israel, the representative nation, but the Jews rejected the king and worked for His execution at the hands of the Romans. The Lord saw beyond all of that. He saw beyond Calvary to the church age and beyond that to the long-awaited kingdom. God's kingdom purposes have not been canceled, only postponed (Rom. 9–11). So we continue to pray, "Thy kingdom come. Thy will be done in earth, as it is in heaven" (Matt. 6:10). And come it will one of these days. In prayer, we are to be occupied with these things.

Then, too, we are to be occupied with the Father's *provision:* "Give us day by day our daily bread." There is to be bread for today, just as there was manna day by day for Israel of old (Exod. 16). We are urged to pray for our current needs, not for wealth and vast cash reserves. After all, we live our lives one day at a time. God has planned it so: "As thy days, so shall thy strength be" (Deut. 33:25).

In prayer, we are to be occupied with the Father's *pardon:* "And forgive us our sins; for we also forgive every one that is indebted to us." When we preach the gospel to those who are outside the kingdom of God, we do not say to the unsaved, "If you promise to forgive, you will be forgiven." We preach an unconditional salvation. We preach the gospel of the grace of God. Grace is unmerited favor; it is getting something that we don't deserve. We preach salvation full and free. However, once a person is in the kingdom of God's dear Son, has received God's grace, has become a child of God, is indwelt by the Spirit of God, is baptized into the mystical body of Christ, and has become an heir of heaven and a joint heir with Jesus Christ, much more is expected of him. Those who are part of the family of God cannot expect to receive forgiveness themselves while they are harboring an unforgiving spirit toward someone else. We must exhibit the spirit of Christ.

In prayer, we are to be occupied with the Father's *protection:* "And lead us not into temptation; but deliver us from evil." From evil! Or as it has been rendered, "from the evil," that is, from the Evil One, from active harm. Certainly, we need to be protected from Satan and from his agents, both demonic and human. We need, just as much, to be protected from the evil that we carry around within our own fallen nature. When a child of God falls into evil, not only is he hurt himself but also he brings discredit to the family of God and does dishonor to the Father.

The Lord Jesus knew exactly about what He was talking. He, as man, had been led by the Spirit into temptation (Matt. 4:1). It had been a terrible ordeal. It came in all of its final force and fury after a forty-day fast. He triumphed gloriously, but it was not an experience that He would like any of His followers to experience. When it was over, He needed the personal ministry of angels to help Him recover.

The Lord continued His teaching on prayer by telling His disciples a story. Picture one of your friends. You go to him in the middle of the night to request the loan of a few loaves of bread. You explain to him that you have unexpected company, someone on a journey who has dropped in on you. The friend to whom you have come is in bed. His family is all in bed. "I can't help you," he says. You refuse to take no for an answer and keep pounding on the door. The Lord makes His point: although the man in bed in the house will not stir himself because he is your friend, he will bestir himself to stop you from pounding on his door. He will even give you more for the sake of peace and quiet. Such was the story (11:5–8).

This parable is difficult because on the surface it would seem that the friend with the plentiful resources is most reluctant to meet the other man's need. We must guard against any interpretation that would teach that the Lord is indifferent to our needs and the needs of the lost. We do not have to keep on pounding on the door of heaven, surely! The Lord is not to be likened to a sleepy man in bed.

The difficulty was not in the matter of giving but of giving *then*. The problem lies with the man who belatedly appeals for help—to cover up his own negligence and unpreparedness. He should have ensured that he was always ready to give the proper answer to whomever asked of him (1 Peter 3:15). He is like Lot running through the dark streets of Sodom to pound at the doors of his lost children's houses, trying—too late—to awaken them to imminent wrath. They thought that he was drunk (Gen. 19).

It is too late in the day to take a crash course on soul winning when we find ourselves suddenly seated alongside someone who urgently needs to be saved. Our most obvious duty is to be ready at all times to meet the spiritual needs of the lost. In the Lord's parable, the man's other friend, his rich friend, responds to this importunate demand by seeming coldness and an apparent unwillingness to help.

"I say unto you," Jesus said, "Though he will not rise and give him, because he is his friend, yet because of his importunity he will rise and give him as many as he needeth" (11:8). In the end, the man gave his friend more than enough bread to enable him to minister to his visitor's needs.

God is a cheerful Giver. He gives generously, not grudgingly. The Lord does not mean to imply by this parable that He is unwilling to answer our prayers and has to be pestered to do so. Nor does He mean that importunity will get an answer to a prayer that otherwise would not be answered. Quite the contrary. Just the same, however, God works according to fixed principles. He does not do for us what we can do for ourselves. He does not give miraculous insights and answers to questions that appear on the examination paper—questions that we should have studied all year but neglected to do so.

God does move, however, when it is a question of someone else's dire needs. We can be sure that the man in the parable made up his mind never to be caught unprepared again.

The context of this parable declares that God, far from being a reluctant Giver, is a ready Giver. Jesus said, "And I say unto you, Ask, and it shall be given you; seek, and ye shall find; knock, and it shall be opened unto you. For every one that asketh receiveth; and he that seeketh findeth; and to him that knocketh it shall be opened" (11:9–10).

In the parable, we see the awakened man running to the house of his rich friend. When his plea was not immediately granted, we see him knocking, refusing to go away, redeeming himself for his past neglect and proving himself to be belatedly in earnest now. Who of God's saints has not had the experience of praying day by day, for weeks, months, or even years with no kind of an answer we would want? God's delays are not denials. He is teaching us something in the delay. George Müller used to say, "The *stops* as well as the *steps* of a good man are ordered of the Lord" (Ps. 37:23).

The Lord continued His commentary on the great goodness and generosity of God (11:11–13). To illustrate, Jesus pointed out the behavior of a human father. Jesus did not have a human father, but He lived in the home of one. Joseph, the village carpenter, was His foster father. "If a son ask bread of any of you that is a father," Jesus said, "will he give him a stone? or if he ask a fish, will he for a fish give him a serpent? Or if he shall ask an egg, will he offer him a scorpion?" (11:11–12). A stone! A serpent! A scorpion! No, never! A man would be a monster to do such a thing.

"If ye then, being evil, know how to give good gifts unto your children: how much more shall your heavenly Father give the Holy Spirit to them that ask him?" (11:13). God is too loving and wise to give us harmful gifts. The greatest gift that God can give to one of His own blood-bought people is the Holy Spirit. The Holy Spirit is the birthright of every believer since Pentecost.

We are moving closer and closer now to the slander. But first Luke shows the Lord Jesus demonstrating the power of the Spirit (11:14). He shows us the Lord casting a demon out of a person. The demon is described as being dumb, meaning that it inflicted that handicap upon its victor: "when the devil was gone out, the dumb spake; and the people wondered" (11:14).

The suggestion that God is a grudging Giver, although not stated in so many words, has been swept away by the Lord Jesus. It is quite unprincipled, and Jesus vigorously denied it in both His preaching and His power.

> 2. A suggestion that was unpardonable (11:15–28)
>   a. The Lord exposes the nonsense of the suggestion (11:15–22)

Luke brings us now to the unforgivable sin. The seriousness of sin must be measured by the rank and dignity of the person against whom it is committed. A soldier in the barracks might hit a fellow soldier and earn some commensurate punishment—fatigue duty, confinement to camp, or some other such appropriate restraint. But suppose that the same soldier were to assault the commanding officer. That offense would bring him a prison term. Suppose that this unruly soldier were to be on parade during a visit to the base by the president. Suppose that he were to try to attack the president. He would be shot to death on the spot by the president's bodyguards. In each case, the actual offense would be the same, attempting to strike someone. And in each case the offense is made more serious by the rank of the person attacked.

Sin is an offense against an almighty, all-holy God. No wonder its punishment is eternal banishment from God's presence! Blasphemy against the Holy Spirit is unpardonable because of the nature of the offense and the awesome majesty and glory of the living God.

In connection with this sin, we note first that Jesus read the evil thoughts of His enemies: "But some of them [the people who were standing there observing the Lord cast an evil spirit out of a man] said, He casteth out devils through Beelzebub the chief of the devils. And others, tempting him, sought of him a sign from heaven" (11:15–16).

Jesus went behind their wicked words and read their even more wicked thoughts.

Matthew defines their sin as blasphemy against the Holy Spirit (Matt. 12:22–32). For someone to have knowledge of the Lord's sinless life, awesome power, and amazing teaching and actually to witness Him perform an unquestionable miracle (in this case, the casting out of an evil spirit) and to declare that He did it in the power of Satan was unpardonable. It displayed a state of soul that was so callous, so beyond divine illumination (the work of the Holy Spirit) as to be hopeless.

This incorrigible state of soul was expressed in two ways. First, they attributed the Lord's miracle to "Beelzebub the chief of the devils." The name comes from an Aramaic word meaning "the Lord of the flies" (2 Kings 1:2), the god of the Ekronites. But the Israelites, in contempt, changed it to a name meaning "lord of the dunghill." In Jewish thought, Beelzebell (Beelzebub) was the worst and the chief of the demons. The Jews thought that he presided over idolatry and incited men to worship graven images. To attribute the mighty works of Jesus to the worst of all of the demons was blasphemy of the very worst kind, blasphemy against the Holy Spirit of God. It was a sin not to be repented of, a sin that assured the blasphemer of eternal torment. It revealed a soul that was too far gone in sin ever to be recalled even by God's amazing grace.

The same spirit of lawless unbelief was expressed in the accompanying demand for "a sign from heaven." Those who made such a demand discounted all of the miracles that He had already performed, day after day, miracles enough and to spare. Worse still, they were tempting Him. What they wanted was some omen in the sky. Even if He had given such a sign, they would not have been satisfied. As it was, He had already given one such sign and was about to give another: when He was born, He put a new star in the sky (Matt. 2:1–10); when He died, He would put out the sun (Matt. 27:45). Not that it made much difference. From that day to this, the majority of Jews have still rejected Him.

So, then, Jesus read their thoughts and answered them. First, He showed the nonsense of what they said: "Every kingdom divided against itself is brought to desolation; and a house divided against a house falleth. If Satan also be divided against himself, how shall his kingdom stand? because ye say that I cast out devils through Beelzebub. And if I by Beelzebub cast out devils, by whom do your sons cast them out? therefore shall they be your judges" (11:17–19). What the Lord's enemies were saying made no sense. No! Satan's kingdom was not divided. It was highly organized from the lowest demon in his domain to the highest principality and power nigh his throne.

As for exorcism in general, if He was supposed to do it by satanic power, by what power did their sons cast out demons?

"But," the Lord continued, "if I with the finger of God cast out devils, no doubt the kingdom of God is come upon you." The Bible speaks of God's arm, God's hand, and God's finger. Each part suggests the putting forth of more power than the other. The Lord needed to put forth but a tithe of His power to play havoc with the kingdom of Satan. The whole demon world went in terror of Him, and they knew who He was and from whence He was. The Jews, of course, would be familiar with Exodus 8:10.

The Lord followed this with one of His apt illustrations. A strongman armed, He said, keeps his palace and its contents, but when one comes along who is stronger than he and overcomes him, then the conqueror takes away all of his armor in which he trusted and divides the rest of the spoils (11:21–22). The strongman, of course, is Satan. His "palace" is the world. His "goods" are the wretched people held under his sway, especially (and there are many of them) those who were demon possessed. The one who is stronger is Jesus Himself, and the wholesale casting out of evil spirits by Christ is one of many demonstrations of Satan's utter helplessness before the Son of God. Satan's only strategy was wholesale and massive retreat.

b. The Lord exposes the nature of the suggestion (11:23–28)

The Lord, having exposed the nonsense that the Jews were talking in attributing His power to Satan, went on to expose the very nature of their unprincipled and unpardonable words. He did so in three steps by means of a principle, a parable, and a proclamation.

Here is *the principle:* "He that is not with me is against me: and he that gathereth not with me scattereth" (11:23). There is no neutrality in this spiritual war. The Lord had but recently taught John that lesson (9:49–50). We are either on His side, or we are against Him. We either help Him gather in His own, or we help Satan scatter them. The Lord had in mind here the wicked leaders of the Jews, who, in opposing Him, were making inevitable the impending agelong scattering of the Jews (Matt. 23). This terrible scattering commenced in A.D. 70 when Jerusalem and the temple fell to the Romans. It was consummated in A.D. 135 at the time of the Bar Cochba rebellion. (Bar Cochba was the first of a line of pseudo-Messiahs who have plagued them down through the centuries. The Jews never had a false messiah until they rejected the true Messiah, then they had a long succession of them.)

Now comes *the parable* (11:24–26). The Lord declared, "When the unclean spirit is gone out of a man, he walketh through dry places, seeking rest; and finding none, he saith, I will return unto my house whence I came out. And when he cometh, he findeth it swept and garnished. Then goeth he, and taketh to him seven other spirits more wicked than himself; and they enter in, and dwell there: and the last state of that man is worse than the first."

This is a terrible picture. The story it tells is on two levels. First, it gives us a fearful glimpse of the peril of demon possession. A disembodied demon is restless. It wanders in "dry places," places devoid of human habitation. We get a picture of this in the prophecy of Isaiah concerning the final fall and utter total desolation of Babylon. The prophet says, "But wild beasts of the desert shall lie there; and their houses shall be full of doleful creatures; and owls shall dwell there, and satyrs shall dance there. And the wild beasts of the islands shall cry in their desolate houses, and dragons in their pleasant palaces" (Isa. 13:21–22). The prophet sees the ruins haunted by hyenas, jackals, and wild dogs. He also mentions satyrs. Some scholars think that this is a reference to goat-shaped demons such as the Edomites worshiped. The word *satyrs* is translated "devils" in Leviticus 17:7. The satyr is a demon that was said to be half goat and half man. The word comes from a Hebrew root meaning "to shudder." The same word is used to describe the idolatry of Jeroboam: "And he ordained him priests for the high places, and for the *devils,* and for the calves which he had made" (2 Chron. 11:15). The word also suggests "hairy ones," goats representing demons. Possibly this is where the world gets its idea of portraying Satan with horns and hoofs and with the leering head of a goat. The whole picture painted by the prophet is one of desolate ruins, a former habitation of man that was haunted by birds, beasts of prey, and evil spirits.

The same prophet uses similar language to describe the desolate ruins of Edom (of which Petra is an example). The word for "owl" in Isaiah 34:11, 13 means literally "a screech owl." The word is used by extension of any creature or being of the night. The Arabs used charms to ward off this night bogey.

The restless spirit in the Lord's parable soon tires of haunting old ruins. It decides to repossess its human victim from whose body it had been expelled. It discovers, however, that the person has been cleaning up his life. The demon has a diabolical idea: why not invite some of its demon companions to join it? It rounds up seven other evil spirits, all worse than it is, and swoops down upon the individual who is immediately held in far worse bondage than before. The Bible gives examples of multiple demon possession, including Mary Magdalene and the Gadarene demoniac. Even when evil spirits are expelled, unless the Holy

Spirit comes in, the unfortunate host can be repossessed. One obvious lesson from all of this is the hopelessness of reformation apart from regeneration.

Beyond all of this is the parabolic aspect of the Lord's teaching. The leaders of Israel had just blasphemed the Holy Spirit; therefore, the parable now focuses on the nation of Israel. The besetting sin of Israel throughout the Old Testament was idolatry and the immorality and cruelty that accompanied it. Aaron, Israel's first high priest, set the pace for it with the golden calf.

The Babylonian captivity cured the Jews of idolatry. They swept and garnished their house and set up in its place a rigid monotheism. Sad to say, however, this monotheism was served by an outward show of ritual buttressed by a religion based upon tradition, upon what the Jews called "the oral law." This tradition was already flourishing in the days of Christ. The Jews would expand it into the vast encyclopedia that became known as the Talmud. Instead of the idolatry that they now abhorred, they had the legalistic formalism of the Pharisees, the agnosticism of the Sadduccees, the fierce nationalism of the Zealots, the worldliness of the Herodians, and the dead ritualism of the priests. The soul of the nation was now possessed by a growing hatred for Christ, whose rejection it has nursed from that day to this.

Then came *a proclamation* (11:27–28). The Lord's foes had gone to one extreme—slander. Now a woman went to the other extreme—sentiment: "And it came to pass, as he spake these things, a certain woman of the company lifted up her voice, and said unto him, Blessed is the womb that bare thee, and the paps which thou hast sucked" (11:27). This was a backhanded compliment, but it was wholly in error because it exalted the Virgin Mary. The statement contained all of the roots of a future development of Mariolatry. The Lord nipped it in the bud, saying, "Yea, rather, blessed are they that hear the word of God, and keep it" (11:28). That is always the answer to the adoration of Mary—the Bible!

C. The sophisticated approach (11:29–52)
    1. In public: the hardness of the people of Israel (11:29–36)

The Lord's exposure of Israel's national unbelief set the stage for a further attack. It began in public "when the people were gathered thick together" (11:29). The Lord took up the demand that had just been made upon Him for a sign from heaven (11:16, 29). "This is an evil generation: they seek a sign," He said (11:29). Then He told them that they would find all of the answers to their doubts and debates right there in the Bible.

There was the case of the *convicted seer,* the prophet Jonah. "For as Jonas was a sign unto the Ninevites, so shall also the Son of man be to this generation" (11:30). Jonah was as displeased by the repentance of Nineveh as the religious leaders of the Lord's generation were at the repentance of people in all parts of the country! Jonah was a sign to the Ninevites. He had been three days and nights in what he called "the belly of hell." When he marched through their streets, it was with a face livid and terrifying from the fierce action of the gastric juices of the great fish. The man himself was as much the message as the words that he proclaimed; he was a sign. "God will punish sin!" It was written all over the disobedient prophet. But there he was, alive from the dead, a living epistle. They could infer from that the fact that "God will pardon sinners."

So! The generation of Jews that He was facing wanted a sign, did it? What an evil generation it was. He had given sign after sign, but signs were soon forgotten. A sign? The very thing—Jonah! That was it! He directed them back to the Book.

Then there was the sign of the *conscientious sovereign,* "the queen of the south," the queen of Sheba. Why! She came from a far-off land just to listen to the wisdom of Solomon. Well, Solomon was all right, but his wisdom was marred by his mistakes. He became a tyrant and an idolater in the end and sowed the seeds of national disaster. A greater than Solomon stood in their midst and they wanted to argue with Him. The queen of Sheba, in the Day of Judgment, would rise up and condemn them. The word used for "condemn" carries the idea of giving judgment or passing sentence, implying the fact of a crime. The Jews must have been angrier than ever to hear Christ comparing them unfavorably with a foreign, Gentile woman.

Then, too, there was the sign of the *converted sinners,* the people of Nineveh. Jonah had to go only a single day's journey into Nineveh, a thoroughly pagan city, and from the king on his throne to the beggar in the street, repentance swept the city.

So the Jerusalem crowds wanted a sign? Well, of what use were signs? They were soon forgotten and they bred a craving for more! Let the people go back to the Book. Back to Jonah, back to the queen of Sheba, back to the Ninevites. The men of Nineveh will rise up in judgment against this generation of Jews. They will condemn it. The Ninevites had no Bible, yet they repented by the thousands at the preaching of Jonah. Probably a million pagans were saved, repenting in sackcloth and ashes! This was probably one of the greatest revivals of all time. "A greater than Jonas is here!" Jesus said. He had something that Jonah did not have—a divine and quenchless love for the lost. Jonah never wept over Nineveh. Jesus wept for Jerusalem. At the Day of Judgment, the queen of Sheba will raise her voice with the voice of Nineveh's throngs to bear witness against these sign-demanding Jews.

Having categorically refused to give the Jews a sign, Jesus gave them a sermon (11:33–36). He began with an *illustration:* "No man, when he hath lighted a candle, putteth it in a secret place, neither under a bushel, but on a candlestick, that they which come in may see the light. The light of the body is the eye: therefore when thine eye is single, thy whole body also is full of light; but when thine eye is evil, thy body also is full of darkness."

A lamp is lighted to be displayed, not to be hidden somewhere. But, even then, the lamp does no good if the man coming toward it is blind! The lamp symbolizes God's Word—in this case, the teaching of Jesus, which the Jewish authorities so bitterly resented, bitterly enough that they accused Him of being in league with Satan. These were those with an evil eye. They saw good and thought it evil. They were blind. Light was before them, displayed where all could see it, but they were blind. Others, equally as bad, distorted what they saw.

The Lord concluded with an *application* (11:35). "Take heed therefore that the light which is in thee be not darkness." The Jews were blinded by the teaching and traditions of their rabbis. What Jesus offered was light—full, glorious light: "If thy whole body therefore be full of light, having no part dark, the whole shall be full of light, as when the bright shining of a candle doth give thee light" (11:36). Only those who have the Lord in their hearts can know such bright light within.

2. In private: the hypocrisy of the peers of Israel (11:37–52)
   a. An unspoken criticism of His manners (11:37–38)

Now comes the attack on the Lord. It was a sophisticated approach. A certain Pharisee asked the Lord to come and have a meal with him. It was the morning meal, which was usually served after they returned from the synagogue. The occasion probably was some time later than the incident just recorded. This particular incident possibly took place on a Sabbath. The Lord Jesus responded to the invitation and deliberately omitted the prescribed ritual of washing His hands. Several such ablutions were attended to during the meal. The Lord deliberately refused to wash His hands as a way of "washing His hands" of a religion that spent itself interminably on trivialities and external rites. Nothing that Jesus could have done could have shocked the Pharisees more, which was exactly what Jesus wanted to do. The Pharisee "marvelled." Other guests were present—lawyers and scribes, for instance (11:45, 53). What Jesus did astounded them. Surely, even a man from Nazareth could not be that ignorant of this most basic custom of polite society.

The Pharisee doubtless felt insulted. The Lord could read his thoughts and launched an immediate denunciation of the man and everything for which He stood.

b. An outspoken criticism of their motives (11:39–52)
(1) Woes upon the formal traditionalists (11:39–44)

Before the Pharisee could say a word, Jesus launched a fearless attack upon religious trivia and Pharisaic hypocrisy: "Now do ye Pharisees make clean the outside of a cup and the platter; but your inward part is full of ravening and wickedness. Ye fools, did not he that made that which is without make that which is within also?" (11:39–40).

Fools! The word used denotes lack of mental sanity. He labeled them "senseless ones." The Lord now certainly had the attention of this Pharisee, a Pharisee who was so careful to keep up a good outward show but who had a heart as untamable as a wolf's. He was like a dish that was carefully cleaned on the outside but extremely dirty on the inside. Did he imagine that God looked on only the outside?

The Pharisees were so conscientious about being outwardly correct that when it came, for instance, to the matter of tithing, they even tithed the herbs growing in their gardens. Tithing, they thought, would make up for their other failures. But what was the use of being so scrupulous over tithing when they neglected the more basic dictates of the Law? "[You] pass over judgment and the love of God," Jesus said. They neglected the most obvious duty to their fellow men. They failed to ensure that justice was served, and they failed to show them the love of God. They should be conscientious when it came to tithing, but they should have been equally scrupulous in treating other people properly (11:42).

"Woe unto you, Pharisees!" Jesus continued, "for ye love the uppermost seats in the synagogues, and greetings in the markets" (11:43). The chief seats in the synagogue were placed in a semicircle around the pulpit, facing the congregation, where everyone could see how important the Pharisees were. Far from loving people, they loved themselves and basked in the adulation they received.

The Lord opened another broadside on this Pharisee. "Woe unto you, scribes and Pharisees, hypocrites! for ye are as graves which appear not, and the men that walk over them are not aware of them" (11:44).

The scribes are among the chief actors in the Gospels. They pop up everywhere as the voice of the people. Along with the chief priests and elders, the scribes were the judges in the ecclesiastical courts. The order of scribes seems to have originated in Babylon. They held office and acquired status. Jesus likened them to graves that had long since overgrown so that people walked over them unaware of what corruption was underfoot. In Jewish law, all contact with a sepulcher, whether conscious or unconscious, involved defilement. Just so, contact with these men, who corrupted God's law by their teaching, was defiling the nation. This was a terrible indictment. It came, we note, from the loving heart of the Son of God, who could read the hearts of these men. He would have saved them, too, if they had let Him.

(2) Woes upon the false teachers (11:45–52)

The Jews' reaction was swift. One of the lawyers in the house spoke up: "Master, thus saying thou reproachest us also." This man was a professional expert in the Law. Probably he and most of his fraternity were Pharisees. These lawyers expounded not only the written law but also the oral law—that encyclopedic mass of tradition and minutia, beloved of the rabbis, that had grown up like a giant weed around God's Word. It probed into every nook and cranny of Jewish life, strangling, choking, and burdening the people with endless rules and regulations. Its proponents prized it above the Mosaic Law. In effect, it annulled God's Word. This lawyer was perfectly right when he protested that the Lord's sweeping denunciation of Pharisaism also embraced him. The Lord responded by expanding on His denunciation, pointedly including the entire lawyer fraternity in what He had to say next.

"Woe unto you also, ye lawyers! for ye lade men with burdens grievous to be borne, and ye yourselves touch not the burdens with one of your fingers" (11:46). Laws concerning the Sabbath, for instance, multiplied and proliferated until that which God had intended as a blessing became a burden. They hedged the Sabbath around with hundreds of restrictions. The rabbis would debate and haggle for years over some small point. No wonder the Lord denounced these lawyers! As for the objecting lawyer, he was a hypocrite. While inventing more and more laws to bind on people's backs, he and his colleagues sidestepped them themselves.

Now comes the second "woe": "Woe unto you! for ye build the sepulchres of the prophets, and your fathers killed them. Truly ye bear witness that ye allow [fully endorse] the deeds of your fathers: for they indeed killed them, and ye build their sepulchres" (11:47–48). The Lord was not impressed by the many gilded tombs around Jerusalem. That was just another show of outward piety, totally devoid of any change of heart. Gilded tombs, indeed! Just another nail in their own coffins.

The Lord continued, pointing out their crowning folly: "Therefore also said the wisdom of God, I will send them prophets and apostles, and some of them they shall slay and persecute . . ." (11:49a). The Lord Jesus Himself was the incarnate "wisdom of God" (Matt. 23:34; cf. Prov. 8:12, 23–31). The Lord's reference here is to a new breed of prophets—the apostles and the prophets of the early church. And, sure enough, the Jews of the establishment hated them, as the book of Acts reveals. The Lord elaborates: "and some of them they shall slay and persecute: That the blood of all the prophets, which was shed from the foundation of the world, may be required of this generation; From the blood of Abel unto the blood of Zacharias, which perished between the altar and the temple: verily I say unto you, It shall be required of this generation" (11:49–51).

The expression *this generation* occurs sixteen times in Scripture. It also occurs with appropriate adjectives: "An evil and adulterous generation" (Matt. 12:39, 45; 16:4; Mark 8:38; Luke 11:29), "a faithless and perverse generation" (Matt. 17:17; Mark 9:19; Luke 9:41), and "an untoward generation" (Acts 2:40). Never was there such a generation. This was the generation that murdered the Messiah. The next closest generation to the one that crucified Christ is the one that will hail the Antichrist (Matt. 24:34).

The generation of Jesus saw His amazing miracles, heard His teaching so full of grace and truth and backed by the authority of His Father in heaven, marveled at His wisdom, traced His sinless life—and then crucified Him. Truly it was an evil, adulterous, perverse, and crooked generation. Nor was it content to reject the Son of God; it went on to reject the Spirit of God, both in the land and throughout the Diaspora.

No wonder Jesus said that all of the shed blood of the martyrs from Abel to Zacharias would be heaped on that generation. The Zacharias to whom the Lord referred was the son of Jehoiada the high priest. He was a preacher and a prophet. King Joash murdered him because he denounced the king's apostasy. His murder was aggravated by the enormous debt that the king owed to Jehoida. The incident is recorded in 2 Chronicles 7:22, the last book in the Jewish cannon of

Scripture. Thus, Abel and Zacharias were the first and last martyrs, respectively, in the Old Testament. The crime that the Jewish nation was about to commit was so stupendous that the generation that did it might as well be guilty of all of the innocent blood that was ever shed upon the earth.

We can imagine the stunned look on the lawyer's face when he heard *that*. The Lord's purpose was to shock and to shake—to shock them out of their complacency about their hypocrisy and to shake them into repentance. The doom that Jesus foretold had its initial fulfillment in the fall of Jerusalem in A.D. 70 and its final consummation in the Bar Cochba rebellion in A.D. 135.

The Lord had one more thing to say: "Woe unto you, lawyers! for ye have taken away the key of knowledge: ye entered not in yourselves, and them that were entering in ye hindered" (11:52). The Jews who had returned to the Promised Land after the Babylonian captivity had been ripe for revival. God sent them gifted and godly men—Zerubbabel, a prince of the house of David, and his friend Joshua, a high priest after the order of Aaron. Then there was Haggai and Zachariah, prophets anointed of God, and Nehemiah, a statesman of courage and conviction. Then, last but by no means least, there was Malachi. Above all, there was Ezra—the scribe. Ezra's great work was to bring the repatriated nation back to the Book (Neh. 8:1–18).

It was a good start, but in time the scribes and their kind monopolized the teaching of the Scriptures. They became increasingly attached to the letter of the law, especially the so-called "oral law." Formalism and hypocrisy took root and came to flower and fruit in Pharisaism. All of this Malachi foresaw and denounced. The Talmud (the oral law) flourished greatly in the four silent centuries between Malachi and Matthew. During that time, the "traditions of the elders," the dead legalism of the scribes, practically supplanted the Scriptures themselves. Jesus scorned these traditions. He brought people back to the Word of God. He adamantly opposed the lawyers. They once had had the truth, but they buried it. They preferred tradition to truth, and they ensured that nobody else should have it; hence, this scathing woe (11:52).

   D. The systematic approach (11:53–13:9)
      1. Total warfare on their part (11:53–54)

The reaction was swift: "And as he said these things unto them, the scribes and the Pharisees began to urge him vehemently, and to provoke him to speak of many things: Laying wait for him, and seeking to catch something out of his mouth, that they might accuse him." Some scholars think that at this point He stood up and walked out. A crowd of angry men pursued Him. Nobody had ever dared speak to them like that in all of their lives. This Galilean had dared to attack them, their schools, their revered rabbis, and their jealously guarded traditions. Their wrath knew no bounds. Now all that they wanted was some careless word that they could use against Him before the Sanhedrin.

Luke piles up the words to describe their goal. They began to "urge him," he says. The word used can be rendered "to entangle." The same word is used to describe the plotting of Herodias against John the Baptist (Mark 6:19). It can be translated "to press upon." They "jostled him" is one translator's offering. Also, they began to badger Him verbally. They began to urge Him "vehemently," that is, "terribly" or "grievously." These clever and unscrupulous educated men, who were used to hairsplitting debate, pressed all around the Lord urgently baiting Him with questions, arguments, and insinuations, all of which were loaded and designed to get Him to express Himself in a hasty or unwise word.

Luke says that they began to "provoke him to speak." The word used commonly meant "to catechize," just as if He were a schoolboy. They were hoping to find some ground for formal accusation in court. Luke adds that they were "laying wait" for Him. (The same word is found in Acts 23:21.) They were trying to "catch" something out of His mouth. The word is used elsewhere of catching wild beasts. They failed. Of course they did, wicked men that they were. They were up against the incarnate "wisdom of God" (11:49).

> 2. Terrible warnings on His part (12:1–13:9)
>   a. Against concealment (12:1–3)

The Lord's disciples must have been aghast at this turn of events. They had become used to opposition, but they had never encountered such venomous hatred. The Lord now sought to prepare them for more and worse ahead.

A crowd had come running, doubtless attracted by the strident voices of the Lord's enemies. The crowd was beginning to degenerate into a mob.

The Lord first warned His disciples against concealment: "Beware ye of the leaven of the Pharisees," He said, "which is hypocrisy. For there is nothing covered, that shall not be revealed; neither hid, that shall not be known" (12:1–2). The Lord had deliberately unmasked the lawyer so that all of the hidden malice in his soul and in the soul's of his fellows might be seen. And how terrible were the sights emanating from those men now! Behind all of their playacting was doctrinal error and moral corruption. The Lord warned His disciples. Such hypocrisy could not long be concealed. For example, even as He spoke, the Lord was reading the soul of Judas. Well He knew what a consummate hypocrite the man was. Judas was putting on a great front, but the Lord read his heart and his dreadful future.

b. Against cowardice (12:4–12)

Now the Lord's enemies would not rest until He was dead. The Lord had already warned the disciples of this eventuality (9:22) and of their own need to prepare themselves for persecution (9:23), but they failed to take it in. The Lord was not handing out attractive, four-color brochures offering health, wealth, and success. They must prepare themselves for persecution and death. The first foe to face would be fear itself. "I say unto you, my friends, Be not afraid of them that kill the body, and after that have no more that they can do" (12:4). The Lord knew perfectly well what horrors awaited Him: mock trials, callous beatings, ribald mockery, a terrible scourging, death by crucifixion, and the ultimate horror of being "made sin" (2 Cor. 5:21). The disciples had best begin preparing themselves to be partakers of His sufferings. Fear? "Fear him, which after he hath killed hath power to cast into hell; yea, I say unto you, Fear him" (12:5). When it comes down to a question of fearing man or fearing God, we had better fear God. In the end, all but one of the apostles became a martyr.

But there is another side to it—God's amazing pity. "Are not five sparrows sold for two farthings, and not one of them is forgotten before God?" (12:6). He sees a sparrow fall from the sky and attends it in its hour of death. Moses tells us that God actually counts how many eggs a bird has in its nest (Deut. 22:6–7). Coming closer to home, God numbers the hairs on our head. The average middle-aged man has about one hundred thousand hairs on his head and another thirty thousand in his beard. He loses seventy-five scalp hairs a day. God does not merely count them; He numbers them. The word is *arithmeo* (from whence comes our word *arithmetic*). The word means that God not only counts our hairs (a virtually impossible task) but also *labels* them. Think of it! God actually knows each separate individual hair on our head as separate and distinct from every other hair. That's our God! If He is that concerned about us, we must trust Him even when persecution comes. We have a God who loves us with an everlasting love. Jesus trusted God down the Calvary road, through Gethsemane, Gabbatha, Golgotha, and the grave—and on into glory.

But there was more: "Also I say unto you, Whosoever shall confess me before men, him shall the Son of man also confess before the angels of God: But he that denieth me before men shall be denied before the angels of God" (12:8–9). In view here are two worlds—*this* world and *that* one. The issue at stake is not salvation but discipleship, not eternal security but status and reward. Stephen comes to mind. He witnessed a good confession before the Sanhedrin with such eloquence and power that they gnashed upon him with their teeth. Stephen had long since renounced *this* world. Even as they threw their stones at Stephen in the place of execution, he caught his first glimpse of *that* world. He saw Jesus, standing to receive to Himself this first martyr of the church (Acts 7:54–60).

But what about those who deny Him? They will be denied and that before the angels, but not by Christ. The verb form implies that the denial will be *self-imposed*. What will it be like to see the Lord in all of His splendor and to be suddenly overwhelmed with shame at having denied Him? Well, Peter could tell us all about that. Thus it was that Peter, having denied his Lord three times, caught the Lord's eye, hurried off to some dark den, and wept his heart out with sorrow and shame. Characteristically, as soon as may be after His resurrection, the Lord went looking for Peter to forgive him and set his feet on a path that eventually led him to a crown of his own.

The Lord continued. There was a very great peril to avoid (12:10): "Whosoever shall speak a word against the Son of man, it shall be forgiven him: but unto him that blasphemeth against the Holy Ghost it shall not be forgiven."

The Bible speaks of three unpardonable sins. Two of them are dispensational and cannot be committed today. Blaspheming the Holy Spirit was the sin of seeing Jesus perform His mighty miracles and then saying that He did it in the power of Satan. Because the Lord is no longer here on earth performing His miracles, we cannot commit this sin. To receive the mark of the Beast in the coming days of the Antichrist is likewise unforgivable (Rev. 13:16–17; 14:9–11; 16:2). The one unpardonable sin that is committed by many people to this very day is the sin of unbelief (John 3:16, 18, 36; Rev. 21:8). The sin of blaspheming the Holy Spirit was a real and terrible sin. It had been committed in the hearing of the disciples a short while before (11:15).

The disciples had one simple principle to remember when facing the fury of the world. When they were hauled into the synagogues and into the presence of magistrates and others in positions of power, they should "take ye no thought how or what thing ye shall answer, or what ye shall say: For the Holy Ghost shall teach you in the same hour what ye ought to say" (12:11–12). The Lord does not say that the supernatural eloquence that the Holy Spirit will bestow upon them will result in their release; more likely, it will infuriate the authorities. What happened to Stephen and Paul illustrates that fact (Acts 21:40–22:23; 23:1–10; 24:10–23; 25:23–32). This bestowal of inspired oratory is not promised for the classroom but for the courtroom. God anoints His preachers, but He does not endorse ignorance, laziness, or lack of study. The divine principle for the pulpit is quite the reverse: "*Study* [be diligent] to show thyself approved unto God, *a workman* that needeth not to be ashamed, rightly dividing the word of truth" (2 Tim. 2:15). The man who does not know what he is going to say five minutes before he gets up can be sure that most people will not remember what he said five minutes after he sits down.

c. Against covetousness (12:13–21)

At this point, the Lord was interrupted. The Lord was earnestly warning His disciples against the hostility of this world and especially to be on guard against the judicial system. As soon as He mentioned the legal system, an anonymous man barged in. He had a grievance. It occurred to him that Jesus could redress a private injustice that he deemed had been done to him. "Master," he said, "speak to my brother, that he divide the inheritance with me."

The Lord cut him off. "Man," He said, "who made me a judge or a divider over you?" (12:13–14). The courts were competent to deal with such secular concerns. The law of inheritance was covered in Deuteronomy 21:15–17. Jesus was on His way to the cross. He washed His hands as far as material things were concerned. He will take up those issues when He comes back to reign. Before we condemn this man too harshly, however, we should examine the petitions that *we* bring to Jesus. All too often, they concern such things as our health, wealth, and welfare in this world.

The Lord followed this exchange with one of the most memorable of His parables—the parable of the rich fool (12:16–21). The man in the parable was not just rich; he was *very* rich. He had just reaped a bumper harvest. He had never had such a harvest. But that raised a problem. What was he going to do with his surplus? That was the question God was asking too—with His eye on the needs of the poor. It did not take this man long to make up his mind. He would build bigger barns. He would store the grain until the commodity was in short supply. Then he would put it up for sale and multiply his gains still more.

The fellow made three mistakes. First, he *mistook his bankbook for his Bible.* He measured success in terms of what he read in his bankbook and on his balance sheet rather than by what he read in his Bible. We note his selfish attitude—"*my* barns, *my* fruits, *my* goods."

Then, too, he *mistook his body for his soul.* He had a little talk with himself. "Soul," he said, "thou hast much goods . . . eat, drink, and be merry." What a way for a man to talk with his soul! What use does a soul have for barns and banquets? Those things have to do with the material side of life; they have nothing to do with the soul. The soul is engineered for the spiritual side of life. The soul needs to be saved and sanctified. The soul needs to be fed from the Bible. But this man had no thought for those things.

Finally, this secular humanist *mistook time for eternity.* He was evidently still a young man. He assured himself that he had "many years," but he was going to be dead before daybreak. Even as he was gloating over his fortune and his future full of fun and frolics, looking again and again at his bankbook and his balance sheet, the voice of God rang forth. God had been looking at the balance sheet that *He* was keeping of this man's life. He wrote across the whole thing one word—*Bankrupt!* "Thou fool. . . ," He said, "So is he that layeth up treasure for himself, and is not rich toward God" (12:21).

So much for squabbling over an earthly inheritance. This man was rich. He had bountiful barns, wide estates, and vast resources—plenty for his relatives to fight over. Not a penny of it could he take with him to the land of the lost. How does a person become rich toward God? By declaring spiritual bankruptcy (Rom. 3:10–20) and turning to Christ (2 Cor. 8:9).

> d. Against care (12:22–32)
>> (1) Our material problems (12:22–31)

Coming back to His disciples, the Lord warned them against the cares of this world. "I say unto you, Take no thought for your life, what ye shall eat; neither for the body, what ye shall put on. The life is more than meat, and the body is more than raiment." Yet, our lives, as a rule, are so taken up with making a living, as we call it, providing for these things. The expression "Take no thought" simply means "Don't be anxious." The Lord knows what it is like to live in this world. He knew, too, what it was like to be poor. The Lord knows we have need of such things. We are not to hide our heads in the sand like so many ostriches and hope that heaven will shower down upon us the money we need as God did the manna in the wilderness (Exod. 16). That is not the thought. Rather, we are not to be anxious. Life is more than food and drink.

"But we have to eat," somebody says. Jesus might well have replied, "On one occasion I did not eat for nearly six weeks. Then Satan came and put Me to the test. He suggested that I perform a miracle that was well within my power and turn some nearby stones into bread. I told him not to tempt God. My Father knew that I was hungry. It was His will for Me to be hungry. He wanted Me to trust Him even when hunger brought Me down to the doors of death. I was right in the center of His good and acceptable and perfect will, right there on the verge of starvation. Better to die of hunger *in* the will of God than to have bread enough and to spare *out* of His will. What happened? After I triumphed over the temptation to move ahead of God's will and take matters into My own hands, God sent an angel from heaven to take care of My physical needs. Was I anxious? Of course not! My Father is absolutely dependable."

Look at the fowls. Jesus continued, "Consider the ravens: for they neither sow nor reap; which neither have storehouse nor barn; and God feedeth them" (12:24). Probably there is no millionaire on earth who could afford to feed the world's bird population for a single day!

A man in England raised a raven, then gave it its liberty. It made its home in some rocks. It would still come to the house where it had been raised to be fed. The man who raised this bird would walk on the nearby hills and the raven would soon appear. The man observed that the raven had caches of food stored up all over the place, hidden in the heather. When the man would feed it, the raven would take a big beak full and stack it away under a stone, covering it so neatly that it was hard for the man to find, even after watching the bird dig it in. The God who taught the raven to cache its food without barns and who Himself feeds the ravens is well able to care for His people.

Look at the facts. "Which of you with taking thought can add to his stature one cubit? If ye then be not able to do that thing which is least, why take ye thought for the rest?" (12:25–26). No one has the ability to increase his stature no matter how hard he thinks about it. By the same token, nobody can add to his allotted span of life. If we cannot change even these basic things, why worry at all?

Look at the flowers. Jesus went on, "Consider the lilies how they grow: they toil not, they spin not; and yet I say unto you, that Solomon in all his glory was not arrayed like one of these. If then God so clothe the grass, which is today in the field, and tomorrow is cast into the oven; how much more will he clothe you, O ye of little faith?" (12:27–28).

Solomon was the most flamboyant of Israel's kings. He was well known for his costly array. Even the queen of Sheba was overwhelmed at his magnificence. The

Lord plucked a wayside weed and held it up for the disciples to see. What was the essential difference between a hedgerow flower and Solomon's vaunted splendor? Simply this: the glory of the lily grows from within; Solomon's glory was all put on from the outside. God, who so arrays the transient, short-lived little flower, can surely be trusted to provide for His own.

"Seek not ye what ye shall eat, or what ye shall drink, neither be ye of doubtful mind" (12:29). We are reminded again of the rich fool and his preoccupation with eating and drinking. The word for "doubtful mind" suggests the rising of the wind. The picture is that of a sailing ship putting out to sea. We must not allow material things to trouble us. A skilled captain knows how to get the most out of the capricious winds and makes even contrary winds move his ship forward. We are not to be tossed and turned by material worries. We are to subdue them and use them to help us grow in grace and increase in the knowledge of God.

"All these things do the nations of the world seek after" Jesus continued, "and your Father knoweth that ye have need of these things" (12:30). The world of lost men and women, who have no heavenly Father, might be excused for their preoccupation with temporal things, but we have a different perspective.

Let us get our priorities right. Jesus said, "But rather seek ye the kingdom of God; and all these things shall be added unto you" (12:31). *Things!* This whole discussion began with *things,* with a man greatly put out because his brother would not share *things.* Our priority must be higher than that. We must seek first the kingdom of God. If we do that, the Lord will see to it that we have what things we need.

(2) His millennial program (12:32)

On the one hand are our material problems and on the other hand are His millennial plans. "Fear not, little flock; for it is your Father's good pleasure to give you the kingdom." What a giant little verse. It belongs with our list of truly monumental texts—John 3:16; Isaiah 53:6; Psalm 23:1; and Hebrews 1:3.

First, there is *a little flock.* The Lord's people on this planet in this age are like the coneys in the wise man's parable. They are "but a feeble folk" (Prov. 30:26). They are at best just a few among so many, a small minority relative to the total world population. There is much to make them afraid, but His sheep are not scattered far and wide on the hostile hills as sheep without a shepherd. They have a Shepherd (Ps. 23:1; Matt. 26:31; John 10:12–16). The people of this world view us as a poor lot but the Shepherd knows each of His sheep by name. And to the utmost bounds of earth's remotest hills, He is shepherding us all toward His home.

Then there is *a loving Father:* "Fear not little flock; for it is your Father's good pleasure to give. . . ." Our Father never stops thinking of us, planning for us, giving to us. Our Father is a living God and a giving God. He knows what is best for us and is resolved to bestow it on us. He has already given us His Word. He has given us His Son. He has given us His Spirit. He has given us His salvation, full and free. He has given us all things that "pertain unto life and godliness" (2 Peter 1:3).

Finally, there is *a large future.* "It is your Father's good pleasure to give you the kingdom." No wonder we should seek first the kingdom of God. He is going to give it to us! No wonder He taught us to pray, "Thy kingdom come." He is going to give it up to us. Satan knows that, and he hates us because of it.

> e. Against complacency (12:33–13:9)
>   (1) The simple command (12:33–34)

The Lord continues to warn His disciples because that kingdom had not yet come and would not come for a very long time. It still has not yet come in its full and final form. We must *live for the right world.* "Sell that ye have, and give alms; provide yourselves bags which wax not old, a treasure in the heavens that faileth not, where no thief approacheth, neither moth corrupteth" (12:33). The disciples at that time were called upon to live like that. The Lord was still on earth, and the message was still restricted to the nation of Israel.

After Calvary and Pentecost, when the church tried to implement communal living, it all broke down. In the end, the Jerusalem church had to receive charity from Paul's Gentile churches. The history of the mendicant friars of the Middle Ages is far from inspiring although those orders were founded by men who practiced poverty and meant well. Paul allowed himself to be beggared for the cause of Christ ("I suffered the loss of all things") and knew what it meant to be in want (Phil. 3:8; 4:11–14), but he nowhere commands us to do what the Lord here commanded the disciples to do. There has been a change in dispensations. The motivating principle is for us to keep our eye on the right world and live accordingly. If we hoard material things, we invite the thief to come and the rust to corrode. And death robs us of it all.

Moreover, we should *live in the right way:* "For where your treasure is, there will your heart be also" (12:34). If we want to have treasure in heaven, we should give something to those who are going there. The rich fool's treasure was down here—so was his heart.

(2) The Second Coming (12:35–48)
(a) Waiting for the Lord (12:35–36)

One reason we should be living for the right world is that is where our Lord has gone and where He is now living. Another reason is that He is coming back, and we surely do not want to be ashamed when He comes (1 John 2:28). "Let your loins be girded about, and your lights burning" (12:35). Loins girded! We must be found *working* when He comes. In Bible times, men wore long flowing garments. When they got down to business, they tucked in the ends so that their robes would not impede them. Lights burning! We must be found *witnessing* for Him when He comes. We are to be "like unto men that wait for their lord, when he will return from the wedding; that when he cometh and knocketh, they may open unto him immediately" (12:36).

The wedding refers to the marriage of the Lamb to the church, His bride. In the background are the Tribulation saints and other heirs of the kingdom. The picture is that of an Oriental wedding and the subsequent marriage feast, all of which could go on for some time. The focus here is on the man's servants, who are expected to stay busy and awake during his absence.

(b) Watching for the Lord (12:37–40)

First, there is *a great promise:* "Blessed are those servants, whom the lord when he cometh shall find watching: verily I say unto you, that he shall gird himself, and make them to sit down to meat, and will come forth and serve them" (12:37). What an extraordinary promise! (See also 17:7–10.)

Someone has called this the greatest promise in the Bible. It is a sure and certain indication of how greatly the Lord loves His servants and appreciates their willing, watchful commitment to His cause.

The Lord next talks about the need for *great preparedness* (12:38–39) and mentions the second and third watches of the night.

It is not always clear in the Gospels as to which coming He has in mind. There are two future comings of the Lord. The first is His coming *for* the church. We call that coming the Rapture. It is a secret coming. The time is not known. That coming is in the air, and its purpose is to snatch away the church (the bride) before the Antichrist comes to play havoc with this world. This coming of the Lord (the Rapture) brings to an end the age of grace.

Millions of souls will be saved after the Rapture (Rev. 7). These Tribulation saints will not be in the church, but they will be in the kingdom—indeed, the gospel preached at that time is called "the gospel of the kingdom" (Matt. 24:14). These post-Rapture believers will face fearful persecution, and most of them will be martyred. These people will also be looking for the Lord's coming. This coming must be distinguished from the Rapture. At this second and final advent, the Lord will come *with* the church (the bride). He will return to earth. This coming will be visible, glorious, invincible, and convened to put an end to the horrors that have engulfed the globe. The date of this coming will be known. It will be 1260 days from the time the Antichrist sets up his image in the rebuilt temple of the Jews in Jerusalem. The day will be known but not the hour.

In Luke 12:38, the Lord mentions the *nearness* of His coming: "And if he shall come in the second watch, or come in the third watch, and find them so, blessed are those servants." The second watch was from 9 P.M. to midnight; the third watch was from midnight to 3 A.M. An Oriental wedding banquet would certainly not be over before 9 P.M. By the time of the fourth watch, day would be breaking. Thus, the two watches that the Lord mentioned emphasize the dark and dangerous night watches. This whole reference, with its emphasis on the hour, has to do with the terrible night season, yet to come, when the Antichrist will be on the rampage (Rev. 13).

The Lord mentions also the *nature* of His coming: "And this know, that if the goodman of the house [in this incident, one of the Lord's servants on earth attending to His affairs] had known what hour the thief would come, he would have watched, and not have suffered his house to be broken through" (12:39). This is probably a reference to the Great Tribulation period on earth, the Lord Himself being away at His wedding and His kingdom people on earth going through the horrors of those days.

The point of the parable is simple enough. A householder gets word that a thief is planning to ransack his house. His informant even tells him the day. What does that householder do? He prepares to give the fellow a warm reception. He redoubles his guard. He urges everyone to watch; the thief is coming.

Just so! Jesus is coming. As far as the Tribulation saints are concerned, He has sent word ahead. He has announced the day—1,260 days after the desecration of the temple in Jerusalem. The countdown begins. The day will be known. He has not advertised the hour, but He has hinted at the watch—it will be after dark, sometime between 9 P.M. and 3 A.M., sometime in that six-hour period. As the time draws near, the believers on earth take fresh courage. They will be living in a nightmare world, and the terror has been going on for years. The householder has been tempted to give up and get out, but he has decided to go on. The day arrives. He alerts his household. This is the day! He puts everything in order. When the heavenly visitor arrives, they'll be ready to give Him a very warm welcome indeed!

In all ages, the Lord's people are to be ready for the coming of the Lord. The word of the apostle is helpful here: "Not forsaking the assembling of ourselves together, as the manner of some is; but exhorting one another: and so much the more, as ye see the day approaching" (Heb. 10:25).

The Lord emphasized the thought: "Be ye therefore ready also: for the Son of man cometh at an hour when ye think not" (12:40). The emphasis is still on the hour of the Lord's return, an unknown hour, similar to the unknown day. Thus, the emphasis seems to be on the final return rather than on the Rapture. The Jews will be in their last extremity. The Tribulation saints will be in hiding and in desperate straits. Jerusalem will be sealed off and its inhabitants being systematically slaughtered. The world's armies will be assembling at Megiddo. All hope of the Lord's return will fade. The world will be mad with lust, rage, and anguish. How to escape the killing, the tortures, and the global holocaust will be the preoccupation of most people. Treachery will be commonplace. Through the din and noise, God's people will hear that still, small voice: "Be ye ready!"

(c) Working for the Lord (12:41–48)

This long discourse is interrupted yet again. Peter, as usual, has something to say. "Lord," he said, "speakest thou this parable unto us, or even to all?"

The Lord disregarded Peter's question and went on with His teaching. Now His focus is on the need for proper stewardship. A great reward exists for faithful stewardship. The Lord will make that man "ruler over his household," with duties to the Lord and to the Lord's people. Indeed, the steward who is standing faithful and true at the Lord's coming will be amply rewarded. The Lord will "make him ruler of all that he hath" (12:44).

But what about the wicked servant? The Lord has three things to say about him. There is the matter of his *skepticism:* "But and if that servant say in his heart,

My lord delayeth his coming . . ." (12:45a). It is easy to see how people can get put off regarding the second coming of Christ. Some people, for instance, set dates for the Lord's return and trumpet their "discoveries." It has happened often. The Jehovah's Witnesses and the Seventh-Day Adventists both did that. When I was young, a man named G. F. Vallance caused a considerable stir that came to nothing. Several years ago, Edgar C. Wisenant attracted media attention with his book *88 Reasons Why the Rapture Will Be in 1988*. All such efforts are in vain, and they invariably produce their casualties.

Then some people embrace the idea that the church is spiritual Israel. That creates all kinds of eschatological problems. Much of the Old Testament has to be allegorized. The literal interpretation of Old Testament prophecies has to be debunked along with clear teaching on the Millennium. The modern rebirth of the nation of Israel has to be somehow explained away.

Along with all this, some people have always picked up bits and pieces of prophetic truth and used them to support some error or other. No wonder many people wash their hands of Bible prophecy altogether and end up becoming skeptics. Some of them use the long-seeming delay of the present age as their excuse for discounting precious truth. The Lord Himself said that His coming would be delayed (18:7; 20:9). Had Israel accepted Him as Messiah, all of the Old Testament prophecies would have been fulfilled then and there. The stubborn rejection of Christ by the Jewish people brought on the church age, a long parenthesis in God's dealings with Israel and the nations.

So the Lord foresaw that some would abandon Advent truth and become skeptical of all prophetic teaching.

Then there is the matter of *his sinfulness,* made all the worse by his abuse of power: "And [he] shall begin to beat the menservants and maidens, and to eat and drink, and to be drunken" (12:45b). Bible truth concerning Christ's coming again ought to to be a sanctifying influence in our lives (1 John 3:3). Men who abandon revealed truth but remain in positions of authority in the church to propagate their unbelief upset the faith of many. Great will be their accountability. Similarly, those who hide behind a cloak of orthodoxy but who actually live scandalously will not escape.

Finally, there is the matter of *his sentence* (12:46–48). Three types of servants are in view here. The first type is the *false* servant: "The lord of that servant will come in a day when he looketh not for him, and at an hour when he is not aware, and will cut him in sunder, and will appoint him his portion with the unbelievers." This servant is no servant at all. Whatever profession of faith the man might have made is annulled by his behavior. The Lord numbers him among the unbelievers. Judas was just such a man.

The second type is the *forgetful* servant: "And that servant, which knew his lord's will, and prepared not himself, neither did according to his will, shall be beaten with many stripes" (12:47). Here is a man who is well schooled in the things of God. He knows what is expected of him. Nevertheless, he wastes his time and talents and ignores God's will for his life. Instead of laying up treasure in heaven, he fritters away his life. He will be "beaten with many stripes." Sometimes those stripes come in this life as God chastises him for his neglect. At other times, God withholds judgment here because He intends to deal with it over there. This brings into view the judgment seat of Christ (Rom. 2:16; 1 Cor. 3:11–15; 2 Cor. 5:10). "[He] shall be beaten with many stripes." He will suffer blow after blow, as it were, as the various affairs of his life are weighed and found wanting and are cast into the fire as wood, hay, and stubble.

Finally, the third type is the *feeble* servant: "But he that knew not, and did commit things worthy of stripes, shall be beaten with few stripes." No excuse will be accepted at the judgment seat for poor performance, but allowance will be made for ignorance. The principle that the Lord lays down is simple: "For unto whomsoever much is given, of him shall be much required: and to whom men have committed much, of him they will ask the more" (12:48b). In other words, the Lord's requirements are similar to those required by a human employer.

(3) The stormy canvas (12:49–59)
    (a) The Master's warning to His men (12:49–59)

The Lord continues His warnings against complacency. "I am come to send fire on the earth," He said. The background bristled with animosity. The Lord's enemies were beating every bush in the hope of flushing into the open some hidden inconsistency in His life. They wanted to get something on Him (11:53–54). Only Luke records this exclamation that escaped the Lord's lips. The context was twofold. The Lord was keenly aware of where this growing hostility of the Jews would end. He was also teaching on the folly of accumulating material things. As Elisha said to his unfaithful servant Gehazi, "Is it a time to receive money, and to receive garments, and oliveyards, and vineyards, and sheep, and oxen, and menservants, and maidservants?" (2 Kings 5:26). Elisha's keen prophetic vision enabled him to see the dreaded armies of Assyria massing far, far away—the terrible scourge that God was going to use to thrash Israel.

The Lord had come to kindle two kinds of fire: Pentecostal fire and punitive fire. The revival fire, foretold by Joel (Joel 2:28–32) would have swept Israel, had the nation responded, and would have ushered in the millennial age. Israel's recalcitrance, however, sealed its doom. The Pentecostal fire came, all right, but instead of bringing in the kingdom, it gave birth to the church. Punitive fire fell on Israel. The Romans came in A.D. 70 and destroyed Jerusalem and the temple. They came back in A.D. 135 and put an end to Jewish national life. The Jews were left to wander the world, constantly hated and hounded.

But now, in God's wisdom, they have been regathered, and their national life has been resumed. The sojourn of the church on earth is about over. The moment the Rapture takes place and the church is removed, God will send Pentecostal fire again. This time the fire will fall on Israel, and Joel's prophecy will have a second and a fuller fulfillment. Millions of souls will be saved despite the rage and resistance of the Antichrist. The 144,000 Jewish evangelists will preach the gospel of the kingdom to earth's remotest bounds, and countless millions of souls will be saved (Rev. 7). But then the Lord will send the punitive fire again, too, to make short work of the Antichrist's sin-soaked world. However, the Lord's disciples at that time did not have an inkling of these events.

The Lord would be the catalyst of these things. At their core would be the cross: "I have a baptism to be baptized with," Jesus declared, "and how am I straitened till it be accomplished!" (12:50). He was referring to His approaching crucifixion. The Lord said that He was "straitened" until that terrible baptism was accomplished.

We are familiar with that old English word *strait*. It appears in our word *straitened*, which means to "make narrow." It is used in the word *straitjacket*, which involves being confined. It shows up on maps as *straits* (the Strait of Gibraltar, for instance), a place where the sea-lanes narrow. The Greek word that Luke used means to be constrained or restricted. Before His resurrection, the Lord had the sense of being increasingly restricted. He could be in only one place at a time, for instance. Now, He can be everywhere, the constant Companion of each of His own (Matt. 28:20), the present Guest at each gathering of His people. Now that His purpose was to go to Jerusalem—there to suffer, bleed, and die—even His movements were restricted.

Moreover, now that the cross was on the distant horizon, the Lord moved to dispel any illusions that the disciples might be entertaining. "Suppose ye that I am come to give peace on earth? I tell you, Nay; but rather division" (12:51). The "peace on earth" heralded by the angels at His birth would now have to be postponed until His coming again. Moreover, the battle would rage in the very homes of God's people: "For from henceforth there shall be five in one house divided, three against two, and two against three" (12:52). Father and son would be at loggerheads; mother and daughter would be at daggers drawn. Once let a member of an ordinary human home become a committed Christian, and the chances of peace will be in jeopardy. The agelong history of the church on earth is proof of that fact.

(b) The Master's warning to the multitude (12:54–59)

Signs of the times were everywhere. The people could see them and were *observant* of them. They could see a cloud rise out of the west. "There's going to be rain!" they say. And right they are. They feel the south wind blow. "It's going to get hot," they say. And they are right (12:54–55). The geographical setting for these forecasts is the land of Israel. To the west was the Mediterranean, from whence came the rain; to the south was the desert, which gave the hot, dry winds. The people could read these signs in the sky. But they were blind to the spiritual signs (12:56). The Lord accused them of hypocrisy.

Why could they not read the plentiful signs of the times? The living God was in their midst. The prophets had foretold His coming. They also had foretold the place (Mic. 5:2), the period (Dan. 9:24–26), and the plan (Isa. 42:1–3). He had Himself demonstrated His deity in countless ways. He had told them who He was and why He was there. A visit to the archives in the temple would have given documented proof that He was descended from David (Matt. 1:1–16). But they were blind to it all.

They were not only blind to what was *apparent* but also blind to what was *approaching* (12:57–59). The whole discussion began when a man asked the Lord to intervene in a legal case. The Lord ended this oration with a legal case, an impending case between themselves and God. He said, "When thou goest with thine adversary to the magistrate, as thou art in the way, give diligence that thou mayest be delivered from him; lest he hale thee to the judge, and the judge deliver thee to the officer, and the officer cast thee into prison. I tell thee, thou shalt not depart thence, till thou hast paid the very last mite" (12:58–59).

Before long, these very people, spurred on by their rulers, would be howling for His death. And what a death! Then the church would be born, and the Jewish rulers would see it as a threat. God would send apostles and prophets. Sanhedrin and synagogue would rise up against them. And still God would hold back His hand. But legal proceedings would soon be under way. The Judge would be on the bench. The Judge would be the Lord Himself, with the nail scars in His hands. But there was still time. The guilty nation of Israel could still make its peace with God. Time, however, would not stand still. All that was required was a national turning to Christ, and the case would be settled out of court.

The nation of Israel refused to come to terms, so it was delivered over to the officer—a veiled reference to the Roman military—God's executioner. By A.D. 135, the Jews were ready to fall for the first of a number of weird false messiahs. He was Bar Cochbar, who led the Jews into an insurrection. The result was the total defeat of the Jews and their complete expulsion from the land. Jewish national life came to an end. For the next two thousand years or so, they would be scattered far and wide. Homeless, hated, and hounded from land to land—"till thou hast paid the very last mite," Jesus said.

(4) The stern conclusion (13:1–9)
(a) Needed repentance (13:1–5)

Some people in the crowd told Jesus about some Galileans whose blood Pilate had mingled with their sacrifices (13:1). The accession of Tiberius to the throne of the empire changed the political climate in Palestine. The mild rule of Augustus gave way to the merciless harshness that characterized the reign of the vile and vindictive Tiberius. The emperor hated Jews and everything for which they stood. The first procurator appointed by Tiberius to bring to heel the troublesome province of Judea changed the Jewish priest four times until he found in Caiaphas the compliant tool he was seeking.

Then came Pontius Pilate. He was far worse than his predecessor. His rule was marked by violence, robbery, bribery, persecution, and gratuitous insults to Jewish religious sensibilities. The actual incident recorded here is not found elsewhere. Likely enough it occurred at one of the national feasts. On such occasions, Jewish nationalism tended to boil over. In any case, the Roman garrison hastened to the scene. Some of the insurgents were caught at the great brazen altar itself. The Romans made short work of them. Their shed blood mingled with the blood of the sacrifices they were offering. This, in the popular mind, was proof that these people must have been notorious sinners. Moreover, they were Galilaeans. They put the incident up to Jesus for His verdict, confident that He would endorse the popular view. "Suppose ye that these Galilaeans were sinners above all the Galilaeans, because they suffered such things? I tell you, Nay: but, except ye repent, ye shall all likewise perish" (13:2–3). And so many of them did when the Romans came. No doubt in that fierce and fanatical struggle many such tragedies occurred.

The Lord continued, "Or those eighteen, upon whom the tower in Siloam fell, and slew them, think ye that they were sinners above all men that dwelt in Jerusalem? I tell you, Nay: but except ye repent, ye shall all likewise perish" (13:4–5). The Jews likely preened themselves when Jesus was told about the incident that befell the Galileans. After all, what would you expect where Galileans were involved? If so, Jesus quickly punctured their balloon. The incident at Siloam took place in the Judeans' own backyard. This incident was well known. The workmen who perished were on Pilate's payroll. A pet project of Pilate's was to build an aqueduct to the pool of Siloam—paid for with money stolen from the Jews' religious treasury. The Jews convinced themselves that this disaster was deserved—it served them right for being in the pay of Pilate.

Jesus brushed aside this attitude. Far from being a singular act of well-deserved judgment, it was quite the contrary. Let the Jews beware. Wholesale judgment was on the way unless nationwide repentance occurred. In the Roman wars soon to come, many people perished in similar ways when Jerusalem fell.

(b) National repentance (13:6–9)

The Lord now draws to a conclusion His warning about repentance. He spoke of *the barren tree:* "A certain man," He said, "had a fig tree planted in his vineyard; and he came and sought fruit thereon, and found none" (13:6). The fig tree was a symbol of the nation of Israel in its Christ-rejecting unbelief (Matt. 21:18–20; 23:13–19; 24:32–33). Normally, fig trees wring their existence from stony and inhospitable soil. This particular fig tree had been given unique opportunities. Everything was done to make it fruitful. Thus, God had dealt with the nation of Israel in contrast to the Gentile nations, which more or less were left to fend for themselves (Rom. 9:1–5). Israel had been blessed with God's covenants and commandments. He had sent them patriarchs, prophets, princes, and priests. What thanks did He get for all of this? None! The tree turned out to be barren.

Next comes *the bitter truth:* "Then said he unto the dresser of his vineyard, Behold, these three years I come seeking fruit on this fig tree, and find none: cut it down; why cumbereth it the ground?" (13:7). The Owner was God. The Vinedresser was Jesus. For three years, He had crossed and recrossed the vineyard, teaching as never man taught, and performing miracles such as no one had wrought. They failed to see the uniqueness of what was happening in their midst

(12:56)—the utter barrenness of the nation of Israel (the fig tree). "Why cumbereth it the ground?" Far from being useful, it was actually spoiling the good land around it. It was intended by God that the nation of Israel be set in the midst of the nations of the earth to be a testimony and a blessing to all mankind. "Cut it down!" That was the word from on high.

The Gardener interceded. Our attention is drawn to *the borrowed time:* "And he answering said unto him, Lord, let it alone this year also, till I shall dig about it, and dung it: and if it bear fruit, well: and if not, then after that thou shalt cut it down" (13:8–9). The nation of Israel was to be given a second chance. The day of Pentecost came, and the Holy Spirit came down. In its very earliest period, the church was composed solely of Jews. The remnant of Israel became the nucleus of the church. But already the nation and its leaders were causing problems. Gentiles were being invited into the church and were already outnumbering the Jews many times over. Having rejected the Son of God, the Jews as a whole were now rejecting the Spirit of God, at home and throughout the Dispersion. The borrowed time ran out, the Romans came, and the *nation* of Israel was no more.

E.   The sermonic approach (13:10–30)
     1. A sympathetic Christ (13:10–13)

The attack against Christ soon broke out again. This time, the opposition took the form of a sermon, brief but bitter, and it was delivered by the ruler of a synagogue. It all began when the Lord's heart went out to a poor woman in desperate need. The whole thing happened in a synagogue in Perea, across Jordan, where the Lord had spent so much of His time during the past six months. The Lord continued His policy of attending the local synagogue on the weekly Sabbath, and He had been asked to preach. He still had a large following among the masses, and it would have been a bold synagogue ruler who would have denied the famous Jesus the pulpit when most of the people were eager to hear Him.

Three great Sabbath controversies are in the Gospels, and the same bitter spirit of hostility toward Jesus can be seen in each of them. In Jerusalem, outright persecution broke out because the Lord had not only healed the man at the pool of Bethesda but also told the man to take up his bed and walk in defiance of strict man-made, rabbinical Sabbath restrictions (John 5:15–16). In Galilee, the opposition began because the Lord's disciples were caught plucking and eating corn on the Sabbath. It came to a head when the Lord deliberately went into a synagogue on the Sabbath and openly healed a man with a withered hand, knowing full well about a plot to kill Him. In the end, no violence was attempted; on the other hand, the common people did not dare to take His side (Matt. 12:1–15).

Now we have another Sabbath conflict, this one in Perea. "Behold," Luke says, "there was a woman which had a spirit of infirmity eighteen years, and was bowed together, and could in no wise lift up herself" (13:11). The poor woman was actually bent double. Moreover, she had been that way for years. The Lord saw Satan's hand in all of this. The woman actually symbolized the nation of Israel, putty in the Devil's hands.

The Lord called her to Him. A sudden stir swept the synagogue. Was He going to perform one of His mighty miracles? Had He forgotten that it was the Sabbath? The jaundiced eye of the small-town synagogue ruler took in everything. He watched the woman make her painful way from her place at the back of the building to where the Master stood. The ruler and the congregation did not have long to wait:

"Woman," Jesus said, "thou art loosed from thine infirmity. And he laid his hands on her: and immediately she was made straight" (13:12–13).

Jesus "loosed her." The word *luo* is used of the untying of a shoe (Acts 7:33), the loosing of a tethered animal (Matt. 21:2), and the freeing of four fallen angels from their incarceration (Rev. 9:14). Only here is it used in connection with a disease, likely because demon activity was involved in her condition.

A word! A touch! And the woman was well. She was "made straight." The word used is used elsewhere for the setting up of a building, or the restoration of a ruin (Acts 15:16).

2. A sanctimonious critic (13:14–16)

The woman "glorified God." The ruler of the synagogue ran to the pulpit. "There are six days in which men ought to work," he fumed, "in them therefore come and be healed, and not on the sabbath day" (13:14). This small-minded man did not dare aim his accusation at Christ. He addressed himself to the crowd. His soul held no joy for the miracle that set this poor captive free. Imagine! Eighteen years of dreadful bondage! Eighteen years! All that this bigoted little man could do was find fault because, in his opinion, the Sabbath had been desecrated. He certainly could not have healed the poor soul, even if she had come some other day. All he could see was someone performing "work" on the Sabbath. Jesus was ready for the fellow.

"Thou hypocrite," Jesus said, "doth not each one of you on the sabbath loose his ox or his ass from the stall, and lead him away to watering? And ought not this woman, being a daughter of Abraham, whom Satan hath bound, lo, these eighteen years, be loosed from this bond on the sabbath day?" (13:15–16). With a few masterstrokes, He exposed the man for what he was. He called the man a hypocrite. He called the woman "a daughter of Abraham." He saw in her the faith that God had seen in Abraham. "Daughter of Abraham! Standing straight and tall! Her face aglow! A song in her soul!

As for the congregation, all of the Lord's adversaries among them were ashamed. Then the synagogue rang with song as "all the people rejoiced for all the glorious things" that Jesus had done. The word for "glorious" *(endoxos)* means "honored," or "distinguished." It is used of those who belong to a royal family and who are splendidly arrayed (7:25). How, we wonder, did the petty ruler of the synagogue digest that sermon when he was left alone?

3. A sobered crowd (13:17–30)

This discomfiture of the Lord's enemies and the corresponding delight of the common people prompted two parables: the parable of the mustard seed and the parable of the leaven. The two parables emphasize Satan's two-pronged attack against God's program on earth during this age. One emphasizes abnormality; the other emphasizes adulteration.

First was the parable of the *abnormal mustard seed:* "Unto what is the kingdom of God like?" Jesus asked. "It is like a grain of mustard seed, which a man took, and cast into his garden; and it grew, and waxed a great tree; and the fowls of the air lodged in the branches of it" (13:18–19). To most people, this result would seem like extraordinary success. Actually, it was weird and abnormal growth. The mustard plant is a shrub, not a tree. This one was frequented by the birds that found lodging in its branches. The birds snatched away the good seed in the parable of the sower (8:5, 12). They symbolize evil spirits, servants of "the prince of the power of the air" (Eph. 2:2).

During this present age, Israel is under the displeasure of God. The church age has been inserted into history as a temporary measure. It, too, has experienced failure. What the Lord is describing here is not the true church but the false church, Satan's counterfeit church. We have here a prophetic glimpse of what we now call Christendom. The parable of the mustard tree shows what happens when people confuse the church with the kingdom. God never intended the church to grow from a shrub into a tree. After the conversion of the Roman emperor Constantine, the church forsook its divine calling and became a great religious kingdom reigning over the nations of the earth. The Roman Catholic Church is a prime example.

The parable of the *adulterated* leaven also foretells failure. Jesus said, "Whereunto shall I liken the kingdom of God? It is like leaven, which a woman took and hid in three measures of meal, till the whole was leavened" (13:20–21). Throughout Scripture, leaven is universally used as a type or symbol of inbred evil. Christendom has been marked by phony development just as it has been marked by phony doctrine. The church today is riddled with it.

The Lord warned against both "the leaven . . . of the Pharisees and of the Sadducees" (Matt. 16:12) and "the leaven of Herod" (Mark 8:15). The Pharisees were *religionists* who promoted dead traditions and empty ritual and religious rules. The Sadducees were *rationalists* who denied the supernatural, the existence of spirits, and the truth of resurrection. They were also wealthy, aristocratic, and powerful. They controlled the temple and the office of high priest. The Herodians were *royalists,* advocating obedience to King Herod and acceptance of anything else that might buy the goodwill of Rome.

The church has had its share of those who would water down and distort its great truths. Often, those who have brought in false doctrine have done so by stealth. The leaven is insinuated into the meal.

The Lord kept on the move now because His time was running out. He went from city to city, "through the cities and villages, teaching, and journeying toward Jerusalem" (13:22). We recall Luke's previous words that the Lord steadfastly set His face to go to Jerusalem (9:51). The statement introduced the Lord's last six months on earth. He was on His way to Calvary. He had been on His way there since before the foundation of the world. But now the shadow of Calvary's hill fell constantly across His path. The Lord spent most of these last six months in Transjordan, a part of the Promised Land corresponding more or less to the Gilead of the Old Testament. The Lord could make His way thus, avoiding both hostile Samaria and Judea.

While on His way, someone asked Him, "Are there few that be saved?" The question seems to have been sincere enough. Perhaps the questioner had noticed the falling away of many people as the Lord's ministry became increasingly controversial and confrontational.

The Lord answered at once: "Strive," He said, "to enter in at the strait [narrow] gate: for many, I say unto you, will seek to enter in, and shall not be able. When once the master of the house is risen up, and hath shut to the door, and ye begin to stand without, and to knock at the door, saying, Lord, Lord, open unto us; and he shall answer and say unto you, I know you not whence ye are . . ." (13:24–25).

"Are there few?" That's your question. "Let me tell you about the many." The important question is not "Are there few or many that are saved?" The important question is "Are *you* saved?" Many will be lost because of being late. They were not serious about their salvation when the door was open wide. They became serious too late.

"Strive!" He said, "Agonize!" Paul uses the word in describing the demands made on an athlete competing in the Olympic games (1 Cor. 9:25). There is nothing lackadaisical about that. The athlete throws everything he has into the race to ensure that he wins. How much more should a man, woman, boy, or girl throw everything they have into the quest for salvation. The old-time evangelists used to hammer away at conviction of sin and genuine repentance as essential to genuine conversion. They preached to the conscience, for a Holy Spirit quickening of the conscience leads directly to salvation. Nathan shows us how it's done (2 Sam. 11:1–12:14). Salvation is free, blessed be God! Satan, however, puts a thousand obstacles in the way for those who hear the call. The Lord underlines here the need for an all-consuming desperate need, a compelling conviction that will overcome all obstacles.

The Lord drew a graphic picture of multitudes who never bothered themselves much about their soul's salvation until the door was shut and it was too late. The time is now! The classic biblical illustration is found in the story of Noah's ark. Too long they scoffed. Too long they sinned away the day of grace. Suddenly, the day came, and the door was shut (Gen. 7:16). Those who were shut in went through the judgment unscathed; those who were shut out were doomed.

The same principle applies to the age of grace in which we live. When the last soul is saved, the door of mercy will be closed. "Then," Jesus continued, "shall ye begin to say, We have eaten and drunk in thy presence, and thou hast taught in our streets. But he shall say, I tell you, I know you not whence ye are; depart from me, all ye workers of iniquity" (13:26–27). They thought that all they needed was a nodding acquaintance. Just because He once had an open-air meeting just down the street from where they lived, they felt sure that was enough to get them in.

I once had a neighbor who came to an evangelistic crusade in town. The message rang out as clear as crystal: "Ye must be born again." I asked him the next morning what he thought of it. "Oh," he said, "a little of that goes a long way with me. Besides, my wife is a descendent of John Wesley."

"It will be too late," Jesus warned, "once the door is shut." "There shall be weeping and gnashing of teeth, when ye shall see Abraham, and Isaac, and Jacob, and all the prophets, in the kingdom of God, and you yourselves thrust out" (13:28). The Lord sees the Old Testament saints feasting with the prophets and the patriarchs. The Lord never treated the dead as being annihilated. They were still alive, in heaven or in hell, for better or for worse. Alas for the lost! They had always known about Abraham. They prided themselves in the fact that they were children of Abraham. They were his descendents. Much good that did them! That only added to their guilt. David and Daniel! Moses and Malachi! Jacob and Jonah! What a gathering of the ransomed that will be. And they, themselves, will be shut out. All of the Bible stories are true! They are not just stories, not just things that happened a long time ago. They are *true*. They deal with real people— alive and singing the songs of salvation. But they themselves, with Jesus in their midst, were unbelievers, procrastinators who were destined to be lost and in anguish for all eternity. Jesus taught us that it is so.

The Lord has one last word: "And they shall come from the east, and from the west, and from the north, and from the south, and shall sit down in the kingdom of God. And, behold, there are last which shall be first, and there are first which shall be last" (13:29–30). So much for Jewish religious and racial pride. Here we have part of the Lord's answer to the question "Are there few that be saved?" (13:23). Few indeed? Who can count the converts of this present age of grace? Who can count the multitudes to be saved in the post-Rapture judgment age? One hundred forty-four thousand Jewish evangelists will be sealed and sent forth to win people for Christ—beneath the nose of the Antichrist himself. This harvest of souls will be great—a multitude that no man can number (Rev. 7).

The Jews despised the Gentiles. They thought that they were unclean (Acts 10:9–22:28), and referred to them as dogs. They refused to enter Gentile homes and regarded what they ate as unclean. They considered themselves to be heaven's favorites (Rom. 2:17–24). Yet, here they come—Gentiles from the four corners of the earth, marching to Zion, crowding into the kingdom, and the Jews were shut out by their criminal unbelief.

    F.   The scare approach (13:31–35)
        1. A warning (13:31–32)

They had snubbed Him, sneered at Him, and slandered Him. Now they tried to scare Him. "The same day there came certain of the Pharisees, saying unto him, Get thee out, and depart hence: for Herod will kill thee" (13:31).

Herod Antipas! It was a name of infamy. He had first imprisoned and then murdered John the Baptist. Doubtless, he had his spies everywhere to tell tales about the new young prophet. If Herod had been afraid of John, he must have been terrified of this new prophet, who was now reported to be in or near Herod's territory. John had performed no miracles, but the whole nation was agog with excitement over the countless signs, wonders, and mighty miracles that Jesus performed. It would be good policy to leave Him well enough alone. Sure, he'd like to see some of the amazing things that Jesus reportedly had done. Some people said that He did them by black magic that was energized by Beelzebub. Others pronounced Him to be the very Son of God.

In the end, Herod decided to try threats. He called for some of the toadies who told him about the preaching and miracles of Jesus, and then he tried to frighten Jesus away. "Tell Him I'm going to kill Him," he said. It was just what they wanted to hear, and they took great relish in telling Him. Plenty of proof existed that Herod was quite capable of doing what he said. After all, he had already murdered John.

If the Lord's foes thought that they could scare Him away, they were very much mistaken. Herod? Murder Jesus? Frighten the Lord of glory? With countless angels encamped around Him? Jesus was not afraid of Herod, Annas, Caiaphas, Pilate, or anyone else. He sent back a message to this murderous man: "Go ye, and tell that fox, Behold, I cast out devils, and I do cures to day and to morrow, and the third day I shall be perfected" (13:32).

Herod probably didn't understand a word of it—except the part about his being a fox. The fox has a reputation as the craftiest creature in the countryside. Countless stories are told of his cunning and how he preys on smaller animals.

The message that Jesus sent to this fox of a man was this that His time was short, and not even Herod could shorten it further. He was not afraid of Herod or his threats. He would continue doing what He was doing. But ahead (after "to day" and "to morrow") lay a "third day" in which He would be "perfected." The reference doubtless points toward His resurrection. From the cross rang out a mighty cry: "It is finished!" (John 19:30). Thus, Jesus dismissed Herod Antipas, the only man to whom He ever addressed a message of contempt. Moreover, He sent the message by the Pharisees. These bitter enemies of Jesus likely used this scare approach to try to draw Jesus to Jerusalem, where the Sanhedrin could control Him. They hoped to frighten Him away from the relative security of the Transjordan region. They need not have been concerned about that; He was on His way to Jerusalem and would arrive there in God's appointed time.

2. A woe (13:33–35)

The Lord had been on His way to Jerusalem for a considerable time. He now had four things to say to that city before He even arrived. First, He had *a fatal denunciation:* "Nevertheless I must walk to day, and to morrow, and the day following: for it cannot be that a prophet perish out of Jerusalem" (13:33). The statement was one of withering sarcasm and scorn. With ironic hyperbole, the Lord accused the Jews of having a monopoly on killing prophets, and He had no intention of depriving them of their most notable victim. The expression "it cannot be" comes from the word *endechomai* ("it is not fitting"), and it occurs nowhere else in the New Testament. The great city where God Himself had once sat between the cherubim in the Holy of Holies had now become the executioner of the prophets and was soon to become the murderer of God's beloved Son.

Second, He had *a factual description* of Jerusalem: "O Jerusalem, Jerusalem, which killest the prophets, and stonest them that are sent unto thee; how often would I have gathered thy children together, as a hen doth gather her brood under her wings, and ye would not!" (13:34). This sad lament was repeated later when He arrived in the vicinity of Jerusalem. He loved that city. He knew every market and stall, every tower and tree. He knew its history from the days of the royal priest Melchizedek to the days of the sly Herod Antipas. He had seen it defiled by foul Antiochus and freed by the mighty Maccabees. The Romans came so that now the synagogue and Sanhedrin ruled the land under the iron scepter of Rome. Many a time, His heart had been broken by the wickedness of those in power. How often He would have sheltered the city from the folly of its ways. But the city would have no part of it.

He moved on. Down the road, there would be *a fearful destruction* of Jerusalem: "Behold, your house is left unto you desolate . . ." (13:35). The siege and sack of Jerusalem was to be one of the most terrible events of history. When it was over, the walls and gates would be reduced to rubble, the temple would be wrapped in flames, and the corpses would be strewn far and wide, and the Romans would be so infuriated by the strength and stubbornness of the siege that they would wreak fearful vengeance on those who were still alive.

But that was not all. Finally, He had *a final destiny* for Jerusalem: "Ye shall not see me, until the time come when ye shall say, Blessed is he that cometh in the name of the Lord" (13:35). This prophecy had a near and partial fulfillment. An immediate fulfillment occurred on "Palm Sunday," when the Lord received the hosannas of the city and especially the cheers of the Galileans who thronged the city in anticipation of Passover. Probably few people realized it, but that Triumphal Entry marked the termination of Daniel 9:22–26b. In keeping with that prophecy, He would be dead within the week. The crowds who thronged and cheered Him would shout just as lustily for His crucifixion.

The real fulfillment went beyond the fall of Jerusalem in A.D. 70, beyond the Bar Cochba rebellion in A.D. 135, on and on, past the two thousand-year church age to the time of His coming again. A blindness has descended on the Jews concerning Christ (Rom. 11:1–10). But when Christ comes back, all of that will change. The first reaction of the Hebrew people to sudden appearing of the Lord in splendor in the sky will be to mourn (Rev. 1:7). But then will come His Triumphal Entry into Jerusalem. Then indeed the Jews will sing their loud hosannas, and Psalm 118:26 (here quoted by the Lord) will come into its own.

G. The subtle approach (14:1–35)
    1. An invitation to dinner (14:1–24)

First, *the table is spread:* "And it came to pass, as he went into the house of one of the chief Pharisees to eat bread on the sabbath day, that they watched him" (14:1). The man was probably well-to-do and a member of the Sanhedrin. The Lord knew all about the insincerity of this man but went to his home because He loved him as He loved one and all. This was the last Sabbath in the Lord's ministry (of which we have record) before His arrival in the city.

"They watched him." The word used implies that they eyed Him with malicious intent. By this time, the Lord must have been quite used to such hostile "hospitality" (6:7; 20:20). Luke used the same word to describe the sharp watch that the Jews kept on the gates of Damascus when they planned to murder the recently saved Saul of Tarsus (Acts 9:23–24).

Soon *the trap was sprung:* "And, behold, there was a certain man before him which had the dropsy" (14:2). Dropsy was the general term for a number of diseases—mostly of the heart, liver, kidneys, and brain—that causes water to collect in the cavities of the body, on its surface, or in the limbs.[1] The trap was twofold: could Jesus heal this man, and, if so, would He do so on the Sabbath? The man seems to have been invited to come to the house but not as a guest.

Jesus was ready. He opened the offensive. Addressing the various lawyers and Pharisees who were in the home as guests and spies, Jesus asked, "Is it lawful to heal on the sabbath day?" They remained silent. Jesus then healed the man and

---

1. Merrill F. Unger, *Unger's Bible Dictionary* (Chicago: Moody, 1957), 266.

let him go (14:2–4). These people, particularly the Pharisees and the lawyers, insisted on the most rigid observance of the Sabbath laws, but they practiced the opposite. They turned the closing hours of the Sabbath into an occasion for feasting. Was it lawful to heal on the Sabbath? Of course it was! But what the Lord described as healing they defined as working.

Then *the tables were turned* (14:5–24). The Lord's enemies maintained their stubborn silence, so the Lord continued, "Which of you shall have an ass or an ox fallen into a pit, and will not straightway pull him out on the sabbath day?" Some commentators claim that the Lord actually said, "Which of you have a son or an ox . . ." The Pharisees would not hesitate to break their absurd rule to rescue a beloved child or a valuable piece of property. They continued their silence, but their eyes spoke volumes. The Lord had unceremoniously thrown out of court their most respected biblical authorities. They were tongue-tied.

The Lord continued His offensive. He shifted His line of attack, but now He displayed their rudeness and pride of place. At this kind of a social function, the couches would be placed thus:

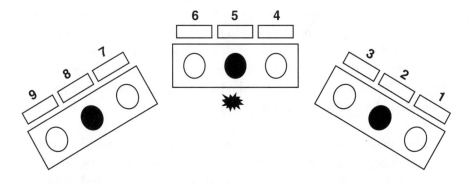

Each table with its accompanying set of three seats was called a triclinium. The center seat of each triclinium was a seat of honor. The host would take seat number nine, the lowest place. The guest of honor at each table would occupy the center seat. The guest seated in the center seat of the middle table would be the special guest of honor.

The Lord had seen these guests pushing and shoving in a scramble for the best seats. So there they sat in whatever seat they had been able to grab or in whatever seat the host had assigned them. They glared at Him. We are not told what seat had been His, but we can be sure that He would not have jostled anyone for a seat.

Again He spoke: "When thou art bidden of any man to a wedding, sit not down in the highest room [couch]; lest a more honourable man than thou be bidden of him; and he that bade thee and him come and say to thee, Give this man place; and thou begin with shame to take the lowest room [couch]" (14:8–9). On the contrary, the Lord advised, "Go and sit down in the lowest room; that when he that bade thee cometh, he may say unto thee, Friend, go up higher: then shalt thou have worship in the presence of them that sit at meat with thee" (14:10).

Jewish doctors of the Law were notorious for their pride. The Lord might well have witnessed just such a scramble for seats and a rearrangement of guests by the host. In the thickening silence, the Lord delivered His conclusion: "For whosoever exalteth himself shall be abased; and he that humbleth himself shall be exalted" (14:11). The Lord repeated this same warning on two other occasions (Matt. 23:12; Luke 18:14).

Taking advantage of the continuing silence, the Lord proceeded to expose the selfishness of the Pharisees just as He had exposed their arrogance and pride. He directed His next remarks to the man who had invited Him to dinner solely to trap him: "When thou makest a dinner or a supper, call not thy friends, nor thy brethren, neither thy kinsmen, nor thy rich neighbours; lest they also bid thee again, and a recompence be made thee" (14:12). That, of course, was just what the man had done. Probably they were all in on the trick to be played on Jesus. "Next time," Jesus said, "when you invite people to your place for supper, invite the poor, the maimed, the lame, the blind. . . ." The man had invited one such poor fellow, the man suffering from dropsy—not to be a guest but to be the bait in a trap.

"Thou shalt be blessed," Jesus continued, "for they cannot recompense thee: for thou shalt be recompensed at the resurrection of the just" (14:14). The Lord Jesus—invited or not—is, as the familiar Christian saying goes, "the Head of this house, the unseen Guest at every meal, the silent Listener to every conversation." He notes everything. He weighs all of our actions. Rebukes and rewards are to be given us at "the resurrection of the just," that is, at the judgment seat of Christ. "And thou shalt be blessed!" The Lord's desire for all of us is that we would do as He says and reap an eternal reward.

At this point, the Lord's comments provoked a response from one of the guests. He picked on the expression "thou shalt be blessed." He liked the prospect of future reward, which he linked with sitting down at the Lord's table in heaven and the prospect of eating bread in the kingdom of God (14:15). The speaker might have been trying to defend the host. Possibly, he felt that he had been picked on unfairly. He said in effect that he, the speaker, counted himself happy ("blessed"—seizing on the Lord's last word) to have been included in the invitation of his host, the Pharisee, and to be eating at his table, to be counted fit for his company and hospitality. How much more, he exclaimed, will be the happiness of those who are counted worthy of the kingdom of God, of being a partaker of resurrection life, and of enjoying the hospitality of heaven itself. Doubtless, the speaker considered himself a prime candidate for such honor, even as he sat there impervious to the Lord's teaching and encased in the armor of his own smug self-satisfaction. The man needed a sharp lesson, and the Lord saw that he received it by telling him a story. The story was designed to emphasize the serious likelihood that many of those who had the best opportunity in the world of enjoying the bliss of glory would not be in the kingdom of God at all, thanks to their own folly.

A certain man, Jesus said, made a great supper and invited many people to come. The invited guests symbolized the Jews to whom God had made so many advances in so many ways over so many centuries. In their own day, they had received the heartiest invitations from John the Baptist and from Jesus Himself. Suppertime came, and the generous host sent his servant to tell the guests to come (14:17). The gospel feast was spread. The invitation held good. The hour was come. The Jews were being urged to come, to flock into the kingdom of God.

"And," said Jesus as He fixed His eye on the man, "they all with one consent began to make excuse." They were of one mind about it. What Jesus had to offer had no appeal to them at all. The Lord picks out three representative excuses. First was the man who was *too big to come*. He had just bought some property, he said. He needed to go and take a look at it. The man was indulging in falsehood or folly. Who buys property sight unseen? In any case, he considered himself too big to be bothered about a mere supper. "You'll have to excuse me," he said.

Second was the man who was *too busy*. He was not a land speculator, wheeling and dealing like the first man. Rather, he was a middle-class workingman. "I've just purchased five yoke of oxen," he said. "I've got to harness them to a plow and try them out. You'll have to excuse me. I can't come." He was just as much a fraud or a fool as the first man. Who, especially in the East, would buy ten oxen sight unseen and wholly untested? The supper? There was no way he could make it. "You'll have to excuse me," he said.

And third was the man who was *too blissful* to come. "I have married a wife," he said, "so I cannot come." This was the silliest excuse of all. He could have gone to the supper regardless of whether he had a wife. He allowed being a newlywed to come between him and a great opportunity to meet important new people. He is the archetype of all people who allow family ties to come between them and God. Abraham, when he was a new believer, nearly made shipwreck on that rock (Gen. 12:1–5; 11:27–32).

The story, however, was only just begun. When the master of the house was told about these excuses, he was angry and told his servant to scour the streets and lanes of the city for the poor, the maimed, the halt (the lame), and the blind. The response was immediate, but still there was room (14:21–22). The word rendered "angry" means literally to be provoked, to be wrathful. It depicts anger as the strongest of all the emotions. It is no light thing to spurn the gospel invitation. The Lord's anger is seen as kindled against those who so lightly made excuses and shrugged off the invitation to the supper of salvation, which was provided at such infinite cost. So, accordingly, the door is slammed on those who shrug off so lightly the opportunity of a lifetime.

Until Calvary, the special apostolic missions were restricted to "the lost sheep" of the house of Israel. This restriction did not last long after Pentecost, although the city of Jerusalem and the nation of Israel were the first to be evangelized and indeed were initially the sole recipients of the gospel. The gospel horizons were soon expanded. First, the Samaritans were invited to the feast, then the Gentiles in ever-increasing numbers began to pour in to the feast. Soon, Gentiles far outnumbered Jews in the church.

In the parable, "the streets" refer to the main thoroughfares, the larger streets. The "lanes" refer to the narrow warrens behind the great boulevards of a large city. The whole picture depicts the gospel invitation going out during this age to wherever people dwell.

So the invitation went forth. Some people refused it. Others responded positively to it. The house began to be filled, but even so there was still room for multitudes more. "Go out into the highways and hedges, and compel them to come in, that my house may be filled," the master said (14:22–23). This probably refers to the final salvation call, which will be made after the rapture of the church (Rev. 7:1–17; 14:6–7).

"For I say unto you," Jesus said to the Pharisee and his guests, "that none of those men which were bidden shall taste of my supper." They refused to come. They were to be shut out and have no part in the great feast that will usher in the millennial age.

2. An invitation to discipleship (14:25–35)

With that telling remark, the Lord rose from the Pharisee's table and walked out of his house. What the conversation was like after His departure we can well imagine. The crowds awaited Him outside. "If any man come to me," He told them, "and hate not his father, and mother, and wife, and children, and brethren, and sisters, yea, and his own life also, he cannot be my disciple" (14:25–26). Love for one's own flesh and blood is proper and commendable. The Lord is not depreciating that love. But if natural love and home ties come between a man and Christ, he must reevaluate his love. Our love for Christ must be so strong that it overrules all other loves. Moreover, to become a disciple of Christ, a person must love the Lord more than he loves himself. The history of the church on earth is filled with stories of such deathless devotion to Jesus.

"Whosoever doth not bear his cross, and come after me, cannot be my disciple," Jesus said (14:27). The words must have struck a most discordant note in the ears of that jostling human crowd. A cross? The cross was the very symbol of Roman oppression and cruelty. It was a gallows, an instrument of unbelievable suffering and shame. Nothing about a cross was glamorous. It was the very symbol of the Curse. "Cursed is every one that hangeth on a tree," declared God's law (Deut. 21:23; Gal. 3:13). The Lord's disciples all reacted against the mention of the cross (Matt. 16:21–25), so we can imagine the astonishment of the crowd. They saw nothing in this message for them. They thought that the procession was marching to Zion to crown Him. The notion that He was heading toward Calvary and a cross never occurred to them in their wildest dreams.

"Count the cost!" Jesus told these willy-nilly members of the throng. A disciple must be like *a man preparing to build.* He has a tower in mind. The first thing to do is ensure that his resources are adequate to the cost he will incur. What mockery he can expect if he runs out of money when the foundation is laid. The place will become a landmark—"So-and-so's folly."

The word *counteth* is derived from a word meaning "a pebble." In those days, calculations were made with the aid of pebbles. The only other place where the word occurs is in connection with the mystical name of the coming Antichrist. People will be able to identify him by "counting" the number of his name—"666" (Rev. 13:18).

The Lord warned the multitude that He wanted no impulsive response to His call. Being a disciple is a costly business. It calls for deliberate serious thought. The mission fields of the world can tell stories of would-be missionaries who, once the glamour wore off and the stark realities became evident, packed up and went back home. John Mark almost became such a "missionary" (Acts 12:25–13:5, 13).

Moreover, a disciple must be like *a monarch preparing for battle* (14:31–32). "What king," Jesus said, "going to war against another king, sitteth not down first, and consulteth whether he be able with ten thousand to meet him that cometh against him with twenty thousand? Or else, while the other is yet a great way off, he sendeth an ambassage, and desireth conditions of peace." The Christian life is a battle. Satan is the foe, the prince and god of this world. It is no light matter to go to war against him. By the same token it is an even costlier matter *not* to go to war against him, strong and mighty in battle as he may seem.

The Lord now summarized these sayings: "Likewise, whosoever he be of you that forsaketh not all that he hath, he cannot be my disciple" (14:33). All about Him was the crowd. Despite the growing opposition of the Jewish establishment, many people were genuinely attracted to Him. He was deliberately separating the wheat from the chaff. He offered no easy path.

"Salt," He said "is good: but if the salt has lost his savour, wherewith shall it be seasoned?" (14:34). It is fit for nothing. Salt that does not do what it is supposed to do—add flavor and arrest corruption—is good for nothing, not even the manure heap.

But there was one more word. The Lord was not trying to frighten away everyone—only those who had not counted the cost and those who would quit when the going got tough. "He that hath ears to hear, let him hear," He concluded (14:35).

    H. The sarcastic approach (15:1–32)
       1. The people (15:1–2)

The net result of all of this down-to-earth teaching is significant. The scribes and the Pharisees were left fuming. The rank and file of the general public were as wishy-washy as ever. But the people on the fringe of society, the "publicans and sinners," those who were generally despised by one and all, were drawn to Him. The Pharisees and the scribes drew their self-righteous robes around themselves, sneered at this sudden move of outcasts and untouchables toward Jesus, and sarcastically jibed, "This man receiveth sinners, and eateth with them" (15:2). No more wonderful thing was ever said about the sinless Son of the living God. They meant to deride Him. The angels in glory must have applauded Him: "This man receiveth sinners, and eateth with them!"

2. The parables (15:3–32)
   a. The lost sheep (15:3–7)

The Lord responded to the sarcasm of the scribes by telling the three most wonderful stories He ever told. Three groups of people were in the crowd. To the publicans and sinners, these stories were parables of *hope*. The religious establishment excommunicated them, but these stories brought hope to their heavy hearts.

The Pharisees and the scribes were there, pulling back from the fallen as though they were lepers, bitterly scornful of a "Messiah" who would befriend such people. Their hard hearts were full of arrogance. To them, these parables were intended to be parables of *love*.

But the Lord's disciples were there too (16:1), taking it all in but not making much sense of it. To them, these parables were parables of *faith*. Much that the Lord was doing and saying mystified them. They needed more faith. They needed to learn that God is no respecter of persons, that He is willing to save one and all, and that salvation is by faith.

"What man of you, having an hundred sheep, if he lose one of them, doth not leave the ninety and nine in the wilderness. . . ." People are lost like sheep are lost, involuntarily; they simply stray. Domestic sheep are not strong, swift, or smart. In fact, they seem to be somewhat stupid. They wander. If a hole is in the hedge and a sheep in the field comes across it, the sheep will go through it. The sheep has everything to gain by staying in the field and everything to lose by poking its way through a hole. It will at once be exposed to its foes. Moreover, once a sheep is lost, it cannot find its way back home. Worse still, once one sheep finds the hole in the hedge, every sheep in the field will follow the leader out through that hole. Similarly, people follow other people—carelessly, foolishly, and without a thought about the perils that surround them as they wander away from God.

Our attention is brought back to the shepherd. Well he knows the perils that lurk out there beyond the fold. He can do only one thing—secure the fold, leave the flock, and search for the lost sheep. Once he has found it, the shepherd "layeth it on his shoulders," Jesus said. He puts it out of harm's way. There is something particularly appealing about that—just one shoulder to bear the weight of government for all of the earth (Isa. 9:6). Two shoulders to secure the saved sheep. Then came the punch line: "I say unto you, that likewise joy shall be in heaven over one sinner that repenteth, more than over ninety and nine just persons, which need no repentance" (15:7).

"The publicans and the harlots go into the kingdom of God before you," Jesus said to the religious leaders of Israel (Matt. 21:31).

b. The lost silver (15:8–10)

People are lost not only the way sheep are lost but also the way coins are lost, through a sudden fall. In this parable, a woman had ten silver coins. She lost one. She lit a lamp to find it. The coin was lost through no fault of its own but through forces over which it had no control. It came under the influence of the power of gravity, and it was gone, lost in the darkness and dirt. The likeness of the king stamped upon it became defiled. Worse still, it had no awareness of being lost.

The woman, however, knew that it was lost. Perhaps it was a piece of silver that she had saved from her meager means, or perhaps it was part of her dowry. Her sense of loss was real. She searched diligently until she found it. This all reminds us of the Holy Spirit's work in this world. He first lights the lamp (2 Cor. 4:6), which represents God's Word (Ps. 119:105), and it dispels the darkness in which people live. The Holy Spirit "sweeps the house," searching diligently for the lost coin.

The parable concludes with joy when the woman recovers the lost coin and restores it to its place. Jesus said, "Likewise, I say unto you, there is joy in the presence of the angels of God over one sinner that repenteth" (15:10).

c. The lost sons (15:11–32)

This parable involves two sons. First, it includes the story of the *scandalous* son (15:11–24). Men are lost like sons are lost—through rebellion, pride, self-will, and deliberate choice. The parable of the prodigal focuses on the publicans and sinners; the story of the elder brother depicts the scribes and Pharisees. We can be sure that both groups easily recognized themselves in the story.

First, there were *the far horizons*. "A certain man had two sons," Jesus said, "and the younger of them said to his father, Father, give me the portion of goods that falleth to me. And he divided unto them his living" (15:11–12). In the parable of the lost sheep, it is the Son who is the active member of the Godhead. In the story of the lost coin, it is the Holy Spirit who is at work. In the parable of the two sons, it is the Father who predominates. Indeed, in this twin parable, the Father is mentioned by name no less than twelve times.

The lure of faraway places took hold of the younger son's soul. Doubtless, he was fed up with the rules, religion, and righteousness of his father. He longed to get away from it all. He approached his father with his heartless demand. In effect, he said, "Let's pretend that you are dead so that I can receive here and now my share of the inheritance." The father, far from indignantly refusing the son's outrageous request, gave him his share. No amount of pleading and reasoning was going to do any good; the father gave in. The young fellow would have to find out the hard way what it was like to be cast adrift in a cold, cruel world.

First, we have the prodigal's going-away prayer—"Father, *give* me." It was the prayer of a heartless young fool. "Not many days after the younger son gathered all together, and took his journey into a far country" (15:13). The expression "took his journey" implies that he went abroad. He wanted to see the world—the great wide, wonderful world—far from the narrow confines of Jerusalem, Judea, and Judaism. If he had headed north to Caesarea, about sixty-five miles away, he could have taken ship to Myra on the coast of the Roman province of Lycia—a giant step of another nine hundred miles. From there, he could have sailed on to Rome, landing at Puteoli. From there, he could have anticipated Paul's route to Rome, heading up the Appian Way another five hundred miles or so. Or he might have journeyed to Rome, marching along the great Roman highways and stopping here and there along the way to sample the world's wicked wares. Or perhaps he headed for Egypt and then on to Carthage or even Tarshish—a far country indeed. One way or another, the distance could have been measured in miles. But that is not how they measure distance going to or coming from the beckoning shore of "the far country." Corinth? Carthage? Crete? The distance as measured by God was expressed in terms of morals, not miles.

He "wasted his substance with riotous living." He abandoned himself to the lust of the flesh, the lust of the eyes, and the pride of life. We see a man throwing his money away, living in debauchery, and surrounded by fast-living companions. "Come on, you fellows, the drinks are on me," he would say. The party girls would add to the fun and frolics of that faraway land.

Then all of his money was gone—and so were his fair-weather friends. God stepped in, doubtless in answer to a living father's heartbroken prayers. "And when he had spent all, there arose a mighty famine in that land; and he began to be in want" (15:14). That was God at work. The far country is no place to be when your funds run out, your friends take off, and famine moves in. "He went and joined himself to a citizen of that country; and he sent him into his fields to feed swine." He was so hungry that he even fished in the hogs' slop bucket and stuffed the muck into his mouth. Working around hogs was an unclean business for a Jew. It would seem that even to get such a vile job he virtually had to force himself on the man who employed him. So much for the far horizons.

At last, he began to think of *the father's house* (15:17–19). "When he came to himself, he said, How many hired servants of my father's have bread enough and to spare, and I perish with hunger!" It was not long after he came to himself that he came to his father. "I will arise and go to my father," he decided. He would make a full confession: "Father, I have sinned against heaven, and before thee, and am no more worthy to be called thy son: make me as one of thy hired servants" (15:18–19). David had prayed a similar sinner's prayer a thousand years earlier (Ps. 51:4). It would have done no good for this young man to have returned home as rebellious and as riotous as he was when he went away. So now we note his coming home prayer: "Father, *make* me!"

"I will arise and go to my father!" That was the moment when the will took over. The gospel invitation first reaches the conscience, then the heart, then the mind, and finally the will (Gen. 24:58; Josh. 24:15; Matt. 23:37; John 5:6).

We can picture the young man as he picks himself up, and, pig pail in hand, bangs on the door of the big house. The owner appears. "Here, Mister, here's your bucket. I'm going home."

The man looks at him in disgust. "Going home are you?" we can hear him say. "By the sight and smell of you, if I were your father, I'd turn the dogs loose on you."

"Mister," we can hear the prodigal say, "you don't know my father."

So off he went, heading for home with a heavy heart but with hope burning brightly in his soul—until at last he topped the last rise, and there it was on the horizon—his father's house. And hope died within him as he looked at himself and thought of the bright lights of home. His footsteps faltered. He sat down on the ground and buried his head in his hands.

"But when he was yet a great way off, his father saw him, and had compassion, and ran, and fell on his neck, and kissed him" (15:20). "But"! Note the marvelous *buts* of the Bible; they always herald a change. "He ran"! God is always swift to forgive and in a hurry to save (Isa. 65:24). He ran! There he goes. Down from his watchtower, out onto the street, and down the road, arms outstretched and garments flapping all about him. He calls! The poor prodigal looks up. Suddenly he is wrapped in his father's arms! "He kissed him"! The text suggests that he kissed him fervently.

"Father, I have sinned against heaven, and in thy sight, and am no more worthy to be called thy son . . ." (15:21). That's as far as the father would let him go. A robe! The best robe! A ring for his hand! Shoes for his feet! Received not as a servant but as a son. The great Pauline parallel is recorded in the story of Philemon and Onesimus, his runaway slave.

So they brought forth the fatted calf! Music! Dancing! The old house had never known such happy, holy, heavenly merriment in all of its days. "This my son was dead," the father exclaimed, "and is alive again; he was lost, and is found." Dead! Alive! Lost! Found! There is the story of the Prodigal Son, the whole story of the ruin and redemption of poor, wayward sinners of Adam's race.

We might well pause here and look at the publicans and the sinners—how they must have smiled! And the scribes and the Pharisees—how they must have scowled! But the Lord did not stop. The story was not yet over. The half had not been told. There was another son, a *sanctimonious older son*. The Lord would have us look at him (15:25–32).

"Now his elder son was in the field: and as he came and drew nigh to the house, he heard music and dancing. And he called one of the servants, and asked what these things meant." This elder brother was one of those pious frauds who never run away and never do anything of a criminal nature, but they do all of the things that their beliefs demand and manage to shed their own sanctimonious gloom over everyone else around them. Their sins arise from their disposition; they are spiteful, moody, touchy, self-righteous, niggardly, and bad tempered.

This particular elder brother was on his way home from the field. Doubtless, he was thinking about his supper to be followed by a restful evening. Then his ear caught an unfamiliar sound. Someone was throwing a party. His brother had come home from the ends of the earth and was thoroughly repentant! Hence, the feasting and the merrymaking. Suddenly, the elder brother realized how much he hated his younger brother. He hated him most not for running away with a large slice of the family fortune and not for the wild excesses in the far country (possibly rumors of his excesses had filtered back home) but for coming back home. More extravagance! More partying! A robe no less! And a ring! New shoes and a banquet fit for a king! He should be banished to the servants' hall, given cast-off clothes, and put to work mucking out the barns!

"He was angry," Jesus said, "and would not go in" (15:28). So his father came out and pleaded with him. Go in? Not him! Let them send a few scraps over to the barn. We are not told all of their conversation, but we are reminded of Dr. Bland, who had the reputation of being the most wicked man in the most wicked town in England. The doctor was dying and knew that he had but a short time to live.

Someone sent for the minister, but he was a liberal who had only bits and pieces of a Bible and knew nothing of God's redeeming grace. The dying doctor soon saw through that fellow and had him chased out of his room. Another minister came and led the doctor to Christ. When the liberal minister heard of what had happened, he was indignant. He couldn't see why the doctor should escape the punishment he deserved. "Do you think," he asked a friend, "that a deathbed conversion atones for a whole life of sin?" The friend replied, "No, but Calvary does!"

This was the elder brother's very problem. He could not see why the repentant prodigal should be instantly ransomed and restored. He knew nothing of Calvary love.

He aired his anger to his father: "Lo, these many years do I serve thee, neither transgressed I at any time thy commandment." Maybe so, but his robe of righteousness was full of holes. It was all *I, me,* and *my.* His self-righteousness was deadly. If he had to share the father's house with that young scapegrace of a brother, he would rather stay outside—exactly what the scribes and the Pharisees were doing.

"Thou never gavest me a kid, that I might make merry with my friends," he complained, showing that he had in his heart all along the far country and a repressed lust for the things that had so ruled the young prodigal's heart. "But as soon as this thy son was come, which hath devoured thy living with harlots, thou hast killed for him the fatted calf" (15:30). "This thy son!" the elder brother jibed. "He's no brother of mine." He was as far away from the father's heart in spirit as his younger brother had been in fact when he was hundreds of miles from home.

Despite his son's sneers, the father loved that mean-spirited, hypocritical elder brother just as much as he loved the prodigal. So he continued, "Son, thou art ever with me, and all that I have is thine" (15:31). This part of the parable was clearly pointed at the scribes and the Pharisees. Israel was the elder brother. The nation occupied a special place in the purposes of God (Rom. 9:4–5), but no reason existed why these special blessings should not continue. But Israel was about to shut itself out by sheer meanness of spirit, just as the elder brother was about to do.

All that the elder brother had to do was come on in and take his rightful place, but not even the father would force him; the decision had to be his. Still pleading, the father continued, "It was meet that we should make merry, and be glad: for this thy brother was dead, and is alive again; and was lost, and is found" (15:32).

The Lord left the story unfinished. The last we see is the father still pleading and the elder brother still pouting. The die was not yet cast when Jesus told the tale. The Jews had not yet finally and irrevocably rejected Christ. The door was not yet shut, but it soon would be. Paul expounded the end of the story later in Romans 9–11.

I. The scoffing approach (16:1–17:10)
  1. The love of money (16:1–13)
   a. A difficult story (16:1–8)

The Lord now turned His attention to His disciples. It is still the same momentous Sabbath in Perea that began with the Lord's invitation to a meal in a Pharisee's house (14:1). The Lord told His disciples a story.

"There was a certain rich man, which had a steward; and the same was accused unto him that he had wasted his goods" (16:1). This steward, or agent, held a responsible position with wide powers of discretion in handling his master's affairs. He was a clever scoundrel who had been using his position to feather his own nest.

Someone accused him of wasting—squandering—his master's goods. The same word was used to describe the prodigal, who "wasted his substance" (15:13). He was summoned before his lord, who demanded a full accounting and then fired him.

At this point, the steward faced a dilemma. He said to himself, "What shall I do? . . . I cannot dig; to beg I am ashamed" (16:3). He dismissed at once any such solution to his problem. Then he had a clever idea. He ran his eye down the list of debtors. He noted what each of them owed. The thing to do was to make friends of these debtors and make them indebted to him.

So he called them all before him and asked how much each of them owed. The first one replied, "An hundred measures of oil."

"I'm calling in all of my lord's accounts," the steward continued. "Settle now, and I'll give you a 50 percent discount. Half price—but you must act quickly." Another man owed a hundred measures of wheat. "I'll give you 20 percent off if you act now," the steward said. He was no fool. He knew just how much he could get in cold cash from each of them. He knew what degree of liberality he would have to show to each to gain his gratitude and goodwill—and hopefully reciprocal generosity later. He was unscrupulous—but clever. He turned accounts receivable into cold cash, which gave him some leverage with his lord. About to be banished from his lord's house, he made friends with everybody, some of whom, at least, he expected would receive him cordially in days to come.

Of course, the thing reached the ears of the man's lord, who viewed the steward's shrewdness with a certain grudging admiration. And the lord (the steward's master) commended the unjust steward for being such a clever rogue. The Lord Jesus added to this story a significant comment of His own: "the children of this world are in their generation wiser [shrewder] than the children of light" (16:8). The Lord told the story to contrast the people of this world and their worldly wisdom with the people of God. The Lord did not say that the children of this world are wiser than the children of light—only for *their* generation. Their native shrewdness does not last very long. It is deeply flawed. It fails to take into account the world to come.

b. A definite statement (16:9–13)

The Lord made a threefold application of the story. First was *a matter of money:* "And I say unto you, Make to yourselves friends of the mammon of unrighteousness; that, when ye fail, they may receive you into everlasting habitations" (16:9). The word *mammon* refers to riches. Just as the steward found a way to guarantee his warm reception into the homes of those whom he had financially benefited, so should we. He did it to secure a temporal benefit; we should do it to secure an eternal reward. If we want to have treasure in heaven, we should give money to those who are going there. The phrase "when ye fail" is generally taken to be "when it fails." The moment death strikes, the power we have to do good with our money ceases, so we should do good with it now. The friends we have made down here because we have ministered to their needs with our means will be waiting for us over there.

This is one of the rare glimpses we get of what things are like on the other side. Dwelling places are over there (John 14:1–3), "everlasting habitations." The redeemed over there are very much alive. Friends will recognize friends. We shall be welcomed into the homes of ones whom we have loved and with whom we have socialized down here. Moreover, our condition over there is directly related to our conduct down here; there is continuity. Our works follow us (Rev. 14:13). We shall meet people from our own generation over there who will receive us warmly because of the lively memory they have of our kindness to them down here.

Then there is *the matter of management:* "He that is faithful in that which is least is faithful also in much: and he that is unjust in the least is unjust also in much. If therefore ye have not been faithful in the unrighteous mammon, who will commit to your trust the true riches?" (16:10–11). Notice the emphasis here on the present tense. The Lord is stating a principle; those who have settled the larger issue of the unseen spiritual world will show it by the way they handle the smaller issues of this temporal world. This principle applies especially to money. A person is careless or unprincipled in money matters in the way he supports or neglects the Lord's work because he is careless in eternal matters. The "unrighteous mammon" to which the Lord refers is God's money that a believer appropriates for his own use. Malachi bluntly calls that kind of thing "robbing God" (Mal. 3:8).

"And if ye have not been faithful in that which is another man's, who shall give you that which is your own?" (16:12). We are on probation down here. We are stewards of divine things (1 Peter 4:10). The time, talents, and treasure allotted to us are ours only on trust. The extent to which we are faithful stewards down here is the extent to which we will be entrusted with things over there.

Finally, there is *the matter of masters:* "No servant can serve two masters: for either he will hate the one, and love the other; or else he will hold to the one, and despise the other. Ye cannot serve God and mammon" (16:13). It comes down to a question of masters—either God masters us or money masters us. We are either going in for something material or for something spiritual. If we are investing for what this world has to offer, we lose sight of God and become the losers when we land on the heavenly shore.

2. The laugh of mockery (16:14)

All of this teaching about money matters produced a mocking laugh: "The Pharisees also, who were covetous, heard all these things: and they derided him." The word translated "derided" here is full of interest. It is used only here and in Luke 23:35, where it is used to describe the scoffing directed at Christ as He hung on the cross. It means literally "to turn up the nose." The Pharisees simply turned up their noses at Christ's teaching. The intensified form of the word here tells us that they were scoffing at Him openly. Luke gives us the reason—they loved money. They looked at Jesus and saw a poor Galilean peasant, and they laughed out loud.

3. The Law of Moses (16:15–18)

The Lord did not let them get away with it. He set before them three aspects of the Mosaic Law—its *essential nature*—which they seemed to have forgotten

(16:15). "Ye," He said, "are they which justify yourselves before men; but God knoweth your hearts: for that which is highly esteemed among men is abomination in the sight of God."

Heaven's values are not the same as human values. Down here, people admire those who are rich. The Lord Jesus, however, read the hearts of those who were scoffing at him. They were saying to themselves, "It's easy to speak so slightingly about money when you don't have any." The Lord's reply exposed their hearts: "You make it your business to pose before men as righteous, but God knows what you are really like. The things that rule your hearts are objects of disgust to God." They are an abomination to Him. The same word for *abomination* is used to describe both the Antichrist's image (Matt. 24:15) and the contents of the golden wine cup in the hand of the great harlot (Rev. 17:4). That is what God saw as He gazed at the scoffing scribes and Pharisees.

Then He added, "The law and the prophets were until John" (16:16). The rabbis and rulers of Israel had built their empire upon their interpretation of the law and the prophets. That interpretation was unsound, so their empire was fraudulent. Its utter wickedness and carnality was about to be revealed at Gabbatha and Golgotha.

The coming of John the Baptist signaled a total change. The kingdom was at hand. The King Himself had come. That changed everything. "The kingdom of God is preached," Jesus said, "and every man presseth into it"—not only the religious elite but also publicans and sinners. The scribes and the Pharisees, however, like the elder brother (15:25–32), were standing on the sidelines sneering.

They were ignorant of not only the Law's essential nature but also its *eternal nature:* "It is easier for heaven and earth to pass, than one tittle of the law to fail" (16:17). The Law was made of the same stuff as eternity because it is the eternal expression of God's holiness, the awesome standard by which the Pharisees and their kind would themselves be judged. The Sermon on the Mount (Matt. 5–7) did not undermine the Law; it simply lifted it to a higher plane. In this current age, grace predominates, but law still undergirds everything (Rom. 13:7–10), especially the law of love. The Law as a *system* came to an end at Calvary with the rending of the temple veil, but the Law as a *standard* remains.

Finally, the Lord underlined the *ethical nature* of the Law: "Whosoever putteth away his wife, and marrieth another, committeth adultery: and whosoever marrieth her that is put away from her husband committeth adultery" (16:18). This statement was in defiance of the school of Hillel, which permitted divorce for all kinds of frivolous reasons. The Lord's standard, as recorded by Luke, was absolute and without exception. We know, however, that exceptions did exist in the Lord's mind, notably where marital unfaithfulness broke the marriage union (Matt. 19:1–12). Nonetheless, we cannot let one verse annul the more complete teaching of Christ. An axiom of Bible interpretation is that "no prophecy of the scripture is of any private interpretation" (2 Peter 1:20). A verse must be considered in the light of not only its immediate context but also other passages that bear upon it. (Here, Luke 16:18 must be modified by Matthew 19:1–12.)

Why, then, did the Lord so abruptly introduce the subject of divorce into this discussion and that so absolutely? Because the Pharisees had just mocked Him for His teaching about money. He was not about to modify His teaching on morality. In this context, He dealt in absolutes. Moreover, He was spelling things out from the standpoint of these "everlasting habitations" (16:9), from the standpoint of heaven, not earth. He is not contradicting the exception clause that occurs in Matthew 19:9–12. It is just not relevant here.

The Lord was not through with the mockers. He pulled back the veil and showed us what awaits people on the other side of the grave. He had just given one glimpse of conditions over yonder (16:9), and His listeners had answered Him with derision. Next, He gave an authoritative statement on what happens after death. This is not a parable (people are not named in the Lord's parables) but a description of something that actually happened to people whom the Lord knew and about things of great importance of which He alone could speak.

4. The lap of misery (16:19–31)
   a. Two deaths (16:19–22)

"There was a certain rich man," He said, "which was clothed in purple and fine linen, and fared sumptuously every day" (16:19). He was very rich and habitually wore the raiment of a king. Indeed, he arrayed himself in radiant splendor, in the kind of robes that Herod Antipas wore, one of which he flung over Christ's shoulders, mocking His claim to be King (Luke 23:11).

In stark contrast, "there was a certain beggar named Lazarus, which was laid at his gate, full of sores, and desiring to be fed with the crumbs which fell from the rich man's table: moreover the dogs came and licked his sores" (16:20–21). Lazarus was a picture of abject poverty. The "sores" that covered his body refer primarily to some kind of a wound or an ulcer. Those who receive the mark of the Beast (Rev. 16:11) will be punished by just such sores when the sores suddenly ulcerate.

The beggar died of want and neglect, which apparently was the rich man's goal. He could have fed the poor fellow with scraps, but that would have encouraged him to stay, and that was the last thing he wanted. He must have hated having to pass him as he went in and out of his house. Or he could have had him hauled away and dumped somewhere, but then some other beggar probably would have occupied the place. No! The best thing to do was let him starve to death, then other beggars would get the message: there are no handouts around here.

b. Two destinies (16:23–31)

The beggar's corpse was carted off to the garbage heap, and the rich man doubtless was pleased by the success of his plan. What the rich man didn't know was that Lazarus was well known in heaven. His name was known, and his "address" was known. A cordon of angels came to take him to "Abraham's bosom," a poetic description of heaven. At death, we are not left to find our own way home. So, poor Lazarus, poor no more, was in paradise in the company of Abraham and in the presence of the Old Testament saints.

Then "the rich man also died, and was buried," the Lord curtly referred to this notable event—notable to men, that is. No doubt, the fellow had an impressive funeral and was buried in a rock-hewn tomb, such as the one that Joseph of Arimathea had prepared for himself (23:50–56). And doubtless the man's five brothers gathered in the rich man's mansion to get their first look at the will.

The rich man himself was in hades and in torment. He saw Abraham afar off. And he saw Lazarus, of all people, reclining on Abraham's bosom. The man was dead. He was buried. But he was still alive. The dead are not dead; they are very much alive. Hades is a real place for real people. It is mentioned various times in the New Testament (here and in Matt. 11:23; 16:18; Luke 10:15; 16:23; Acts 2:27–31; 1 Cor. 15:55; Rev. 1:18; 6:8; 20:13–14). In hades, the rich man could see, hear, and speak. He could feel. He could reason, and, above all, he could remember. Before the Lord's resurrection and ascension, hades was located in "the lower parts of the earth" (Eph. 4:9). It comprised two regions separated by a vast, impassable gulf. The disembodied soul seems to have some kind of interim body that enables individuals to be recognized (1 Sam. 28:13; 2 Cor. 5:1–10).

Anguish filled the former rich man's soul. In his torment, he saw two people, one whom he had known and whom he recognized as Lazarus, the former beggar. The other person was a man about whom he had heard all of his life but whom he now saw for the first time—Abraham, a real person.

The Bible was right. God is the God of the living, just as Jesus had said (Matt. 22:29–33).

The rich man prayed. He had never given much thought to prayer. He had never had much need for prayer. He had been rich, and rich people can buy most of the things they want. But he believed in prayer now. *He* was the beggar now. "Father Abraham, have mercy on me, and send Lazarus, that he may dip the tip of his finger in water, and cool my tongue; for I am tormented in this flame."

Request denied! The role reversal of Lazarus and the rich man was based on unchangeable decrees. The rich man did not love God; otherwise, he would have had compassion on poor Lazarus. Lazarus was a believer for in no other way could he have been on the happy side of hades. Our eternal destiny is based on our love for God and our faith in His Son. It is fixed at death and brooks no change (Rev. 22:11). As for the rich man's prayer, the request was denied.

First, Abraham reminded the sufferer that he was reaping what he had sowed, that there was an unalterable continuity between what he once had been and what he now was. Like the prodigal in his affluent days, he had spent everything.

"Son, remember!" thundered Abraham. All of the wasted years of his life rose up before him. He saw himself as a boy, as a teen, as a young man, and finally as a hardened old sinner making bets with his friends, perhaps on how long it would take that pious old fool Lazarus to die. How terrible will be the moment for each lost sinner at the Great White Throne when God awakens his memory. He will remember his sins, pride, wickedness, bitterness against God, and opportunities to be saved.

The rich man prayed, but he was too late. He knew nothing of prayer. Praying to one of the saints is useless, even if it is to one of the greatest saints such as Abraham. With all of the will in the world, even so great a saint as Abraham was powerless to answer the tormented man's despairing cry. "Beside all this," Abraham said, "between us and you there is a great gulf fixed." No traffic moves between heaven and hell. Mark well that word *gulf (chasma),* which gives us our word *chasm*. It is a medical word and can be rendered "an open wound." *That* explains it! "Between me and thee is an open wound." What keeps a lost person in hell? An open wound! The wound, thrust deep into the Savior's side. God sees that wound, and His wrath burns. What keeps a saved person in heaven? An open wound that pleads the blood of Christ to cancel God's wrath.

> God will not payment twice demand
> First at my Savior's pierced hand,
> And then again at mine.

Moreover, when the rich man awoke in hell, he suddenly was a believer in preaching. He had never had much use for preachers in his former life, but he had a use for one now! Lazarus would make an excellent preacher. When he lived on earth, the rich man had doubtless scoffed and sworn at Lazarus. No more! He sought and solicited him now. A fine preacher Lazarus would be, emerging from his tomb, alive to the horrors of the damned and to the happiness of the saved.

"I pray thee therefore, father, that thou wouldest send him [Lazarus] to my father's house: for I have five brethren; that he may testify unto them, lest they also come into this place of torment" (16:27–28). He had never believed in hell. Had he believed in hell, that belief would have quickened his conscience and changed his behavior. He believed in it now, but it was forever too late. He had five brothers, and they didn't believe in hell either. They needed a preacher!

Nobody other than disease-ridden, starving, dying Lazarus had ever stabbed his conscience. Abraham *must* send Lazarus. He uttered his plea, but it was set aside. "They have Moses and the prophets; let them hear them," Abraham replied. There is enough Bible truth in David and Daniel, in Ezra and Ezekiel, and even in mighty Isaiah alone, for them to know the truth about such things. And then, too, there is Job and Jeremiah. How many more witnesses must God send? No! They have God's Word in their own mother tongue; let them believe that.

The once-rich man reacted to that refusal. "Nay, father Abraham: but if one went unto them from the dead, they will repent." A miracle! That's what those brothers of his needed most, a miracle. Someone they knew, someone they could not forget, someone like Lazarus, someone to come back for a moment from the edge of eternity—that was what they needed! That would do it! Repentance would follow as a matter of course.

But Abraham knew better. "If they hear not Moses and the prophets, neither will they be persuaded, though one rose from the dead" (16:31). And that was the end of the matter. Abraham had no more to say. The man himself was silenced. God shuts people up to His Word. And Abraham was right. The very next person Jesus raised from the dead was *a man named Lazarus* (John 11). Far from believing, the members of the Jewish religious establishment added to their plot to murder Jesus a plot to murder Lazarus too (John 11:47–54).

5. The life of ministry (17:1–10)
   a. Its special relationship (17:1–2)

The Lord had read their hearts aright. Luke now records the closing events of that astonishing Sabbath afternoon in Perea. It had begun with an invitation to dinner that was really a plot to snare Him. He had ended with the solemn unveiling before the souls of everyone there in the crowd of the eternal destiny of the lost and the redeemed. The Lord now turns to His disciples. His focus is on the life of ministry to which He has called them. It involves a special relationship, one that was both perilous and precious.

The fact that all kinds of danger marched beside them must have been dawning on the disciples. If their Lord had not earned the malice and hatred of the scribes and the Pharisees already, He had most certainly earned it now. Unflinchingly, He turned on these enemies of truth and denounced them to their face. He addressed His remarks to His disciples, but He clearly meant His words for His foes: "It is impossible but that offences [stumbling blocks] will come: but woe unto him, through whom they come!" (17:1). The disciples must be prepared. Traps would be set for them. That fact was inevitable given the nature of the battle in which they were engaged. They were up against the very Devil himself. The scribes and the Pharisees were but pawns on the chessboard of time. But woe to them and their like! Deliberately to set traps to stumble others, especially children (Matt. 18:6) and God's people, is a terrible thing in the eyes of heaven. They are the special objects of God's care. The "little ones" mentioned here are those who are taking their first steps in the Christian faith. Woe to those who cause them to stumble! They are under the penetrating eye of God. They would be better off to have a millstone hanged about their neck and to be cast into the sea. The word for "millstone" is literally "an ass-millstone," a great millstone requiring the strength of an ass to turn it. Jesus said that it would be better for a person to be drowned than for him to stumble someone under the burning eye of God. The actual woe is not described, but the proximity of this statement to what the Lord had just been saying about the rich man and Lazarus suggests that Jesus had hell itself in mind. The same divine wrath awaits pedophiles.

b. Its spiritual resources (17:3–6)

The life of ministry draws upon spiritual resources for both its forgiveness and its faith. Jesus, still talking to His disciples, turns to the question of *forgiveness:* "Take heed to yourselves: If thy brother trespass against thee, rebuke him; and if he repent, forgive him. And if he trespass against thee seven times in a day, and seven times in a day turn again to thee, saying, I repent; thou shalt forgive him" (17:3–4).

The Pharisee who had that very afternoon asked Jesus to supper to set a trap for Him was a case in point. The Lord had taken heed to Himself. First, He did not let the man intimidate Him so that He would be unable to deal with the man with dropsy. On the other hand, His attitude toward the Pharisee who had set the snare was one of gentleness. He rebuked the man but was perfectly willing to forgive him if the Pharisee had shown the slightest sign of repentance. The fact that the Pharisee and his friends did not ask for forgiveness but continued sneering and setting traps did not alter the Lord's attitude. He employed both grace and truth in dealing with them. He was even willing to go to Calvary and die for them (23:34). Although the Lord's enemies had trespassed against Him several times that Sabbath afternoon, He had been willing to forgive them. Their response was to continue rejecting Him.

How can we possibly forgive someone several times a day? Is it impossible? Not to those who draw on the spiritual resources available to them in Christ.

The disciples listened to all of this in complete astonishment. "Increase our *faith*," they said. "If ye had faith as a grain of mustard seed, ye might say unto this sycamine [mulberry] tree, be thou plucked up by the root, and be thou planted in the sea; and it should obey you" (17:5–6). No wonder the disciples asked for more faith! The Lord bluntly told them that they did not need more faith. The smallest amount of faith could accomplish the miraculous. Faith is not measured by its bigness or littleness. What is needed is not so much a *large* faith as a *living* faith—faith in the Lord Himself and in His indwelling Holy Spirit. Surely, that is an infinite resource suitable for any occasion!

c. Its special responsibilities (17:7–10)

The Lord drew this lengthy, wordy encounter to a close by warning His disciples against any form of conceit. Suppose that they could wield the kind of faith that could uproot and transplant trees. The very possession of such power might go to their heads; hence, the warning. The Lord then told them a story.

"Which of you, having a servant plowing or feeding cattle, will say unto him by and by, when he is come from the field, Go and sit down to meat? And will not rather say unto him, Make ready wherewith I may sup, and gird thyself, and serve me, till I have eaten and drunken; and afterward thou shalt eat and drink? Doth he thank that servant because he did the things that were commanded him? I trow [think] not."

No Eastern master in olden times would dream of allowing a bond slave to take priority over himself—nor would the slave expect that he would. The slave would take no credit to himself for simply having done his duty. He would not expect special consideration, treatment, or reward for that. Besides, his duties were not yet done; he now had household duties that demanded his attention. Not until all of his chores were finished could he expect to take care of his own needs. His master would not applaud him just because he had done his duty in the field. On the contrary, work would go on according to standing orders. That was the story.

"So likewise ye," Jesus said, "when ye shall have done all those things which are commanded you, say, We are unprofitable servants: we have done that which was our duty to do" (17:10). The point is that the most outstanding of the Lord's servants, when they have done all that is expected of them, have done no more than their duty after all. In a sense, we are not needed at all. Service is a rare privilege. The Lord could have dispensed with it altogether had He so decided. What a blow to our spiritual pride!

J.   The selfish approach (17:11–19)
    1.   The meeting (17:11–12)

The Lord was still in Perea when word reached Him of the serious illness of His friend Lazarus of Bethany. A few days later, He went to Bethany, raised Lazarus, and, because of the increasing plots against Him, retired to an unknown location. He took the disciples into retirement before going to face the final storm in Jerusalem.

The incident that Luke records here took place at the beginning of the Lord's last journey to Jerusalem. "As he entered into a certain village, there met him ten men that were lepers, which stood afar off." Perhaps their common misery had drawn these ten men together. That lepers tended to flock together we learn from 2 Kings 7:3. Even a Samaritan had joined himself to this sad company and was accepted by the Jewish sufferers as one of themselves. This woeful group kept their distance as the Mosaic Law commanded. As their forlorn fellowship stood rooted to their place, the Lord's company stopped. Hope revived in their hearts. This was Jesus! He had healed many lepers; maybe He would heal them.

    2.   The Master (17:13–14a)

"And they lifted up their voices, and said, Jesus, Master, have mercy on us." The doleful chorus awoke the echoes and then died away. Have mercy? Of course, He would have mercy. But He would also put their faith to the test.

"Go show yourselves unto the priests," He said. Perhaps, like Naaman of old, they expected Him to come and strike His hand over the place and thus perform one of the mightiest of all of His miracles—healing ten lepers with one blow (2 Kings 5:11). But Jesus did no such thing.

According to the Old Testament Law, a person who was cleansed of leprosy had to present himself to a priest, be thoroughly examined, and follow up this procedure by following a long, involved, and costly sacrificial ritual (Lev. 14:1–32). It was no light thing for these ten men to seek out a priest and pronounce themselves to be cleansed lepers. As yet their condition remained unchanged. In their condition, it was virtually a death sentence for them to approach other people.

Moreover, no recorded incident exists of this ritual ever being performed. Therefore, the Lord's requirement was no small test of their faith. They went.

3. The miracle (17:14b)

Their first steps in the life of faith and obedience were rewarded immediately. As they went, they were cleansed! All ten of them, including the Samaritan! The dread disease was gone. They examined themselves. They examined each other. It was like being raised from the dead. Then, whooping and laughing, off they went as fast as their legs would carry them to find the nearest priest.

4. The man (17:15–19)

The Lord saw them go, but already their fellowship was breaking up. No doubt the Samaritan's former companions told him that no Jewish priest would pronounce absolution over him. As for them, they had no wish to show up at the synagogue in the company of a Samaritan. Where could he go? Who would pronounce him to be clean? Jesus, of course!

Let the others go to a priest. He would go back to the Savior. Meanwhile, Jesus was left with the feeling of not being thanked by so much as even one of them. Then He heard him. One could have heard the Samaritan praising and glorifying God miles away! He flung himself in praise and worship at Jesus' feet.

Jesus accepted his worship. "Were there not ten cleansed?" He asked, "but where are the nine?" The only one to thank Him, He observed, was "this stranger" (literally, "this alien").

K. The snobbish approach (17:20–19:27)
1. The demanding attitude (17:20–18:8)
a. The character of the kingdom (17:20–21)

The Lord is still on His way to Jerusalem, teaching as He goes. Various attitudes are adopted toward Him. Take, for instance, the attitude of His constant foes the Pharisees. Luke says, "And when he was demanded of the Pharisees, when the kingdom of God should come, he answered them and said, The kingdom of God cometh not with observation: neither shall they say, Lo here! or, lo there! for, behold, the kingdom of God is within you."

The religious establishment was looking for a visible, material, temporal, and worldly kingdom. They wanted a militant messiah, one who would smash the power of Rome and found a new global empire with Jerusalem as its capital and them as its officers. With snobbish arrogance, they wanted to know when He was going to start moving in that direction. The Lord ignored their demand for a date and described instead the spiritual kingdom that He had come to build.

"The kingdom of God cometh not with observation," He said. The word for "observation" here emphasizes "hostile watching" and is always used in a bad sense. They were always watching Him thus (Mark 3:2; Luke 6:7; 14:1; 20:20). The word has a sinister connotation about it.

Moreover, there would be no saying, "Lo here! lo there!" God's plan for a visible, millennial kingdom was dependent upon the Jews' accepting the spiritual truths of the kingdom as preached by John and Jesus (John 3:1–12). The mystery parables of Matthew 13 reveal that the plan to establish an earthly kingdom was postponed because of the Jews' attitude toward the King. All rumors about the Messiah's being here or there should be written off as untrue.

"The kingdom of God is within you," Jesus declared (17:21). Thus, He taught the open-minded Pharisee, Nicodemus, that we need to be "born again" if we are ever going to see the kingdom of God. The Lord is referring, of course, to the spiritual kingdom (John 3:3). The Lord and His enemies were at cross-purposes. They were talking about a material kingdom; He was talking about a spiritual kingdom. They demanded that He tell them just when He proposed to set up His kingdom. He told them, and they failed to understand.

b. The coming of the kingdom (17:22–18:8)

The Lord now addressed His disciples. They were in almost as much a fog about eschatology as were the scribes and the Pharisees. Indeed, it is not always clear to us with the full blaze of New Testament revelation in our hands, just exactly where we are. Is the Lord talking about the impending fall of Jerusalem or about the second coming of Christ?

First, the Lord talked to the disciples about *a day of visitation.* There would be a *rejection* (17:22–25), a *return* (17:26–32), and a *rapture* (17:33–37). "And he said unto the disciples, The days will come, when ye shall desire to see one of the days of the Son of man, and ye shall not see it." Rumors will be flying everywhere—"The Lord is here! The Lord is there!" He warned, "Go not after them, nor follow them." His coming will be like lightning blazing across the sky. "But first must he suffer many things, and be rejected of this generation" (17:22–25).

Calvary changed everything. In Matthew 23, the Lord pronounced a series of terrible woes upon His generation, climaxing with the overthrow of Jerusalem and the temple and concluding with the dissolution of Jewish national life, which took place at the time of the Bar Cochbar rebellion. By that time, the church was well established and had spread widely. The true believers among the Jews ("the Israel of God") were incorporated by the Holy Spirit into the church. All of these things came upon that generation as the Lord foretold. That generation is mentioned frequently in the Gospels, often accompanied by scalding adjectives.

In Matthew 24, the Lord mentioned a different generation, one that would witness the rebirth of the state of Israel and Jewish national life. These events would herald the approach of the end times. In neither case are we expressly told how long the respective generation would last. The generation in Matthew 23 lasted about a hundred years.

Matthew makes these events much clearer than Luke does. The Lord began this instruction by telling the disciples that many times in the days to come they would wish that they could see again the wonderful days of the Lord's first advent (17:22). It would be a barren wish. They would encounter false Christs, but those people would quickly be exposed as frauds (17:23). He pointed them to His return, to His coming as swiftly as a lightning flash, as terrible as a drawn sword, and glorious beyond compare. But first must come the *rejection* by the generation that even then was scheming and plotting His death.

The Lord then turned to the question of His *return* (17:26–32). Passing over the centuries of the church age and the global scattering of the Jews, the Lord pointed His disciples back to two climactic periods of ancient history that would throw light upon the end times. They would be like the days of Noah. People would be carrying on with their ordinary, everyday affairs, oblivious of the doom that hovered over their heads (17:26). Mention of "the days of Noah" takes us back to Genesis 4–6. The picture that Moses painted depicts a pornographic society, fast paced and clever but filled with violence and advanced occultism. It was an utterly godless society, despite Noah's warnings of wrath to come.

Mention of "the days of Lot" (17:28–29) takes us back to Genesis 19. We have a similar picture of a materialistic society that is totally given over to its daily affairs and steeped in sin. It would be a perverted society, carrying on with the ordinary affairs of life, blind to reality, stone deaf to Lot's sudden warnings, and living in debauchery even as the fire and brimstone were descending in fiery judgment from on high. "Remember Lot's wife," the Lord cried. Virtually dragged out of Sodom by angel hands, Lot's wife escaped by the skin of her teeth, only to look back and perish with the ungodly.

So we get two glimpses of the careless evil world that we see all about us today. The days of Noah and the days of Lot describe the days in which we live, days ripe for the Lord's coming again.

Having talked to His disciples about His rejection and His return, the Lord now talks about the *Rapture* (17:33–37). First, He talks about the reality of it: "Whosoever shall seek to save his life shall lose it; and whosoever shall lose his life shall preserve it. I tell you, in that night there shall be two men in one bed; the one shall be taken, and the other shall be left. Two women shall be grinding together; the one shall be taken, and the other left" (17:33–35).

The Lord sets the globe before us. It is nighttime in half of the world, so the Lord shows us two people in bed. It is daylight in the other half of the world, so the Lord shows two people grinding at the mill. At the same moment, on a global scale, in each of the groups, the reemedmed will be raptured and the lost will be left behind.[2] The church will be gone! The apostate church, Israel, and the nations of the world will be left for judgment. That will be the global *result:* "And they answered and said unto him, Where, Lord? And he said unto them, Wheresoever the body is, thither will the eagles [vultures] be gathered together" (17:37). The rapture of the church is by no means the end. It clears the way for the coming of Antichrist and all of the wars and woes that will follow.

The Lord turns now to a description of *a day of vengeance* (18:1–8). He tells the disciples a story. We note first the *purpose* of the parable: "And he spake a parable unto them to this end, that men ought always to pray, and not to faint." The Lord's thoughts are still focused on the days just before His coming again.

---

2. For a more complete discussion, see John Phillips, *Exploring the Gospel of Matthew* (Grand Rapids: Kregel, forthcoming).

The background of the parable is provided by the days of Noah and Lot, which describe the dangers and decadence of the end times after the Rapture and before the Lord's final return. Men's hearts will be failing with fear. His own people, however, have an unfailing resource. They must pray, not faint.

Now let us look at the *pieces* of the parable. First, there was the unjust judge. He feared neither God nor man; he had no reverence for God and no respect for people. "There was a widow in that city; and she came unto him, saying, Avenge me of mine adversary" (18:3). Widows in the East have frequently been exploited, as was the case of this woman, despite the fact that the Law itself noted her condition (Exod. 22; Deut. 10:18). The force of the text indicates that she kept coming back repeatedly.

For some time, the judge ignored the woman, but he finally changed his mind. Although he boasted of his utter disregard for the opinion of God or man, he would consider this woman's case because of her continual coming to his bench. (The text suggests that she had made up her mind never to give up.) The judge was shrewd enough to see that he had met his match. Such are the pieces of the parable.

This brings us to the two *points* of the parable. "Hear what the unjust judge saith," Jesus declared. "Shall not God avenge his own elect, which cry day and night unto him, though he bear long with them? I tell you that he will avenge them speedily" (18:6–8a). The Lord is no unjust judge. We do not need to be importunate with Him. God does not have to be persuaded or pestered. He responds when the proper time comes like a lightning flash—although, of course, His answers might not always be what we expect.

Behind all of this is a deeper teaching. The widow represents God's people in this world, helpless against the assaults of the adversary. The word used is *antidikos*, a word used of the Devil (1 Peter 5:8). The parable, therefore, pictures a child of God who has suffered at the hands of Satan but who, as a believer, does have a place to go; there is a court.

In the unseen world is a high court of angels. The four and twenty elders (Rev. 4:1–11) seem to be members of a similar court. Other angelic beings seem to have functions connected with that court (Matt. 18:1–7). Human kingdoms come under its supervision (Dan. 4:13–17, 31–33), as do their rulers (Acts 12:21–23). God Himself presides over its affairs (Ps. 82:1). Satan has access to that court (Rev. 12:10) and is subject to its power (Rev. 17:7–10).[3]

---

3. See also 1 Kings 22:18–25; Job 1:6–12; 2:1–7; Daniel 7:9–14; 12:7–12; Zechariah 3:1–10; Revelation 7:1–3, 10–12; 8:1–6; 11:15–19; 15:6–8; 20:11–15.

The conclusion of the parable focuses on two things—the compassion of Christ and the coming of Christ: "Nevertheless when the Son of man cometh, shall he find faith on the earth?" (18:8). The answer is "yes!" He will find those who dared all to be true to Him. As for the faith itself, it will be under severe attack. This entire line of teaching underlines the dangers and difficulties of the coming judgment age.

    2. The disdainful attitude (18:9–30)
        a. The man who disdained the prayer of a publican (18:9–14)

We are now introduced to two men, one a Pharisee and the other a publican. The prevailing sin of the Pharisees was a fussy, self-righteous, hypocritical, religious smugness. Throughout the Gospels, they were the Lord's chief foes. That people could be so bigoted and so blind is incredible. God incarnate was in their midst. Who had ever taught such magnificent truths? Who had ever performed so many mighty miracles? Yet, all they could think of was His utter rejection of the endless religious taboos that they used to hedge around God's sublime but simple law. Again and again, the Lord had sought to pierce the armor of their false religion. Now He tries again. The purpose of the parable was plain: "He spake this parable unto certain which trusted in themselves that they were righteous, and despised others" (18:9).

"Two men," Jesus said, "went up into the temple to pray; the one a Pharisee, and the other a publican." We can be quite sure that they did not go up to the temple together.

The very word *Pharisee* became the Hebrew term for one who was *separated* by his beliefs and practices. That sect originated in the time of Jonathan, the successor of Judas Maccabee, in the troublesome intertestamental period. They were not overly numerous, about six thousand of them. Their goals were to observe in the strictest manner all of the requirements of the traditions of the elders and of the Levitical law and to be scrupulous in carrying out all religious duties. They disdained those who were ignorant of the law and the traditions. As a group, they were most noted for their hypocrisy. Many Jews despised them. The rabbis spoke scathingly of them from time to time. It was said that they tormented themselves in this world only to gain nothing by it in the next. They were the incarnation of legalism, and they have many heirs in the church.

By sharp contrast, the publicans were the tax collectors. They owed their power, wealth, and privileges to the occupying Roman rulers. They were dishonest and

232 Exploring the Gospel of Luke

unscrupulous and despised by one and all. They were regarded as traitors and were treated as untouchables. The outstanding characteristic of the Pharisee as he took his place in the temple court and began to pray was his self-righteousness. With fine sarcasm, Jesus said that "[he] prayed thus with himself" (18:11). "I thank thee, that I am not as other men are," he told God. Other men are "extortioners, unjust, adulterers, or even as this publican. I fast twice in the week, I give tithes of all that I possess" (18:11–12). He stood there in the temple, posturing as the people passed by, congratulating himself on his goodness. He used the word *I* five times in a single breath. He boasted that he tithed *all*. The Mosaic Law required only tithes of corn, wine, oil, and cattle. The Pharisee threw out his chest.

The outstanding characteristic of the publican was his repentance. Jesus said that the publican stood "afar off." He "would not lift up so much as his eyes unto heaven, but smote upon his breast, saying, God be merciful to me a sinner" (18:13). All he could do was plead for mercy. He availed himself, though he did not know it, of the coming work of Christ on the cross.

"I tell you," Jesus said, "this man went down to his house justified rather than the other: for every one that exalteth himself shall be abased; and he that humbleth himself shall be exalted" (18:14).

b. The men who disdained the challenge of a child (18:15–17)

The next oblique attack upon the Lord's ministry came from a sad source—His own disciples, who again showed how very little they understood of the Lord's great love for people. What they did was about as bad as the Pharisee who looked down his nose at the praying publican. They were just as much out of touch with the Lord's loving heart.

First, there were *the mothers* who "brought unto him also infants, that he would touch them" (18:15a). It was a common enough practice for Jewish mothers to bring their little ones to famous rabbis to be blessed. The word for "infants" suggests newborn babes or very small children. The word *also* implies that they had other children with them. They wanted Jesus to touch them. His was the touch that could cleanse the leper and raise the dead. His touch could multiply loaves and fish. It could give sight to the blind. These were sensible women! What might it mean for any people if *all* mothers wanted their children to know the touch of God upon their lives?

Then along came the disciples. Note that the mothers didn't want their children touched by *them*. The disciples "rebuked" them. That is a strong word in the original. It is used of the Lord's rebuke of evil spirits, of His rebuke of the winds, and of His rebuke of a fever. The disciples figured that the Lord was too busy to be bothered by mere babes. What a bossy band of bunglers these disciples seemed to be. What a wrong impression they gave of Jesus. They shoved them away.

Jesus saw what was happening. He "called them unto him, and said, Suffer little children to come unto me, and forbid them not: for of such is the kingdom of God. Verily I say unto you, Whosoever shall not receive the kingdom of God as a little child shall in no wise enter therein" (18:16–17). Mark adds that Jesus was "much displeased," or "indignant" (Mark 10:14), one of the rare occasions when the Lord is said to have displayed deep emotion. Nothing could have displeased Him more than this officious act.

Jesus loved those little children. They were artless, unsophisticated, trusting, and unspoiled. "Of such is the kingdom of God," Jesus declared, thus exposing the blindness of the disciples to true spiritual values. Children are naturally drawn to Jesus.

c. The man who disdained the demands of discipleship (18:18–30)

We begin with *the ruler*. This is the last incident recorded by Luke before he tells us of the Lord's final journey to Jerusalem, the final example of that snobbish attitude toward Christ that leads a person, for one reason or another, to turn away from Him. Such people think that they know better than He does what life is really all about.

In the crowd was a rich young ruler. The word for "ruler" suggests someone in power or with authority, a lord. He addresses Jesus as "Good Master." The word can be rendered "teacher," or, as we would say today, "Doctor." The Lord was addressed thus in the Gospels thirty-one times. As drawn to Jesus as he was, however, this rich young man had a fatal flaw in his thinking; he thought that he would have to *do* something to inherit eternal life (18:18).

Jesus challenged him at once. "Why callest thou me good? none is good, save one, that is, God" (18:19). Would this young man accept the fact that Jesus was God, absolutely good? The Lord said that He was indeed God (John 8:46; 14:30). Later, Pilate would declare, "I find in him no fault at all" (John 18:38). The dying thief suddenly realized the difference between Jesus and other people, himself included (Luke 23:41). "Well, young man," Jesus implied, "am I absolutely good? Am I God?"

The Lord continued. The man wanted to *do* something. The Lord obliged him: "Thou knowest the commandments, Do not commit adultery, Do not kill, Do not steal, Do not bear false witness, Honour thy father and thy mother" (18:20). These were all commandments dealing with man's duty to man.

The man responded quickly and easily. He said, "All these have I kept from my youth up" (18:21). He was quite sure that he passed that test with flying colors.

But Jesus promptly showed him that he had done no such thing. "Yet lackest thou one thing: sell all that thou hast, and distribute unto the poor, and thou shalt have treasure in heaven: and come, follow me" (18:22). The word for "poor" refers to those who are destitute. It is the word used to describe the beggar Lazarus in the story of the rich man (16:20, 22). What had this rich, young ruler done for the likes of Lazarus? The Law of Moses required a man to love his neighbor as much as he loved himself (Lev. 19:18).

The Lord put the rich young ruler to the test. In effect, He said to him, "You say that you have kept the commandments conscientiously. You claim to love your neighbor as yourself. Prove it! Sell everything. Find some of this world's desperately poor. Give your money to them. And come, follow Me!" What a challenge to a man who wanted to *do* something—*that* is God's irreducible minimum.

"When he heard this, he was very sorrowful: for he was very rich" (18:23). The word used to describe his sorrow suggests that he was very sad, exceedingly sorrowful. The superlative is used. He was shaken to the core of his being. Perhaps, too, one of the factors in this equation was that Jesus and His disciples were so obviously poor. And he seemed to look down his nose at the poor. He certainly did not want to be one of them.

So much for the ruler. Next comes *the reality* (18:24–27). It was written all over the rich young ruler's face: surprise, struggle, surrender! Just for a moment, he felt the pull of Christ's glorious personality. Life with Him could be a great adventure. Then he thought of his fields and farms. He looked at Jesus and saw a man as good as God—because He was God. No! It would never work. He was too used to being rich. He was sorry. Very sorry. But not sorry enough.

The Lord turned back to His disciples as the rich man presumably drifted away. "How hardly shall they that have riches enter into the kingdom of God! For it is easier for a camel to go through a needle's eye, than for a rich man to enter into the kingdom of God" (18:24b–25). The Lord was deeply moved. The rich young man was a poor young man after all. He went home to his plentiful riches to be forever haunted by all that he had just thrown away. He had a full safe but an empty soul.

Jesus made him an object lesson: the eye of the needle described him exactly. The needle's eye was a small gate fixed in the great main gate. Once the big gate was closed for the night, the only way into the city was through the small gate. But to pass through that little gate, the needle's eye, the camels would have to be unloaded. A rich man's heaping wealth proved to be an encumbrance. The rich young ruler's wealth was just that—an encumbrance.

This teaching brought an immediate reaction from those who were standing by. "Who then can be saved?" they asked.

The Lord dismissed the remark. He said, in essence, "Nothing is impossible to God." It takes a miracle, indeed, for anyone to be saved.

But what about *the reward?* Some people there had paid just such a price for discipleship. Peter spoke up, and, as so often happened, he said the wrong thing. "Lo," he said, "we have left all, and followed thee." He stopped there, but we can know what he was thinking: *What are we going to get out of it?* Peter, Andrew, James, and John gave up a prosperous business. Matthew gave up a lucrative career and all of the ill-gotten gains that he had amassed, we can be sure. They had all given up homes and families.

The Lord answered Peter's unspoken question: "Verily I say unto you, There is no man that hath left house, or parents, or brethren, or wife, or children, for the kingdom of God's sake, Who shall not receive manifold more in this present time, and in the world to come life everlasting" (18:29–30). The word for "more" here means "many times more." Matthew's account reads "an hundred fold," or as we would express it, 10,000 percent! The Lord has ways to even things out down here. More! When the eternal world encroaches on this one, as it will in the millennial reign (Rev. 21–22), great indeed will be their reward: "And in the world to come life everlasting."

> 3. The derogatory attitude (18:31–19:27)
>   a. The shadow of the Savior's passion (18:31–34)

First, there is the *inevitable* (18:31–34). The derogatory attitude toward Christ that casts its shadows as it were over this section of the gospel is not so much overt as covert. It comes out in the Lord's warnings about what lies ahead for this Christ-rejecting nation and to others who turn their back on Him. It comes out with the warning that begins this section and in the parable that ends it.

"Then he took unto him the twelve, and said unto them, Behold, we go up to Jerusalem, and all things that are written by the prophets concerning the Son of man shall be accomplished . . ." (18:31). He had been studying these Scriptures since His childhood. He knew them by heart. There was to be the Triumphal Entry into Jerusalem (Zech. 9:9); the betrayal by Judas (Ps. 41:9); the cross with all of its terrors (Ps. 22; 69; Isa. 53); His death and burial (Ps. 16:10); His resurrection (Jonah 2; Matt. 12:40); His ascension back home to heaven (Ps. 24); and His enthronement in glory (Ps. 45:6–7), to be followed by the outpouring of the Holy Spirit (Joel 2:28–29) and His Melchizedeken priesthood (Gen. 14; Ps. 110:4). He knew every detail. He knew "all things that are written by the prophets."

But He knew much more than that. He added some details: "For he shall be delivered unto the Gentiles, and shall be mocked, and spitefully entreated, and spitted on: and they shall scourge him, and put him to death: and the third day he shall rise again" (18:32–33). Thus, He added detail after detail. The whole scene lay before Him as an open book.

To the disciples, it was *incredible.* The Jews would have put Him to death themselves, but then He would have been stoned, not crucified—and the Scriptures cannot be broken (John 10:35). The establishment was afraid of the common people, many of whom believed in Him, and multitudes of whom from all parts of the country were in Jerusalem for the feast of the Passover and were eager to see more of His miracles and hear more of His words. Besides, by handing Him over to Pilate, they could get him to do their dirty work for them. Moreover, this One whom they hated without a cause would suffer a much more excruciating death and would die under the curse of God (Gal. 3:10, 13).

The disciples were stunned. Jesus saw it as inevitable; they saw it as incredible. They simply blocked it from their minds. "This saying was hid from them, neither knew they the things which were spoken" (18:34). It was beyond their comprehension, beyond all belief. He had told them already some of these things. The more details He gave, the more they disbelieved.

b. The showing of the Savior's power (18:35–43)

He had now arrived in the environs of Jericho. A blind man sat by the wayside begging. The Lord had now crossed Jordan. This famous Old Testament city of Jericho (Josh. 5:13–15) was a resort town in Jesus' day and a bedroom community for people who worked in Jerusalem. It was a favorite dwelling for many of the priests—and the publicans. Jerusalem was only fifteen miles away, but the road to the capital was not only uphill but also transported the traveler from one weather zone to another. Jerusalem was two thousand three hundred feet above sea level; Jericho was in a hot trench one thousand three hundred feet below sea level, and the heat there was fierce. The north-south highway twisted and turned between high cliffs and yawning ravines. It was surrounded by a trackless wilderness, where caves yawned and brigands lurked. Jericho itself abounded with tropical vegetation. Herod had a winter palace, an amphitheater, and a hippodrome a couple of miles away. He died in this city some time after the birth and attempted murder of Christ. He was eaten up by disease and haunted by his crimes.

As the Lord approached Jericho, He was accosted by the blind beggar. In Bible times, such unfortunates were on their own. No institutions or social programs existed to help them. They begged.

The blind man heard the commotion which heralded the approach of Christ. A person in the crowd told him: "Jesus of Nazareth passeth by . . ." (18:37). He would never pass that way again. It was now or never for that poor blind man. He raised his voice. "Jesus, thou son of David," he cried, giving Jesus His full messianic title, "have mercy on me." He raised his voice again, louder, shriller, until he annoyed those round about. They told him to hold his peace. But not him! He cried so much the more. The time had come for his great decision to be made and for the world's callous opposition to be braved. Such a moment came to Pilate when he came face-to-face with Christ. It came to Felix and King Agrippa (Matt. 27:22; Acts 24:22–27; 26:24–29). Just a short while before, it had come to the rich young ruler. Now it had come to this beggar. Others let the golden moment pass because their sense of need was not as dire as his. He cried again and again.

Jesus came to a stop and commanded him to be brought to Him. He asked him to put his request in words. His need was obvious to everyone, surely! Nevertheless, the Lord wanted his request to be voiced. After all, perhaps he was just begging. But not him! He wanted to be saved. He wanted to see! No one ever appealed to Jesus in vain. "Him that cometh to me I will in no wise cast out," He said. So runs the eternal promise of Christ. The man expressed his need: "Lord, that I may receive my sight!"

Jesus said, "Thy faith hath saved thee." That was the living link between the need and the cure. Instantly, "he received his sight" (18:43a). That was "the word of his power" (Heb. 1:3)—the same Word spoke the worlds into space. The living link of this beggar's faith released all of the omnipotent power of Christ into his life. At that moment, the man's eyes were opened—and he looked into the face of Jesus. And he followed him! Of course he did! What else could he do? And "all the people, when they saw it, gave praise unto God" (18:43b).

c. The shining of the Savior's presence (19:1–27)

First, *false ideals* are exposed (19:1–10). Again we look at the place: "Jesus entered and passed through Jericho" (19:1). Once many years before, the prophet Elisha had healed Jericho's bitter water (2 Kings 2:15–22). Jesus would have healed its lost soul. Instead, He simply "entered and passed through" the place. It was known as the city of palm trees (Deut. 34:3; Judg. 1:16), located about six miles from the river Jordan and about eighteen miles or so from Jerusalem. It was the gateway to Judea from the east, straddling the caravan road from Damascus to Arabia. It was a prosperous center of commerce, a military outpost, and close enough to Jerusalem to be the last stopping place for pilgrims on their way to the Holy City. Jesus was making His way through Jericho, followed by a jostling crowd when it happened: He met Zacchaeus.

A publican! A rich man. One who collected taxes for Rome and who waxed fat and prospered in the process. The Jews, rich and poor alike, hated and feared the fraternity of publicans, especially Zacchaeus. He had the dubious distinction of being chief of the publicans.

He was a small man, a characteristic that on this occasion presented a problem. He wanted to see Jesus. He had heard about Him, heard that Jesus cared little about the rigid social taboos that governed Jewish life. But how could he ever get where he could see this heralded Messiah for himself? The crowds—big people, strong people—were pushing him. What could he do? Why, climb a tree, of course!

As soon as he discovered that Jesus was on His way through Jericho, Zacchaeus ran ahead of the crowd and found a sycamore (fig) tree, a tree of considerable size. Jesus knew all about it because "when Jesus came to the place, he looked up, and saw him, and said unto him, Zacchaeus, make haste, and come down; for to day I must abide at thy house" (19:5).

When Jesus stopped, everyone else stopped. To everyone's astonishment, Jesus called the man in the tree by his name and invited Himself home to the man's house! Zacchaeus wasted no time. Down he came, full of joy at this unexpected turn of events.

The crowd watched all of this with growing astonishment. "When they saw it, they all murmured, saying, That he was gone to be guest with a man that is a sinner" (19:7). They were outraged. What kind of a messiah could this be who would actually invite Himself into the home of a *publican?* A *chief* publican no less? Just a few moments earlier, they had been praising God for Him (18:43); now they were murmuring against Him. Such was the crowd. The Lord was neither impressed by the one attitude nor depressed by the other.

Nobody can invite Christ into his life and not be changed. We read, "And Zacchaeus stood, and said unto the Lord; Behold, Lord, the half of my goods I give to the poor; and if I have taken any thing from any man by false accusation, I restore him fourfold" (19:8). This response was required by the Law of Moses (Exod. 22:1). It was the penalty that David had pronounced on the man in Nathan's parable (2 Sam. 12:1–5) and the penalty that God imposed on David himself (2 Sam. 12:10).

"This day is salvation come to this house," Jesus declared. The willingness to give and to make abundant restitution to those he had wronged was evidence of a new heart and a saved soul. Jesus called him "a son of Abraham," that is, a true believer. The Lord explained just why He had "gone to be guest with a man that is a sinner." It was because "the Son of man is come to seek and to save that which was lost" (19:10). Incidentally, this is *the key verse* in the gospel of Luke. And note that not a single two-syllable word is in the sentence.

The Lord continued His teaching, now exposing *false ideas* (19:11–27). Note *what was thought:* "And as they heard these things, he added and spake a parable, because he was nigh to Jerusalem, and because they thought that the kingdom of God should immediately [at any moment] appear" (19:11). The Lord had just emphatically declared that His primary purpose on earth was to save sinners, Zacchaeus being a prime example. He was both able and willing to do just that. The kingdom of God was about to be set aside in the eternal counsels of God because the Jews had rejected God's plan (Matt. 13). The people were still unable to grasp what He was saying. Note what *was taught* (19:12–17): He was going away.

"He said therefore, A certain nobleman went into a far country." There was to be a prolonged absence and an eventual triumphant return. The kingdom that He had refused to receive at Satan's hands and on his terms He would receive from His Father in heaven.

First, there was the preparation: "And he called his ten servants, and delivered them ten pounds, and said unto them, Occupy till I come. But his citizens hated him, and sent a message after him, saying, We will not have this man to reign over us" (19:13–14).

The word *occupy* here means "to be pragmatic, to trade." They were to get busy, to take a pragmatic business approach to their responsibilities.

This parable must be distinguished from the parable of the talents (Matt. 25:15). That parable placed the emphasis on the differing gifts and abilities of the Lord's servants: we do not all have the same talents. In the parable of the pounds, each servant received the same trust—one pound. The one parable emphasized the development of gifts; the other parable emphasized common and equal responsibility. Until the Lord comes back, it is our responsibility and privilege to get on diligently with His interests in the world.

But what is meant by a *pound*? What do all believers have in common? The word itself simply suggests a sum of money. The important thing here is not so much the amount as the fact that each of the ten servants received the *same* amount. The pound represents the gospel itself. However different our skills and abilities are, we all have the same gospel truth to impart. The most brilliant orator in the most prestigious pulpit in the world does not have a better gospel than the most fumbling, bumbling of preachers. The message of the gospel is the same.

But only a *pound*? It seems such a paltry sum. Paul dealt with the issue of its value (Rom. 1:16–17). He labored under no illusions, however, as to where it stood in the world's system of values. To the clever and conceited Corinthians, he confessed, "We preach Christ crucified, unto the Jews a stumblingblock, and unto the Greeks foolishness; but unto them which are called, both Jews and Greeks, Christ the power of God, and the wisdom of God . . ." (1 Cor. 1:23–24). When he preached the gospel on Mars Hill, the Greek intellectuals mocked (Acts 17:32).

So the lord entrusted one "pound" to each of his servants. "There!" he said, "you have all you need." The world boasts of its politics, culture, and religion. It parades its great Goliaths of Gath who breath out threatenings and slaughter. God's answer is a despised gospel communicated by some humble believers. Against all of this world's great names and all of its mighty men, God puts up His David, a mere lad with a slingshot and a stone, to make short work of them.

So we have all that we need—a *pound,* the gospel. The departing lord went on his way leaving behind him a handful of men called and commissioned to make capital for their lord while he is away. But if the lord had those men to help him, he left behind also those who hated him, and they sent an insulting message after him: "We will not have this man to reign over us" (19:14). Nevertheless, the lord is receiving a kingdom (19:15), and there is nothing that his enemies can do to stop it.

In due time, the lord came back. The ten servants were summoned to give account of their stewardship. The lord wanted to see what each had "gained by trading," what each had accomplished with the truth entrusted to him. The first had gained ten pounds. "Well," the lord said, "thou good and faithful servant: because thou hast been faithful in a very little, have thou authority over ten cities" (doubtless a reference to the kingdom of God). Similarly, the second servant had used his opportunities and had made five pounds. He, too, was rewarded in the kingdom and was given authority over five cities (19:16–19). Both of these servants did what they could with their respective "pounds" (their gospel opportunities). One was more successful than the other, but the lord had no trouble evaluating and rewarding their differing abilities, opportunities, and activities.

Thus was the gospel spread during the early days of the church. Luke charts the progress in his day (Acts 6:7; 9:31; 19:20). That was how the "pound" increased. People were saved, churches were founded, and revival fires gave rapid expansion to the work.

Then another man stepped forward. "Behold," he said, "here is thy pound, which I have kept laid up in a napkin: for I feared thee, because thou art an austere [hard, harsh] man: thou takest up that thou layedst not down, and reapest that thou didst not sow."

The lord gave him no quarter. The man's assessment of the lord's character was false, and the lord threw it back into the fellow's face. No one ever had a more loving lord than Jesus. He is righteous and penetrating in His judgment, indeed, but never harsh or hard. "Out of thine own mouth will I judge thee, thou wicked servant," the master said. In essence, he said, "If you knew about me what you say about me, why did you not put my money in the bank so that, when I came back, I might have received my own back with at least some interest?"

There was no failure on the part of the pound. Everyone who traded with it made some profit. Nobody had to confess that he had lost the pound entrusted to him or that he had squandered it. We have the Holy Spirit's word for it that God's Word "shall not return unto me void" (Isa. 55:11). The unfaithful servant's indictment was that he made no attempt to do anything at all with what had been entrusted to him.

He suffered loss when the lord came back. "Take from him the pound, and give it to him that hath ten pounds. (And they said unto him, Lord, he hath ten pounds.) For I say unto you, That unto every one which hath shall be given; and from him that hath not, even that he hath shall be taken away from him" (19:24–26). Some people were surprised that the servant who had the ten pounds was given the extra one, but that was plain good sense. He had already proved himself to be the most diligent and most successful of the lord's servants. He would do far more with that extra pound than even the next best investor, the one who had made five pounds. The lord was simply employing the same diligence, wisdom, and pragmatism for which he looked in his servants.

As for the unfaithful servant he was stripped of all power, privilege, and position and was allowed to enter the kingdom "so as by fire" (1 Cor. 3:15). The parable includes a picture of the coming judgment seat of Christ.

Next came the turn of "those citizens" who had sent their insulting message after the lord when he went away. "Bring [them] hither, and slay them before me," the lord demanded. This is a sobering warning to all Christ rejecters.

    L.   The straightforward approach (19:28–20:19)
        1. Coronation (19:28–44)
           a. Jerusalem's crowning day (19:28–40)

Now comes the Lord's triumphal entry into Jerusalem. This was, or should have been, the crowning day. Instead of its witnessing the homage of the Jewish leaders, however, it provoked a straightforward and outspoken hostility toward the Lord Himself—an unequivocal rejection by the establishment of Jesus as their Messiah.

First, our attention is drawn to *the coming* (19:28–29): "And when he had thus spoken, he went before, ascending up to Jerusalem. And it came to pass, when he was come nigh to Bethphage and Bethany, at the mount called the mount of Olives, he sent two of his disciples. . . ." The city was spread out before Him as He crested Olivet. Bethphage is thought to be a precinct of Jerusalem that spread eastward over the Mount of Olives as far as Bethany. The enormous crowds at the annual feasts camped out all over this district. This enlarged area was called Bethphage. Bethany was the beginning of this district. It was from here, from this area, which was annexed by Jerusalem for the Passover, that the Lord began His entry on what we now call Palm Sunday. Within the week, He would be dead.

Luke now tells us about *the colt*. The Lord had already sent two of His disciples to secure this creature for Him (19:29–30). That colt has a threefold message for us. First, it had to be *redeemed:* "Go ye into the village over against you; in the which at your entering ye shall find a colt tied, whereon yet never man sat. . . ." The Law of Moses had something to say about this: "Every firstling of an ass thou shalt redeem with a lamb; and if thou wilt not redeem it, then thou shalt break his neck" (Exod. 13:13).

The colt, moreover, had to be *released*. It was tied to a post. It had life, but it did not have liberty (19:33–34). It was still in bondage. When the Lord's servants were challenged about their loosing of the colt, they said, "The Lord hath need of him."

But that was not all. They brought this redeemed and newly released creature to Jesus. It had to be *ruled*. It had not been released simply to kick up its heels and gallop off to faraway fields. On the contrary, it was brought under the authority of the Lord Jesus. The disciples "cast their garments upon the colt, and they set Jesus thereon." It surrendered its will to His. It went where He wanted it to go and did what He wanted it to do. Its one supreme task was now to lift up Christ where everyone could see Him. It is a marvelous snapshot of the Christian life.

The multitudes saw Jesus. They "began to rejoice and praise God with a loud voice for all the mighty works that they had seen." They shouted, "Blessed be the King that cometh in the name of the Lord: peace in heaven, and glory in the highest" (19:37–38).

Then Luke turns our attention to *the critics* (19:39–40): "And some of the Pharisees from among the multitude said unto him, Master, rebuke thy disciples." There was nothing devious about that statement; it was a blunt demand that He tell His disciples to be quiet. An old prophecy was being fulfilled (Ps. 118:26). He was doing what the prophet had foretold (Zech. 9:9). The scales swung now back and forth. It was Jerusalem's moment. Some people sang. The Pharisees sneered. The Lord's foes won.

b. Jerusalem's coming doom (19:41–44)

As Jesus reached the edge of the plateau, the city lay before Him. Luke draws our attention to *a weeping Savior:* "And when he was come near, he beheld the city, and wept over it, saying, if thou hadst known, even thou, at least in this thy day, the things which belong unto thy peace! but now they are hid from thine eyes" (19:41–42). The word for "wept" means "to wail," or "to weep out loud." He loved that city. He loved every stone, every street, every man, every woman, and every child. He even loved Caiaphas and his gang of thieves.

It is amazing that Jerusalem should ever have been built at all. Most of the world's great cities are built on rivers. Jerusalem had none. Hills hemmed it in on every side. Its water supply came from afar. It was perched high above deep ravines. It was a city of ghosts and memories. The entire Old Testament story revolved around this city. It was where Abraham met Melchizedek. There David seized the hill of Zion. There lay the valley of the Kedron, where Solomon and successor kings bowed the knee to Baal and Moloch and other gods of many kinds. There Greek, Roman, and Jew elbowed their different ways.

It was Passover time, the annual birthday feast of the Jewish nation. Every sepulcher was newly whited so that careless pilgrims could avoid walking on them and becoming ceremonially defiled. Above everything stood the temple, rebuilt and embellished by Herod. He had begun this enterprise some twenty years earlier. It would finally be finished in A.D. 64, half a dozen years before the Romans came and burned it to the ground. There, too, were the money changers. There, too, proudly displayed, were the rags and tatters of a worn-out religious system of dos and don'ts. Yonder were the enormous flocks of sheep ready for sale for the Passover, thousands upon thousands of them.

So Jesus gazed down upon Jerusalem. Its name means "Peace!" but the city did not even know the things that belonged to its peace. At least thirty major sieges can be counted in its history, some of them numbered among the most terrible events in recorded history. Jesus Himself was the "Prince of Peace" (Isa. 9:6). Him they were about to cast out and crucify. How blind! How blind!

There was also *a woeful sight*. The Lord could see ahead to the siege and sack of Jerusalem by the Romans (A.D. 70). He saw the thoroughness of the Romans as they dug trenches, built towers, and brought up great catapults to hurl massive stones against Jerusalem's towering walls. He saw the squabbling factions in the besieged city, fighting against each other instead of engaging the foe. He saw famine and pestilence reaping their own horrifying harvests. He saw escaping Jews caught by the hundreds and crucified within sight of the walls (19:43–44).

2. Confrontation (19:45–48)

The Lord now went into the temple courts. What caught His eye there was the money market that the authorities had set up in the Court of the Gentiles. The money changers were there, their sharp minds calculating how much to fleece this one and how best to cheat that one. The animal barons were there with all of the sheep to sell to pilgrims from near and far. Inflated prices and fat profits would exist there. The Lord's anger was kindled. He "began to cast out them that sold therein, and them that bought; saying unto them, It is written, My house is the house of prayer: but ye have made it a den of thieves" (Isa. 56:7; Jer. 7:11). These merchants and money changers owed their concessions to the temple officials. These officials, in turn, skimmed off a handsome percentage of the profits for themselves. Annas, the infamous high priest, seems to have owned the bazaars. The Sanhedrin held its meetings in some of the adjacent rooms. No wonder Jesus called the place (literally) "a den of brigands."

Having rid the temple courts of these robbers, Jesus began to teach there daily. "But the chief priests and the scribes and the chief of the people sought to destroy him. And could not find what they might do: for all the people were very attentive to hear him" (19:47–48). Jesus knew that He had no more implacable enemies than the wicked men who comprised the Jewish religious establishment. However, they were obliged to bide their time. They knew that Jesus had awesome power at His disposal. No one could deny the countless miracles He had performed. Besides, the common people hung upon His words, and no one wanted to incite them into a mob—yet.

3. Condemnation (20:1–19)
a. How they wickedly assailed His authority (20:1–8)

The next move was theirs: "And it came to pass, that on one of those days, as he taught the people in the temple, and preached the gospel, the chief priests and the scribes came upon him with the elders" (20:1). This was the third day of the last week of the Lord's life.

The day before, the authorities had been afraid to interfere with Him and watched with silent rage His cleansing of the temple. But this was a new day. They had spent the night debating their options. Their decision was to accost Him first thing the next morning, as soon as He set foot in the temple, before the crowds could gather. And so they did. The expression "came upon" implies suddenness and hostility. It was a straightforward attack upon His right to do and say the things He did.

"Tell us, by what authority doest thou these things? or who is he that gave thee this authority?" Essentially, they were asking, "Who gave you a license to preach? Where did you go to school? What degrees have you earned? Where is your certificate of ordination?"

The word for "authority" is *exousia,* which suggests "delegated authority." He was not a priest. He was certainly not a scribe. He was no trained rabbi. So where were His diplomas? What right had He to come riding into Jerusalem as though He were a messiah? And, above all, how dare He attack the legitimate business concessions endorsed by the authorities and conducted in the appropriate temple court?

He was ready for them: "I will also ask you one thing; and answer me: The baptism of John, was it from heaven, or of men?" (20:3–4). It was a clever reply. His authority and John's authority came from the same divine source. The people had flocked to hear John. He had baptized people by the thousands upon their confession of sin and repentance. The nation's religious and political leaders had rejected John's preaching and his baptism. They had sent a similar delegation to John and had come away with their ears scorched by John's fierce woes.

The Sanhedrin now faced a dilemma. Far from their delegates intimidating Jesus, He intimidated them: "And they reasoned with themselves, saying, If we shall say, From heaven; he will say, Why then believed ye him not? But and if we say, Of men; all the people will stone us: for they be persuaded that John was a prophet" (20:5–6). The word for "reasoned" occurs only here. It suggests that they went into a close huddle. The comment "the people will stone us" likewise occurs only here means literally "stone to death." The word for "persuaded" implies that the common people had long been firmly convinced that John was a God-anointed prophet.

Finally, they came to a decision. "They answered, that they could not tell whence it was" (20:7). It was a pitiful confession of their cowardice, unbelief, and wickedness. They were the people who claimed to have jurisdiction over all religious and political issues in the country. For them to say publicly, "We cannot tell" was a tremendous blow to both their reputation and their pride. "You can't tell?" Jesus said. "Then I won't answer you, either."

b. How they wickedly asserted their authority (20:9–19)

The Lord now told His graphic and prophetic parable of the vineyard. It was designed to force His foes to face their terrible and chronic unbelief. The parable made it very evident, indeed, just how they were exercising their own authority. The parable itself was addressed to the common people so that they could be informed of the wickedness of the ruling religious and political parties. The vineyard was obviously the nation of Israel (Isa. 5:1–77; Jer. 2:21; Ezek. 15:1–6). The husbandmen were the nation's religious leaders. The owner left everything in their care while he "went into a far country for a long time" (20:9). The period envisioned corresponds to the Old Testament period and on into the period of the Gospels. There had been all kinds of husbandmen—lawgivers like Moses; conquerors like Joshua; judges like Jephthah, Gideon, and Samson; prophets like Samuel; kings like David and Hezekiah; scribes like Ezra; and reformers like Nehemiah. Sometimes, the husbandmen were good, godly stewards of the vineyard. At other times, they were godless, unregenerate individuals. By the time of Christ, those who wielded the power were corrupt, cruel, and callous worldlings, calculating and merciless men.

The men who ruled the vineyard had invariably treated as meddlers the prophets whom God sent. They beat them up, imprisoned them, and, all too often, murdered them. The nation's rejection of these God-sent ambassadors revealed a growing boldness, as the parable shows (20:10–12).

But now came a great change. The lord in his far country decided to send an ambassador extraordinary—his own son. "I will send my beloved son: it may be they will reverence him when they see him" (20:13). That was the Lord's answer to his enemies' question: "By what authority doest thou these things? or who is he that gave thee this authority." He threw the answer back in their faces.

His Father was the Owner of the Vineyard. God Himself had vested Jesus with full authority. He was God's only begotten and well-beloved Son. His authority came from above, from a country far, far away, from God Himself. They were accountable to Him for their wicked behavior. "It may be they will reverence my son," the father said. The expression "it may be" occurs only here. It means "surely." Surely they will stand in awe of My Son!

And so Jesus laid aside His glory and came down to earth. The demon world stood in awe of Him. Pilate stood in awe of Him (John 19:8). But will the lords of the Sanhedrin stand in awe of Him? Not them! Before long, they overcame their initial fears and conceived and executed the most horrendous crime ever committed by men. They murdered *Him.*

For "when the husbandmen saw him, they reasoned among themselves, saying, This is the heir: come, let us kill him, that the inheritance may be ours. So they cast him out of the vineyard, and killed him" (20:14–15) on a cross.

"What therefore shall the lord of the vineyard do unto them? He shall come and destroy these husbandmen, and shall give the vineyard to others. And when they heard it, they said, God forbid" (20:15–16). In time, the Romans came and took away their place and nation (John 11:48). The vineyard was given to others (the word *others* here is *allos,* "another of the same kind"). This is a veiled reference to the church, which now holds the place of spiritual and religious privilege once held by the Jews.[4]

The hint that the nation of Israel might lose its place drew a spontaneous "God forbid" from the Jews. The expression can be rendered "Perish the thought." It occurs only here in the Gospels but ten times in Paul's epistles (see, for instance, Rom. 11:1, 11).

The Lord ignored this exclamation and ended the parable with a warning: "And he beheld them, and said, What is this then that is written, The stone which the builders rejected, the same is become the head of the corner? Whosoever shall fall upon that stone shall be broken; but on whomsoever it shall fall, it will grind him to powder" (20:17–18). The quotation is from Psalm 118:22. We can be sure that the rulers of Israel knew this great psalm by heart. The cheering crowds of yesterday had proclaimed it as they cheered Him on His way at the beginning of this momentous week. The whole psalm should be read in the light of Calvary. The Lord quoted from it even as He was singing the last Hallel and prepared to move out from the Upper Room to go to Gethsemane.

The Lord concentrated on the part of the psalm that foretold the dreadful role being played by the Sanhedrin. A cornerstone forms the bond between the two most important walls of a building. From it all of the lines of the building run. Length, breadth, and height are angled from this stone. If this stone is out of square, the building will be out of square. This stone was always cut with meticulous care and was laid with special ceremony.

Jesus Himself was the Cornerstone to which the psalmist referred. It would have been considered incredible to build without first laying the cornerstone. To throw it away as useless would have been the very epitome of folly. Yet, that is just what these "builders" (the Sanhedrin) were doing. They had already stumbled over that Stone (Christ), and they have continued to do so to this day. One day that self-same Stone will fall upon them, grinding them to powder (20:18).

The shots went home. "And the chief priests and the scribes the same hour sought to lay hands on him; and they feared the people: for they perceived that he had spoken this parable against them" (20:19).

Well, they would succeed. It was only a matter of a day or so now. They would have Him on the cross. But they would not be through with Him. Back He would come from the dead. The half had not been told.

---

4. This topic is discussed further in John Phillips, *Exploring Romans* (Grand Rapids: Kregel, 2002), chaps. 9–11.

> M. The seductive approach (20:20–21:38)
> 1. The plot of the adversaries exposed (20:20–21:4)
>   a. They question Him (20:20–40)

For the moment, the Sanhedrin was bound by its own fears, but they kept a close watch on Him and hired spies, "which should feign themselves just men [i.e., pretend to be honest men], that they might take hold of his words, that so they might deliver him unto the power and authority of the governor" (20:20).

The raising of Lazarus of Bethany, recorded by John, increased the Sanhedrin's determination to get rid of Jesus. It was in their own self-interest to do so (John 11:50), and what better way than by tripping Him up and provoking Him into making a compromising statement that they could use against Him in a Roman court. The word for "spies" occurs only here and means "sitting in ambush," or "lying in wait." Job used the word, or its equivalent, to describe the craftiness and cunning that an evil man employs when he plans the seduction of his neighbor's wife (Job 31:9). The word for "feign" gives us our word *hypocrite*. It has to do with acting a part on the stage. How deep are the depths of wickedness in a human heart that would actually design and deploy such tactics against God's beloved Son! They wanted to hand Him over to Rome and to ensure that He was condemned to death—on a cross.

So they planted their spies and asked Him a question: "Master, we know that thou sayest and teachest rightly, neither acceptest thou the person of any, but teachest the way of God truly: Is it lawful for us to give tribute unto Caesar, or no?" (20:21–22). If He said yes, they would undermine His standing with the common people. The tribute to which they referred was the detested poll tax, which the Pharisees in particular paid only under bitter protest. They took the position that, as the people of God, they had no right to be paying taxes to pagan Rome. On the other hand, if He said that it was not lawful to pay taxes to Caesar, the Pharisees would applaud Him, but the powerful politically oriented Sadducees would report Him to the Roman governor.

"But he perceived their craftiness, and said unto them, Why tempt ye me?" (20:23). Their plot was as transparent as daylight. It was almost childish. Others would have taken refuge in the words *No comment!* Not so Jesus.

"Show me a penny," He said. In those days, a penny was a small silver coin that was the equivalent of a workingman's daily wage. On one side of the coin was an image of Tiberius Caesar, one of the most depraved men ever to sit on a throne. On the other side was the title "Pontifex Maximus," Supreme Pontiff, the head of the Roman pagan religious system. The very coin itself was an affront to a Jew. Jesus held up the coin. "Whose image and superscription hath it? They answered and said, Caesar's. And he said unto them, Render therefore unto Caesar the things which be Caesar's, and unto God the things which be God's" (20:24–25). The Lord's enemies were dumbfounded. They could not find fault with a single word He had said. Indeed, "they marvelled at his answer, and held their peace."

Now it was the Sadducees' turn. They were the skeptics. They denied the existence of angels and demons and the possibility of resurrection. This sect kept in the background in the Gospels, but they took the lead in persecuting the infant church. They were not a large party, but they were wealthy and powerful. They were the party of the high priests. The question they now put to Jesus was one of their stock-in-trade arguments against belief in the supernatural.

They began by quoting Scripture: "Master, Moses wrote unto us, If any man's brother die, having a wife, and he die without children, that his brother should take his wife, and raise up seed unto his brother" (20:28). The Sadducees referred Jesus to the Old Testament law of Levirate marriage (Deut. 25:5), which was given to protect widows who were often neglected, victimized, and abused in Eastern lands.

They told Jesus a story: "There were therefore seven brethren: and the first took a wife, and died without children. And the second took her to wife, and he died childless. And the third took her; and in like manner the seven also: and they left no children, and died. Last of all the woman died also" (20:29–32). What a tale of woe! The unhappy woman spent her life going to weddings and funerals. One could write a novel about this poor widow. Was she under some kind of a curse? Were the husbands increasingly apprehensive about marrying her? After all, every husband in turn died before long.

The Sadducees gleefully came to the punch line. Perhaps they chanted it out in chorus. They were sure that it would stump this country preacher from the backwoods: "In the resurrection whose wife of them is she? for seven had her to wife" (20:33). The seven had her! And they had Him!

"None!" The answer was bold, blunt, and unexpected. He had lived in both worlds. He knew the answer right well. He could speak with authority. The Sadducees denied that there was life after death. Their rationalism taught them that falsehood. But they were wrong. Their views were based on ignorance, as Jesus now told them (20:34). He tore aside, for a moment, the veil between this world and that world. He said, "They which shall be accounted worthy to obtain that world, and the resurrection from the dead, neither marry, nor are given in marriage: Neither can they die any more: for they are equal unto the angels; and are the children of God, being the children of the resurrection" (20:35–36). What a revelation of things unseen! What a slap in the face to the Sadducees! What an awesome and authoritative utterance.

Jesus would have us know that not everyone goes at death to that land of light and love. All who die go somewhere. The destination of some people is that "place of torment" about which the Lord had already spoken (16:19–31). Only those who are "accounted worthy" will obtain access to the glory land. The "just" are those who, like Abraham, are made just by God (Rom. 4:1–3) and who, like David, discover how to have righteousness reckoned to them by faith (Rom. 4:6–8). Certainly, that ruled out the Sadducees and their like, blinded as they were by their own rationalism.

In the world to come, there will be no need for marriage or for people to propagate. For one thing, our bodies will be changed (1 Cor. 15:35–57). In this regard, we shall be like the angels, who have no need to reproduce their kind. Also, those who gather around the throne of God (Rev. 4–5) will be beyond the reach of sin and death.

So much for the Sadducees and their silly question! Matthew tells us that the Lord prefaced His remarks by telling the Sadducees, "Ye do err, not knowing the scriptures, nor the power of God" (Matt. 22:29). The expression *ye do err* can be rendered "ye deceive yourselves." Rationalism and liberal theology rest upon self-deception (Rom. 1:21–22), ignorance of the spiritual character of God's Word (Acts 13:27), and ignorance of God's power and His ability at any time to intervene in both the ordinary laws of nature and human affairs (2 Peter 3:5–9).

The Lord still was not through with these sneering Sadducees. "The dead are raised," He said (20:37). That is a tremendous statement that we ought to underline. It was a flat contradiction of the rationalism of the Sadducees. The dead are raised! He ought to know. The whole country rang with the news that every once in a while He Himself actually raised the dead.

Then the Lord backed up His exposure of the ignorance of the Sadducees with a Bible lesson. They had taken Him back to Moses (20:28); now He took them back to Moses. The passage to which He referred them was Exodus 3:6. He said, "Now that the dead are raised, even Moses showed at the bush, when he calleth the Lord the God of Abraham, and the God of Isaac, and the God of Jacob. For he is not a God of the dead, but of the living" (20:37–38). "The dead are raised," Jesus said. The word used refers to corpses. Moses "showed" this,

Jesus said. The word for "showed" is *mēnuō,* which can be rendered "disclosed." It refers to things revealed that before were unknown. When Moses met God at the burning bush, the patriarchs were long dead. Jacob had been dead for 198 years, Isaac had been dead for 225 years, and Abraham had been dead for 330 years. That was from our human point of view. "Dead. Of course they were dead!" the Sadducees would say. No, very much alive, Jesus declared, because God is the God of living people. He is not the God of people who no longer exist. "For all live unto him," Jesus added. So much for liberal and Saduccean skepticism. Awed in spite of themselves, some of the scribes acknowledged, "Thou hast well said. And after that they durst not ask him any question at all" (20:39–40).

b. He quells them (20:41–21:4)

The Lord now went on the offensive. "How say they that Christ is David's son?" He asked. Well, that was an easy one! Of course He had to be David's Son! The Davidic covenant guaranteed that (2 Sam. 7:8–12). He was to be born in David's city (Mic. 5:2), and He was to sit on David's throne (Isa. 9:6–7). And He it was who stood before them.

The Lord continued. If the Messiah was to be David's son, there was a problem because David himself said in Psalm 110, "The LORD [Jehovah] said unto my Lord [Adonai], Sit thou on my right hand, till I make thine enemies thy footstool. David therefore calleth him Lord, how is he then his son?" (20:42–44). In Psalm 110, David freely acknowledged the fact that the promised Messiah was his Lord. No Hebrew father would call his son his Lord. Moreover, this coming Messiah, who was to be David's Lord, was to sit on not only David's throne but also God's throne. More still! He was to be something that no Hebrew king could ever be—He was to be Israel's great high priest. He also was to be both a royal priest and an eternal priest (Ps. 110:4).

What was the Lord doing? He was forcing the scribes and the Sadducees to acknowledge from the Scriptures that the Son of David was also the Son of God. That He was truly the Son of David they could not deny. He was often called that (Matt. 9:27; 15:22; 21:9, 15). The temple records would prove it. So then He who stood before them was indeed both Son of David and Son of God, and that priest according to Melchizedek (Ps. 110:4), the King-Priest to whom even Abraham gave his tithe (Gen. 14). His enemies said nothing; they were once again rendered speechless.

He now appealed to the people who had heard all of this and also witnessed the eloquent silence of the scribes and their like. "Beware of the scribes," He said, "which desire to walk in long robes, and love greetings in the markets, and the highest seats in the synagogues, and the chief rooms at feasts; which devour widows' houses, and for a show make long prayers: the same shall receive greater damnation" (20:45–47).

Matthew tells how this public exposure of the pride, greed, doom, and hypocrisy of the scribes was part of a greater denunciation of the Sanhedrinists—the rabbis, the Pharisees, and the whole official religious establishment of Israel in general (Matt. 23). The Lord delivered this teaching in the temple. The challenge by the Sadducees had been all about a widow. The Lord had silenced them. Now He accused them of exploiting helpless widows to line their own purses. Then He saw a widow who, far from begging importunately for someone to help her in her deep poverty, actually gave her all (21:1–4). She stands in stark contrast to those religious teachers who had just tried to trap the Lord, some of whom actually exploited widows.

The Lord seems to have moved on to get away from the unceasing contentions of His foes. He found a vantage point where He could see into the Court of the Women and watch the passing crowds. Under the colonnades that surrounded the Court of the Women were thirteen trumpet-shaped boxes for receiving the donations of the people. Among the inscriptions on the boxes was one labeled "for the poor"; another was labeled "for the sacrifices."

Then something caught the Lord's eye. It was the fanfare and the flourish with which the rich cast their handsome gifts into the various chests. Then something else attracted His attention. A widow, obviously very poor, was hovering between two boxes. She was having trouble making up her mind. In her hand she held two mites, two very small coins. They were all that she had. As poor as she was, she understood the plight of the poor. She would put one of her coins into the box for the poor. The other she would keep for herself. She would give half and keep half. Then she saw the box marked "for the sacrifices." She looked at the coin in her hand. Maybe she should give her coin to help with the cost of maintaining the sacrificial system. It was a costly business to keep all of that going. Besides, if she put her money into *that* box, it would be like giving something directly to God. Should she give her coin to God or to man? Her hand, holding the coin, hovered back and forth. At last, she made up her mind. She dug into her sparse purse and extracted the other coin. Then, hastily, hoping that no one would notice how small was her gift, she threw in *both* coins—one to buy a glass of milk for some poor widow's child, the other to help some poor soul buy a dove for sacrifice. The disciples were taken up with the lavish gifts of the rich, but Jesus was taken up with the struggle and glorious victory of the poor, destitute woman.

"I say unto you," Jesus said to His disciples, "that this poor widow hath cast in more than they all: for all these have of their abundance cast in unto the offerings of God: but she of her penury hath cast in all the living that she had" (21:3–4). "All her living!" The word translated "living" is *bios*. She has cast in her *life*, Jesus said.

The Lord is no man's debtor. We cannot help but wonder what that poor widow found on her doorstep when she arrived there, hungry but happy, having unknowingly made the Lord happy too.

2. The plan of the ages exposed (21:5–38)
   a. Events leading up to the collapse of Jerusalem (21:5–24)
     (1) A question of pride (21:5–7)
      (a) The limited view of the crowd (21:5)

The Lord now came back to the situation in which He found Himself. All about Him were the hurrying throngs, pouring through the temple courts bent on enjoying the national holiday. Some people were pointing out the marvels of the temple itself, drawing attention to the massive stones that formed its foundation and to gifts that bedecked the walls. The Lord was unimpressed by it all. It was the work of a man who tried to murder Him, a man who was determined to build a temple that was more imposing than Solomon's. Herod had prepared a thousand vehicles to carry the stone to the site. He had recruited ten thousand workmen, under the supervision of a thousand priests, to do the work. And the Jews hated him. He was an Edomite and a mass murderer. But if he thought he could ingratiate himself with the Jews by building them a temple, he was mistaken. The Jews were proud of their temple but despised its builder.

(b) The larger view of the Christ (21:6–7)

Outwardly, the temple was impressive enough. Herod had begun work on it in 20 B.C. It was still under construction even as Jesus sat there listening to the chatter of the crowd. There it stood, all magnificent granite and gold, pillared cloisters, and towering walls. Indeed, it seemed to grow out of the very bedrock on which it stood.

As for the "gifts" that Luke mentions, they would be its ruin. The Roman conqueror Titus, during the siege of Jerusalem, ordered that the temple was to be spared. His edict ran counter to the word of Christ who had decreed its utter ruin. The word of Christ prevailed. As the terrible battle raged toward its end, the temple somehow caught fire. Its vast treasure of gold melted in the flames. Some of the gold found its way into the crevices between the massive stones. The Roman soldiers, hungry for spoil, tore the stones apart.

This prediction of Christ astonished the Jews. It led them to ask Him some questions: "Master, but when shall these things be? and what sign will there be when these things shall come to pass?" (21:7).

(2) A question of prophecy (21:8–24)
(a) A preliminary view of subsequent events (21:8–11)

First, there would be *false Christs* (21:8). The Lord's teaching as recorded by Luke focuses on the destruction of Jerusalem, which occurred in A.D. 70 and climaxed in the final rebellion under Bar Cochbar in A.D. 135. It also centers on end-times events that are coming into focus today. It is not always easy to be sure whether events described belong to the impending fall of Jerusalem or to the end-of-the-age catastrophes. Probably many of them focus on both because both events have features in common.

The Lord began by drawing attention to coming false Christs: "Take heed that ye be not deceived: for many shall come in my name, saying, I am Christ; and the time draweth near: go ye not therefore after them" (21:8). The Jews had no false messiahs until after they rejected Christ, the true Messiah; then they had many, the first being Bar Cochba. He led a vigorous rebellion against Rome, but the Romans suppressed it with great severity in A.D. 135. They then banished all Jews from their homeland on pain of death. They changed the name of Jerusalem and built a temple to Jupiter on the temple site. They changed the name of the country to Palestine, after the name of the Philistines, the ancient foe of Israel. Thereafter, Jerusalem passed out of history for centuries—no Jew being allowed to approach it and the Jews themselves becoming wanderers in countless Gentile lands, where they are found to this day.

After that, the Jews, in their ghettos and enclaves of Europe and elsewhere, settled down to make the Talmud their spiritual home and to entertain a host of colorful characters, each of whom conned them into believing that he was the Messiah. The Lord's reference here in Luke, however, probably refers to end-times pseudomessiahs.

The Lord moves on to depict *fearful crises* as an end-times herald (21:9–11). There would be *national calamities:* "But when ye shall hear of wars and commotions, be not terrified: for these things must first come to pass; but the end is not by and by [i.e., not yet, or not immediately]." The word for "commotions" refers to unrest, instability, disorder, and confusion. Paul told his friends at Corinth that God is not the author of such things. The Corinthian church was a veritable battlefield when Paul wrote to them. Here the Lord told His people that such upheavals would be common enough down through this age. But His people must not be alarmed. Wars and rumors of war and such like would become more and more severe and frequent. When end-times events begin to cast their shadows before them, wars will become apocalyptical and global—"Nation shall rise against nation, and kingdom against kingdom" (21:10). World War I heralded the change. Until the 1914–1918 conflict, war had always been army against army. The "Great War," as it has been called, however, changed that. Now we face "total war," whole nations harnessed for the all-consuming business of slaughter. Now a growing number of nations and terrorists have weapons of mass destruction.

Not only would national calamities occur but also *natural calamities* as well: "And great earthquakes shall be in divers places, and famines, and pestilences; and fearful sights and great signs shall there be from heaven" (21:11). Earthquakes! Famines! Pestilences! All nature will begin to run amok. Although such things have always been endemic in the world, they are now becoming epidemic. Earthquakes are becoming more frequent and more severe. Famines are more evident, some of them caused by changing weather patterns, others by man's own folly. As for pestilences, not only have new potent and deadly viruses appeared, but also man's accelerating defiance of God's moral laws is causing the widespread dissemination of venereal diseases. Modern man has added to all of his other insanities the folly of stockpiling chemical and biological weapons of enormous potential destructiveness. Moreover, as the end times draw closer, terrifying signs will appear in the sky and in the heavens (21:11).

> (b) A protracted view of sequential events (21:12–24)
>   i. Beware of intolerant adversaries (21:12–19)

The emphasis in this paragraph seems to refer primarily to the events leading to the fall of Jerusalem. However, similar conditions on an aggravated scale will be symptomatic of the end days.

There will be *persecution:* "But before all these, they shall lay their hands on you, and persecute you, delivering you up to the synagogues, and into prisons, being brought before kings and rulers for my name's sake" (21:12). The Lord now warns His disciples to expect persecution for His sake. The book of Acts chronicles the persecution of the early Christians at the hands of the Jews (Acts 4:19–21; 5:17–18; 7:54–60; 8:1, 3; 12:1–10; 13:50; 14:2–5, 19; 17:5, 13; 18:6, 12; 21:27–32; 23:1, 10, 12–17; 24:1). But these were only the beginning of sorrows because then the Romans took over, and wave after wave of immeasurable suffering washed over the church from the days of Nero until the coming of Constantine.

There would be *prosecution* (21:13–15). The believers were not to hire attorneys or prepare briefs. They were simply to show up in court filled with the Holy Spirit, as Stephen did (Acts 7) and as Paul did time and time again.

"And it shall turn to you for a testimony" (21:13). The court appearances would be an opportunity to witness to Christ before men in high places. Paul often seized on such contacts with people in positions of power actually to preach to them (Acts 24:1–17; 25:1–26:32). The Lord did not promise that the inspired defense of the Christian prisoners would secure their release. But He did promise that even their most bitter and brilliant prosecutors would be unable to refute their testimony. Books of church history are full of such tales (21:14–15).

Then, too, there would be *provocation:* "Ye shall be betrayed both by parents, and brethren, and kinsfolks, and friends; and some of you shall they cause to be put to death. And ye shall be hated of all men for my name's sake" (21:16–17). Family, friends, and foes alike would join forces against the innocent believers. Often, as we have seen them do in their attacks upon Christ, they would provoke the believers to get them to say something that could be used against them.

Also, thankfully, there will be *preservation* (21:18–19). "But there shall not an hair of your head perish. In your patience possess ye your souls" (21:18–19). The hairs of our head are numbered (Matt. 10:30–31). The Lord's promise here is obviously not a guarantee that His faithful witnesses will escape martyrdom. It *is* a pledge, however, of their eternal security and that, like Stephen, they will enter into their reward unscathed (Acts 7:54–60).

ii. Beware of invading armies (21:20–24)

This doubtless refer to the invasion of Judea by the Roman armies in A.D. 70. But that was only a preliminary and partial fulfillment. The prophecy focuses ultimately on the end times: "When ye shall see Jerusalem compassed with armies, then know that the desolation thereof is nigh" (21:20). Those who had been eye witnesses of the Roman army on the march would know that even before the clash of arms began, the very sight of the power of the invading force would strike terror into many a heart.

The defenders would see the endless columns of infantry and cavalry from the towers and battlements of the doomed city. The banners, the golden eagles, and the standards held high bore witness to the discipline and order of the foe. Rank after rank they came—the engineers, the pioneers, the baggage trains, all of the impedimenta of war as waged by Rome, the siege equipment, the battering rams, the catapults, and the endless columns of marching men.

The Romans were experts at subduing even the most stubborn cities. When the beat of drums echoed across the valleys of Judah, the whole world knew that Jerusalem was doomed. Jesus warned, "Then let them which are in Judaea flee to the mountains; and let them which are in the midst of it depart out; and let not them that are in the countries enter thereinto" (21:21). Luke was antici-pating the war of A.D. 70. Luke had in mind the drawing of the military cordon around the city. Once that dread circle was complete, flight would be too late. The warning to flee, however, is linked by Matthew to the day when the Anti-christ will put his image in the temple and demand that all people receive his mark (Matt. 24:15–17).

Jesus continued, "For these be the days of vengeance, that all things which are written may be fulfilled" (21:22). The focus turns for a moment to the Jerusalem of Jesus' day. Vengeance! The curses of Matthew 23 had swift and fearful fulfill-ment. The murder of Christ on Calvary's hill called for retribution. So simulta-neously two days were introduced—a day of vengeance on the Jews and their leaders for the crime of crimes. Swift and sure it came. Upon that very generation it came. Out of the west it came, and by the time it was finally over, the nation of Israel was scattered far and wide in an exile that lasted two thousand years until the present.

Launched at the same time was the day of grace. The cross became the means of "so great salvation" (Heb. 2:1–4) being offered to all, and Calvary became the place where God meets the guilty sinner in peace! Amazing grace indeed! Be-cause of Calvary, Jew and Gentile alike became one in Christ and members of the mystical body of Christ, the church (1 Cor. 12:13; Eph. 2:11–22).

However, the destruction of the city and the temple and the dispersal of the Jews to many lands in Bible times does not exhaust the following statement:

"that all things which are written may be fulfilled" (21:22). All of the events connected with the first coming of Christ awoke to fulfillment at that time. But many more prophecies continue to slumber in the tomb of time, howbeit they are now stirring and anticipating full, fast, and fearful fulfillment. The day of grace is about to give way to the day of wrath.

The Lord came back, at once, to a description of the impending fall of Jerusalem in A.D. 70. His eye saw it, and His heart broke over it. "But woe unto them that are with child, and to them that give suck, in those days! for there shall be great distress in the land, and wrath upon this people" (21:23).

Rome had no mercy. A million Jews are said to have perished in this war. The Romans crucified them by the thousand. It has been said that every time the Romans caught a Jew, they crucified him—in all kinds of ways—some of them upside down or sideways or at other angles to add to their sufferings. One report is that the Romans stopped crucifying Jews only when they ran out of wood. The city finally surrendered, and the Romans deported ninety-seven thousand Jews and sold them into slavery or shipped them off to the various areas of the Roman world to be slaughtered in the arena.

Meanwhile, the people in the besieged city suffered from starvation and pestilence and from the fierce squabbles of roaming gangs. Jesus said, "And they shall fall by the edge of the sword, and shall be led away captive into all nations" (21:24). So began the second great exile. The history of their sufferings is spread out over most of the world for more than two thousand years. They have been hated and persecuted from that day to this. Now Jerusalem is again in the spotlight. Jews themselves are disliked and hated around the world. Islamic hatred of the Jews has become a major factor in global Gentile anti-Semitism.

Before moving on to the climax of this prophecy, the Lord paused to make a statement of great significance that only Luke preserved: "and Jerusalem shall be trodden down of the Gentiles, until the times of the Gentiles be fulfilled" (21:24). And so it has been, century after century, starting way back in the days of Nebuchadnezzar. Jerusalem has been held by the Babylonians, the Persians, the Greeks, the Romans, the Crusaders, the Arabs, the Turks, the British, and the United Nations. For the moment, the Jews hold it and vow never to let it go. Just the same, the Antichrist will hold it for a time. He will have three capital cities: Rome will be his political capital, Babylon will be his commercial capital, and Jerusalem will be his religious capital. The rebuilt temple will house his image (Rev. 13).

Two prophetic periods are connected with Jerusalem and the Jews. When

Israel became an elect nation, it was entrusted by God with two spheres of ascendancy over the Gentiles—political ascendancy and spiritual ascendancy. For two thousand years, beginning with Abraham, if God had anything to say, He said it in Hebrew. Gentiles who wanted to know God had to go to a Jew. He gave Israel His laws, His temple, and His Word. He signed a treaty with this people (Gen. 12:1–3; 15:1–21; 18:1–33), something that He has done with no other nation. Israel was to be schoolmaster to the world to teach all peoples God's ways.

Israel failed, so God summoned Nebuchadnezzar of Babylon to execute judgment on the apostate people. The Jews were deported to Babylon, and "the times of the Gentiles" began. Jerusalem has been in Gentile hands ever since. God has given *political* ascendancy to various Gentile world powers "until the times of the Gentiles be fulfilled." It will be in the hands of the last Roman emperor, the Antichrist, when Jesus comes back to reign.

When God took away Jewish political ascendancy in the days of Nebuchadnezzar, He left spiritual ascendancy in their hands. Daniel and his friends, for instance, became tremendous witnesses for God. The captivity ended. Idolatry was burned out of the Jewish soul. They were commissioned to build again the temple in Jerusalem. A handful of Jews took up the challenge under the guidance of a number of great men of God, and the Jews were given a second chance to bear witness to the nations.

Then came the long, slow decline and the rise of rabbinical Judaism and those parties and institutions that so dreadfully opposed Christ and brought about His crucifixion. So God took away Israel's *spiritual* ascendancy. On the Day of Pentecost, with a "rushing mighty wind" (Acts 2:2), and with flames of fire and the coming of the Holy Spirit, God brought in the church. The church (the mystical body of Christ) now has the spiritual ascendancy that the Jews forfeited by their rejection of Christ (Rom. 11:25). That is soon to end. As the church was supernaturally injected into history on the Day of Pentecost (Acts 2), so it will be supernaturally ejected out of history at the Rapture (1 Thess. 4:13–5:11). The Jews will then have their *spiritual* ascendancy restored. The evangelists of the Apocalypse will be Jews (Rev. 7). When Christ finally comes back to earth to reign, He will overthrow the Antichrist and the False Prophet, trample down all Gentile power and rule, and bring in the millennial age. The Jews will then gain back their *political* ascendancy, gladly owning at last the fact that Jesus is absolutely sovereign, Savior and Lord.

b. Events leading to the coming of Jesus (21:25–38)
   (1) The signs (21:25–26)

The Lord now returned to end-times events: "And there shall be signs in the sun, and in the moon, and in the stars" (21:25). Let the world beware. Catastrophic upheavals will occur in the heavens. Because Jesus created all of the suns and stars of space, and because He upholds "all things by the word of his power" (Col. 1:16, Heb. 1:1–3), it will be no big thing for Him to shake the very heavens themselves when He returns. If, as many people believe, He originated the Creation with a Big Bang, it will not be hard for Him to herald His coming with a few more big bangs along the way. After all, when He was born, He put a new star in the sky, and when He died, He put out the sun (Matt. 2:2; 27:45).

"And upon the earth distress of nations, with perplexity; the sea and the waves roaring" (21:25). There will be widespread panic at these ominous omens, when so-called "natural laws" are suspended. The word *perplexity* here has been translated in various ways—"at a loss for a way," for example, or "at their wits end." It depicts the utter moral and mental bankruptcy of even the global superpowers when they are confronted by these coming extraterrestrial upheavals. "The powers of heaven shall be shaken" (21:26). People will be terrified.

These mighty shakings in the heavens could also involve those cosmic beings who rule with Satan in the heavenlies (Eph. 6:12–13). The apocalypse describes such warfare in outer space (Rev. 12:1–5, 7–17).

Again the Lord paused. He wants us to see the following things.

   (2) The Son (21:27)

"And then shall they see the Son of man coming in a cloud with power and great glory." He went home in a cloud when His work on earth was done (Acts 1:9). He will come back in the clouds to receive to Himself His bride (Acts 1:11). He will be back yet again in the clouds when He comes back here to reign (Rev. 1:7). Clouds! He wrapped Himself in a glory cloud in Old Testament times when He marched ahead of His people on the desert road to Canaan (Exod. 13:21). He sat enthroned in glory on the mercy seat upon the ark between the cherubim when He pitched His tent among His chosen people long ago (Exod. 40:34–38).

There Jesus stood that day in His homespun peasant robes. All about Him were the restless crowds. He poured out these great truths, but few, if anyone, understood. But this comment was loud and clear: "And then shall they see the

Son of man coming in a cloud with power and great glory." *He* was "the Son of man." He often referred to Himself as such. In fact, the title occurs about eighty times in the New Testament. The first reference is to His poverty: "The foxes have holes, and the birds of the air have nests; but the Son of man hath not where to lay his head" (Matt. 8:20). The last reference is to His power and His coming again in dazzling glory: "Behold a white cloud, and upon the cloud one sat like unto the Son of man, having on his head a golden crown, and in his hand a sharp sickle" (Rev. 14:14). It will be "this same Jesus," but now with all of His might and glory revealed (Acts 1:11).

(3) The sermon (21:28–36)

"When these things begin to come to pass, then look up, and lift up your heads; for your redemption draweth nigh" (21:28). The word for "look up" suggests "watching with outstretched neck!" Disasters will abound on every hand. The economy and ecology of the planet will be in chaos. War after war and pestilence after pestilence come and go. The Antichrist will be battling his numerous foes, and the nations will be drawn to Armageddon. The final countdown has begun. And from their holes and hideouts, those who still believe will begin to crane their necks toward the eastern sky.

"Watch the fig tree," Jesus said. "Watch all the trees!" Several trees are used symbolically in the Old Testament for Israel, notably the vine, the olive, and the fig. The fig tree speaks of the nation of Israel during this age. The first mention of the fig tree is in connection with the fall of Adam and with his own efforts to cover his shame—totally ineffective attempts they turned out to be (Gen. 3:7). God had a different and better plan (Gen. 3:21). On the way toward Jerusalem, the Lord cursed a barren fig tree that bore nothing but leaves, a symbolic act depicting graphically the condition of the nation of Israel at the time of the Crucifixion—full of outward show but totally devoid of anything for Jesus. Barren! That fig tree, cursed by Christ, died within the day. The rebudding of the fig tree would be *the sign* of Christ's coming again (Matt. 24:33–35). The rebirth of the state of Israel in our generation heralds the approach of end-times events.

"And all the trees," Jesus added. Israel is not the only nation to watch. Suddenly, there has been a global surge of nationalism. Minorities march for independence. Scores of little nations have asserted themselves. All of Israel's ancient foes have been revived and are vociferous in voicing their bitter hatred of Israel.

The Lord has advised us to keep an eye open regarding these signs. They herald end-times events. "Know ye that the kingdom of God is nigh at hand" (21:31).

"This generation shall not pass away, till all be fulfilled" (21:32). Obviously, this statement did not have in mind the generation *to* which He was speaking because that generation has long since passed away. That was the generation that witnessed the death of the nation of Israel. It must, therefore, refer to the generation *of* which He was speaking—the generation that would witness the rebirth of the fig tree and all of the trees, Israel and many other nations besides. A word of caution is in order here. A "generation" is not a hard and fast unit for measuring the passing of time, such as an hour, a day, a month, or a year; it is flexible. The generation that witnessed the demise of the nation of Israel ran from the time Christ spoke to A.D. 135 (approximately one hundred years). The Lord never intended us to use a generation as a means of dating His coming for the church.

The date for the *rapture* of the church is settled in heaven, but it is a secret date. All speculations and guesses as to that day and hour are doomed to fail.

Also settled in heaven is the date of the Lord's *return* to rescue Israel and rule the world. That date, however, is *not* a secret. It will be 1,260 days from the time the Antichrist sets up his image in the temple. Luke does not address this matter. We must seek details in the book of Daniel, the Olivet discourse as recorded by Matthew, and the book of Revelation.

What is the practical value of all of this information? Jesus said, "And take heed to yourselves, lest at any time your hearts be overcharged with surfeiting, and drunkenness, and cares of this life, and so that day come upon you unawares. For as a snare shall it come on all them that dwell on the face of the whole earth" (21:34–35).

The post-Rapture world will be one of unrestrained wickedness. The Antichrist will be known as "the man of sin" (2 Thess. 2:3). He will be wickedness incarnate and will encourage all kinds of evil. Fearful penalties will be imposed on those who do not wholeheartedly fall in step with the times. The removal of the church and the cessation of the Holy Spirit's restraining control will give the Antichrist full rein.

Those who are saved as a result of the kingdom preaching of God's witnesses will face immediate and terrible persecution. The unregenerate will fall in with the Antichrist's policies, and believers will be under fierce pressure. They must not give in (Matt. 24:12–14). Things will happen quickly, universally, and diabolically. It will be all too easy to believe the buttered lies of the Beast, so easy to give in and follow the world into all sin (Ps. 73:2; Prov. 5:14). The word for "surfeiting" here is one of Luke's medical words. Technically, it refers to nausea, giddiness, and the headaches (hangovers) that accompany drunkenness. The word for "cares" suggests being drawn in different directions, being driven to distraction.

"Watch ye therefore, and pray always," Jesus warns, "that ye may be accounted worthy to escape all these things that shall come to pass, and to stand before the Son of man" (21:36). We see two classes of people here: those who have a sure standing before God and those who don't. The true believer's standing is never questioned. He stands before God as perfect in Christ and robed in the very righteousness of Christ. His state might fluctuate, but his standing is as sure as the throne of God. Those who have only an empty profession of faith in Christ have no standing at all before God.

(4) The Savior (21:37–38)

Thus ended the sermon. Luke gives us one last look at Jesus before the dark shadows close around Him: "And in the day time he was teaching in the temple; and at night he went out, and abode in the mount that is called the mount of Olives. And all the people came early in the morning to him in the temple, for to hear him" (21:37–38). The whole world was His. He could have turned His back on Jerusalem and gone anywhere He wished. But no! It had been decided long, long ago and far, far away, in the council chambers of eternity, that all things would come to a head in Jerusalem. Besides, He was the Passover Lamb. The lamb had to be taken on the tenth day, a male without spot or blemish. It had to be kept until the fourteenth day to ensure that it was without spot or blemish. Thus, the Lord tethered Himself to Jerusalem and allowed events to take their course. The countdown to Calvary had begun.

PART 4

Events Relating to the Savior's Cross

Luke 22:1–24:53

Section 1: The Table (22:1–38)
  A. The last Passover (22:1–18)
   1. The date (22:1)

"Now the feast of unleavened bread drew nigh, which is called the Passover" (22:1). Everyone was thinking about that event. It was the annual birthday celebration of the nation of Israel. All roads leading to the capital were thronged with pilgrims hurrying with set faces, eager to get to Jerusalem in time. But not just Jerusalem! All over the country those who could not make the pilgrimage were inspecting their lambs. On the given day, three hundred thousand lambs would die in the Promised Land alone. But all across the vast length and breadth of the Diaspora, thousands more lambs would die. Wherever Jews were found, from the fourteenth day of the first month (Nisan) to the twenty-first day, they kept Passover and the accompanying Feast of Unleavened Bread. In Jerusalem, the Jewish leaders were preparing to kill Jesus, the true Passover Lamb.

   2. The Devil (22:2–6)

Now the Lord's foes come into focus: "And the chief priests and scribes sought how they might kill him; for they feared the people" (22:2). It was no longer a question as to whether they should kill Jesus, but when, where, and how. The Sanhedrin now took up the lead. It had seventy-one members, its president was the high priest, and it met in one of the temple's chambers. Twenty-three members were required to make a quorum. It was made up of the chief priests, the elders of the people, and the scribes. Many of the chief priests were Sadducees by persuasion and were nominated by Herod. The high priest was under the thumb of Herod and the Roman procurator. The scribes were doctors of the Law and delighted in subtleties and sophistries. They bitterly hated Jesus because He repudiated "the traditions of the elders." When the Sanhedrin was in session, the judges sat in a semicircle. Two court reporters took down the proceedings. Voting began with the youngest to avoid their being influenced by their elders. In capital cases, the accused could be pronounced "not guilty" on the same day that he was tried, but if the verdict was "guilty," sentence could not be pronounced until the next day.

Such was the Sanhedrin, a powerful politico-religious body. They had a problem, however, in the case of Jesus. He was popular with the people. They feared a popular uprising and a swift and sure Roman response. How could they arrest Jesus without starting a riot? Then Judas showed up. Luke says, "Then entered Satan into Judas surnamed Iscariot, being of the number of the twelve" (22:3). He was a Judean, the treasurer of the group, and a thief. He seems to have become a disciple in the hope of attaining a high office in the coming kingdom. He became increasingly disillusioned by the mystical side of the Lord's kingdom purposes. And all of this talk about a cross! Judas decided to cash in and get out. Then Satan took possession of him.

He went to the authorities and bargained with them. How much money could he get for betraying Jesus into their hands (22:4)? A deal was struck, and thereafter Judas actively sought means to deliver the Lord into their hands "in the absence of the multitude" (22:6). So he sold the Savior to the Sanhedrin, and he sold his soul to Satan.

3. The decision (22:7–13)

Meanwhile, the Lord gave Peter and John instructions regarding a place to prepare the Passover: "Then came the day of unleavened bread, when the passover must be killed" (22:7). The Lord, of course, knew all about the treachery of Judas, which is probably why He gave His messengers such roundabout instructions (22:10–11). They were to look for a man who was carrying a pitcher. In that day and age, women were responsible for drawing and carrying water. A *man* carrying a pitcher would be very noticeable, so they had no trouble identifying him, following him (22:10), and making contact with the master of the house.

Peter and John were soon on their way. The area to the southwest of Jerusalem was within the wall and was the oldest part of the city, the original "City of David." It was a prosperous area. Possibly the disciples entered this part of the city by the Water Gate, which led to the Gihon, Jerusalem's most ancient water supply, the most likely place for the disciples to spot a man carrying a pitcher of water. It would have been a hard climb up the steep hill of paved terraces to the house itself.

The owner of the house had everything ready (20:12–13). It is not at all improbable that the large Upper Room was where the early believers met. The room set aside for Jesus was the best room in the house, the Upper Room, the most private room, a room with direct access from the outside stairs. The owner had provided wine, the four cups, the unleavened bread, the bitter herbs, the sauces, the table, and the required number of couches. All Peter and John had to do was make ready the Passover lamb. Evidently, there was a believing remnant in Israel made up of people who loved the Lord and who gave lavishly to His cause.

4. The desire (22:14–18)

"And when the hour was come, he sat down, and the twelve apostles with him. And he said unto them, With desire I have desired to eat this passover with you before I suffer" (22:14–15). The hour! The Lord had been moving forward toward this hour from before the beginning of time. The hour drew closer when Adam fell and God clothed him with animal's skins. It moved closer still when He stooped down to this planet to be born. It came closer still when He put away His carpenter's apron to go down to Jordan to be baptized of John. It came closer when He came down from the mount and set His face toward Jerusalem. Now the hour had come.

The Passover lamb was slain, its blood poured out, and its body put on a spit. One length of pomegranate wood was thrust through the lamb horizontally and another thrust through it vertically, so it was impaled upon a cross of wood and then roasted in the fire.

Christ's heart's desire was to gather with His people with He Himself in the midst, partaking of the feast that so vividly proclaimed His own impending death. One more time! The next time would be in the kingdom of God (22:16).

But there was more: "And he took the cup, and gave thanks, and said, Take this, and divide it among yourselves: for I say unto you, I will not drink of the fruit of the vine, until the kingdom of God shall come" (22:17–18). Thus, the Lord brought the Old Testament Passover ritual to an end. Later, Paul would put it thus: "Christ our passover is sacrificed" (1 Cor. 5:7). The symbolic Old Testament feast, repeated year after year for hundreds of years, was replaced by the once-for-all sacrifice of Christ.

B. The last provision (22:19–20)

Now came the founding of a new feast, one that the church has commemorated for the past two thousand years and will do until Jesus comes again. "And he took bread, and gave thanks, and brake it, and gave unto them, saying, This is my body which is given for you: this do in remembrance of me" (22:19). What startling words: He took bread . . . He gave thanks . . . He broke . . . He said, "this is my body." What an awesome thing! He actually gave thanks for the breaking of His body, which would occur in just a few short hours. He was to be beaten and bruised. He was to be scourged and spiked and stabbed. And yet He gave thanks. So should we.

But there was more: "Likewise also the cup after supper, saying, This cup is the new testament in my blood, which is shed for you" (22:20). The "new covenant" was foretold by Jeremiah (Jer. 31:31; Heb. 8:8, 13; 12:24). It contained various clauses. The *eschatological* clauses belong exclusively to the nation of Israel and anticipate the nation's complete regeneration and its millennial blessings at the second coming of Christ. The *soteriological* clauses belong to Israel too, but the saints of this age are included in them. The new covenant, for believers in this church age, was thus proclaimed in the Upper Room. The Lord pledged it in the cup of outpoured wine, and He purchased it at infinite cost at Calvary.

    C. The last protests (22:21–38)
       1. The disclosure (22:21–23)

All of this time, Judas was sitting there, badly wanting to get out. By now, he probably knew that Jesus was going to Gethsemane once the gathering broke up. He was in a fever to cover up his guilt and guile. The Sanhedrin would be getting impatient. All of this talk about eating and drinking in the kingdom of God—he was not going to be fooled by that anymore. Then came the bombshell! Almost casually, Jesus announced, "Behold, the hand of him that betrayeth me is with me on the table" (22:21). He froze. How many hands were on the table at that moment? But the moment passed. Jesus continued, "And truly the Son of man goeth, as it was determined: but woe unto that man by whom he is betrayed!" (22:22).

Calvary was foreknown to God. When it was decided in the high halls of heaven to act in Creation, it was foreknown that the time would come when God would likewise need to act in redemption. They knew to what dizzying heights sin would soar and to what abysmal depths it would sink. It was determined that God would make the very cross itself evidence of how far man would go in sin and make it, the instrument of His grace, evidence of how far God would go in salvation.

Later, Peter put it thus: "Ye men of Israel, hear these words; Jesus of Nazareth, a man approved of God among you by miracles and wonders and signs, which God did by him in the midst of you, as ye yourselves also know: Him, being delivered by the determinate counsel and foreknowledge of God, ye have taken, and by wicked hands have crucified and slain" (Acts 2:22–23).

One of these wicked hands was on the supper table that night. No sooner did Jesus issue His warning than "they began to inquire among themselves, which of them it was that should do this thing" (22:23). It was incredible. No one suspected Judas. In the confusion, he snatched his wicked hand from the table and lifted his voice to protest his innocence along with the rest of them. He stolidly ignored the Lord's "woe."

> 2. The dispute (22:24–30)
>   a. The disciples and their conflict (22:24)

It was at this solemn moment that an argument broke out. "And there was also a strife among them, which of them should be accounted the greatest" (22:24)—this, after having had this very question settled for them months earlier (Matt. 18:1–4; Luke 9:46). This was the very spirit of Antichrist: who should be the greatest? This was the very sin of Lucifer: who should be the greatest?

But there was worse! The word for "strife" indicates "*love* of strife." Right there, with the shadow of the cross lying across the table with its broken emblems, the disciples began a squabble. Who should be the greatest! One lexicon says that the word used can be rendered "to be eager of contention." It must have stabbed Jesus to His heart.

> b. The disciples and their conversion (22:25–27)

How patient Jesus was. He said, "The kings of the Gentiles exercise lordship over them; and they that exercise authority upon them are called benefactors. But ye shall not be so: but he that is greatest among you, let him be as the younger; and he that is chief, as he that doth serve" (22:25–26).

When he was a prisoner on the small island of St. Helena in the Atlantic, Napoleon, reflecting on his career, made the following observation:

> Everything in him [Christ] astonishes me. . . . Alexander, Caesar, Charlemagne, and myself founded empires. But on what did we rest the creations of our genius? Upon force. Jesus Christ alone founded his empire on love; and to this hour millions of men would die for him.[1]

---

1. Philip Schaff, *The Person of Christ* (New York: George H. Doran Co./American Tract Society, 1913), 138.

The disciples thought of a kingdom. In their hearts arose a vision of Rome, with its marching men, its countless conquests, and its iron rule. All about them was the might and majesty of an empire of pomp and splendor. They thought of lofty positions in such an empire, global and glorious, and they coveted such seats of splendor for themselves. Jesus said "No!" to all that. The Devil had offered Him that years earlier (Matt. 4). The kingdom of God was not to be made of such stuff. He curbed again the soaring, worldly ambitions of His men.

"For whether is greater, he that sitteth at meat, or he that serveth? is not he that sitteth at meat? but I am among you as he that serveth" (22:27). What more could be said?

c. The disciples and their coronation (22:28–30)

Dim indeed was the disciples' grasp of these things. There would be a crowning day, but not now—indeed, not for a very long time. John tells us how He taught them about the Holy Spirit and how He prayed for them. "Ye are they which have continued with me," He said. By this time, Judas was gone, hurrying through the city to collect both his money and a mob.

Then He drew aside the veil and gave them a glimpse of a distant day: "And I appoint unto you a kingdom, as my Father hath appointed unto me; that ye may eat and drink at my table in my kingdom, and sit on thrones judging the twelve tribes of Israel" (22:29–30). This statement is to be taken literally. It points ahead to the millennial age. Every time we pray the pattern prayer, we repeat the request: "Thy kingdom come."

3. The deceiver (22:31–34)

Something alien was still in the air. Judas was gone, but all was not well. This time the focus turned to Simon Peter. Jesus spoke to him: "Simon, Simon!" The double use of a name was intended to arrest attention. The device is used ten times in the Bible. Jesus used it on the cross (Matt. 23:37). Here, the Lord used the duplication of Peter's old name not only to arrest him but also to impress upon him his danger. Peter must have been startled when the Lord called him by his old name, the name of his unregenerate days. Peter was not only vulnerable but also was being stalked by the Evil One. "Behold, Satan hath desired to have you, that he may sift you as wheat" (22:31). Evidently, Satan had been sizing up Simon. He must have sensed something of Peter's greatness. On the Day of

Pentecost alone, Peter would bring three thousand souls to Christ. Before that happened, however, Satan would like to do to Peter what he was about to do to Judas—turn him into a suicide. He had already been given permission to try him. Little did Peter know how greatly he was about to be tempted.

"But I have prayed for thee, that thy faith fail not: and when thou art converted, strengthen thy brethren" (22:32). That is part of the wonder of the Christian life; we have the Lord Jesus to be our Great High Priest and to pray for us as our Advocate with the Father (1 John 2:1). We can be sure that His prayers are always effectual.

During the next three days, all of the disciples would be tested to the very limits of their faith. Their Beloved would be arrested that very night and hauled here and there, being beaten and bullied and falsely condemned. He would be crucified and buried. And their whole world would fall apart. They would lock themselves in the Upper Room in fear for their own lives.

Peter was to be a special target. Jesus knew how badly he would fall. But why did Jesus allow Satan to attack Peter so severely? So that he might emerge stronger on the other side and be in a position to strengthen the brethren (22:32).

Peter was indignant. "Lord," he said, "I am ready to go with thee, both into prison, and to death" (22:33). It was just as well that the Lord was not counting on Peter's good intentions. Peter had completely underestimated the fierceness of Satan's coming attack and overestimated his own personal courage and commitment.

"I tell thee, Peter," Christ responded, "the cock shall not crow this day, before that thou shalt thrice deny that thou knowest me" (22:34).

Peter! The Lord addressed Peter in this way only once before—when He changed his name from Simon to Peter as a result of his great confession. A few minutes later, Peter had rebuked the Lord for prophesying His death. The Lord instantly rebuked him: "Get thee behind me, Satan . . ." (Matt. 16:18, 23). Now the Lord used the name Peter for the second time. It was a warning. Satan was still on the prowl. Peter had succumbed to Satan before, even becoming his tool! "I have prayed for thee," He said.

4. The dispensation (22:35–38)

The Lord turned His attention to other matters. He had in mind the change in dispensations now instituted. Periodically in history, God has changed His way of doing things, of administering human affairs.[2] The Lord was now going to set just such a change in motion.

---

2. John Phillips, *The Bible Explorer's Guide* (Grand Rapids: Kregel, 2002).

"And he said unto them, When I sent you without purse, and scrip, and shoes, lacked ye any thing? And they said, Nothing" (22:35). That was when He sent them to "the lost sheep of the house of Israel" (9:1–9; Matt. 10:6), at a time when there was still a possibility that national revival might occur.

"But now," He said, "he that hath a purse, let him take it, and likewise his scrip: and he that hath no sword, let him sell his garment, and buy one" (22:36). Times had changed. The marching orders for the church in the world are quite different than those for the ministry to Israel in the land. Christians even have the right of self-defense under the appropriate conditions. The offer of the kingdom was now postponed, so the Lord prepared His servants for a different war and a different world. The gospel of the kingdom was to be replaced by the gospel of the grace of God (Acts 20:24; Eph. 3:2). The gospel was to go out to all the earth (Acts 1:8). All was changed. Reasonable preparations must be made to secure an income and ensure a measure of protection. No ordinary prudent steps must be omitted. Church history tells of such times when the church took steps to protect itself from a hostile world. The times are rare, but they are appropriate when they come.

The Lord's thoughts went back to the prophet Isaiah: "For I say unto you, that this that is written must yet be accomplished in me, And he was reckoned among the transgressors: for the things concerning me have an end." The quotation is from Isaiah 53:12. Numbered among the transgressors! He, the Holy One of Israel, numbered among the transgressors! He, before whose burning eye even the sinless seraphim seek shelter in their wings, numbered with the transgressors! He could see what they could not see. Judas had rounded up his toughs and troops and was marching forward to a crisis confrontation in Gethsemane (22:37). The things concerning Him were at an end. Before another day was done, He would call out from a cross the word *Finished!*

Then came the last misunderstanding of this tragic day: "And they said, Lord, behold, here are two swords" (22:38). Two swords! If there was any thought of armed resistance, they would need many more swords than that! Two swords, when Judas had a detachment of Roman soldiers marching as to war. But the Lord had no intention of waging war. Besides, had He so desired, He had twelve legions of angels to summon to the scene. Not, of course, that He had any need for them. Two swords? "It is enough," He said with a trace of irony. Two swords indeed. Peter still didn't get it. The Devil was already after him. He had two swords!

Section 2: The Tears (22:39–53)

    A.   The agony of Jesus (22:39–46)

Luke now takes us to *Gethsemane:* "And he came out, and went, as he was wont, to the mount of Olives; and his disciples also followed him" (22:39). It was His custom to go to this quiet garden just across the Kidron at the foot of Olivet. Judas was sure that he would find Him there—a nice quiet spot to arrest Him. The name Gethsemane means "the oil press," so called because of the olive trees that grew there.

Next, there was divine *guidance:* "And when he was at the place, he said unto them, Pray that ye enter not into temptation" (22:40). And what temptation! Temptation to cowardice and to flight. The only way to fight such a foe was by prayer.

And then came *grief:* "And he was withdrawn from them about a stone's cast, and kneeled down, and prayed" (22:41). A stone's cast! The Jews executed criminals by stoning them to death. "A stone's cast" was the distance of death. He was that close to it now. And what a death! He was soon to be "made sin" for us, He who knew no sin (2 Cor. 5:21). His whole being shrank from it. No wonder He wept.

"Father," He cried, "If thou be willing, remove this cup from me: nevertheless not my will, but thine, be done" (22:42). What He saw when He gazed into the dark depths of that cup is set before us throughout the Bible (Isa. 51:17; Rev. 14:10; 18:5–7). He saw! He spoke! He surrendered! He shrank from that dreadful cup but yielded to His Father's perfect will just the same. He "became obedient unto death, even the death of the cross" (Phil. 2:8).

Then there was *grace.* God gave Him respite. "And there appeared an angel unto him from heaven, strengthening him" (22:43). There was no one here on earth able to strengthen His hand in God, so an angel came. The mental, emotional, and spiritual anguish completely drained Him. Satan would have killed Him then and there had he been able. Instead, an angel came. The unjust steward of our Lord's parable, when weighing his options, said, "I cannot dig." The word he used meant "I do not have the strength to dig." An intensified form of the word is used here to describe the supernatural strengthening of the Lord.

Then there were the *groans:* "And being in an agony he prayed more earnestly: and his sweat was as it were great drops of blood falling down to the ground" (22:44). The Holy Spirit employed here a word used solely to describe the Lord's agony. It stands for severe emotional strain and anguish along with violent struggle and physical strife. Strengthened, the Lord broke out into a passion of prayer. He "prayed more earnestly" Luke says. The word used here is found nowhere else in the New Testament. It means "to stretch." Every nerve was stretched to the breaking point.

The sweat poured down, sweat mingled with blood. We cannot imagine, still less describe, the intense pressure and agony that produced such extraordinary woe.

Luke then drew attention to another ingredient in this recipe of suffering—the *guilt* of the disciples in going to sleep when they should have been agonizing in prayer. "And when he rose up from prayer, and was come to his disciples, he found them sleeping for sorrow, And said unto them, Why sleep ye? rise and pray, lest ye enter into temptation" (22:45–46).

Luke does not give us the whole story. Matthew does that (Matt. 26:36–46). But Luke explains why the disciples fell asleep: they were overcome by sorrow; they were utterly exhausted. Maybe Satan lulled them to sleep as a balm for their woes. It was a strange, heavy sleep that held them so tightly—the Lord Himself woke them up two or three times, but the moment His back was turned, they fell asleep again.

The Lord rebuked them gently. His hour of temptation was over; theirs was about to begin. He had won His battle—on His knees. They were about to lose theirs—by taking to their heels.

B. The arrival of Judas (22:47–53)
   1. The betrayal in the garden (22:47–48)

Time was up. "And while he yet spake, behold a multitude, and he that was called Judas, one of the twelve, went before them, and drew near unto Jesus to kiss him. But Jesus said unto him, Judas, betrayest thou the Son of man with a kiss?" (22:47–48). This was no unorganized mob that now materialized out of the gloom. We learn from John's gospel that Judas "received a *band* of men" (John 18:3). The word used means a cohort, the tenth part of a legion, some six hundred men. Evidently, the Sanhedrin was afraid of serious trouble. At the head of the cohort was the commander of the Twelfth Legion, the officer commanding the Jerusalem guard. No doubt, the instructions given to Judas told him to identify Jesus promptly so that He could be arrested and whisked away to the high priest's palace. Once they had lost their leader, budding opposition from the disciples would be cut off. Judas would kiss Jesus. And that would be that.

As the traitor approached Jesus, the Lord called him by his name, Judas, for the last time: "Judas, betrayest thou the Son of man with a kiss?" (22:48). And the Lord used His favorite title in challenging the traitor—"the Son of man." The last time Judas had heard that title was an hour or so earlier in the Upper Room when Jesus had said, "And truly the Son of man goeth, as it was determined: but woe unto that man by whom he is betrayed!" (22:22). This loving attempt to call Judas back from the Abyss failed. The Lord abandoned him to his doom.

2. The battle in the garden (22:49–53)

Then Peter barged in: "When they which were about him saw what would follow, they said unto him, Lord, shall we smite with the sword? And one of them smote the servant of the high priest, and cut off his right ear" (22:49–50). The action was completely foreign to the Lord's will. Perhaps Peter thought that now that the first blow had been struck, the Lord would call down fire from heaven or summon a cohort of angels. Maybe it was Peter's way of making good on his boast that he would stand for Jesus at all costs.

Something about the whole episode is ludicrous. Peter did not smite a soldier but a slave, the high priest's servant, Malchus. Even then, it was wholly ineffective. No doubt, Peter intended to cut off the fellow's head, but all he did was smite off his ear! Jesus interfered at once. "Suffer ye thus far," He said to the man who was doubtless carrying on, crying in pain and covered with blood. Always the gentlemen, Jesus excused Himself and went to work. "And he touched his ear, and healed him" (22:51). "Love your enemies," Jesus had said (Matt. 5:44). And beside all that, it was a marvelous miracle. Who but Jesus could in an instant pick up a severed ear and put it back where it belonged?

By now, "the chief priests, and captains of the temple, and the elders" showed up. Out of hatred or curiosity, they had tagged along with the troops. They were the very people who should have taken the lead in welcoming to earth the Son of the living God. Jesus challenged them: "Be ye come out, as against a thief, with swords and staves? When I was daily with you in the temple, ye stretched forth no hands against me" (22:52–53).

On the sixth day before the Passover, the Lord had approached Jerusalem from Jericho, entered the city, and cleansed the temple. Why had they not arrested Him then? On the fourth day before the Passover (our Palm Sunday), He rode boldly into Jerusalem as the Messiah. Why had they not arrested Him then?

The next day, He had cursed the fig tree, entered the temple, and faced their hatred. Why had they not arrested Him then? Again, the next day it was the same. Why had they not arrested Him then? Instead, under cover of darkness and with numbers of people tagging along and marching men fully armed, they arrested Him. Why did they not arrest Him in broad daylight? Why wait until dark?

"But this is your hour, and the power of darkness," Jesus added (22:53). The hand of Satan was in all of this. He is the prince of darkness (Eph. 6:12; Col. 1:13). Satan had been waiting for this hour. The forces of darkness, both human and demonic, would have their moment of triumph. It would be brief. The lights would go out—but then would come the perfect day (Prov. 4:18).

Section 3: The Trials (22:54–23:25)
   A. The trial before the Hebrew priests (22:54–71)
      1. Jesus is denied (22:54–23:25)
         a. Peter's terror (22:54)

"Then took they him, and led him, and brought him into the high priest's house. And Peter followed afar off" (22:54). It was not far. They probably went back through the same gate by which the Lord a short while before had led His disciples on the way to Gethsemane. The palace of the high priest stood on the slopes of the southern hill not far from the house of the Last Supper, on the slope between the upper city and the Tyropoen. It was now about three o'clock in the morning.

The palace of Annas was well known. The Gospels do not tell us why Jesus was first taken to the house of Annas, who was the former high priest. Probably it was because Annas pulled the strings. He was the most powerful man in Jerusalem. The cynical Caiaphas was really the high priest, but everyone knew who held the power. Annas was enormously wealthy, much of his money coming from the traffic in the temple. He had liberal religious views and no conscience. He was friendly to the Romans and knew how to use his money to make friends and influence people.

Luke was more interested in people. He shows us Peter, for instance, tagging along afar off, keeping a safe distance between himself and the soldiers. He had no intention of intervening. He was afraid. Torn between curiosity and cowardice, between fear and love, he plodded on. Afar off! That is a most dangerous place to be.

b. Peter's trial (22:55–60a)

When the attendants arrived at the palace, they kindled a fire and sat down to await events. "And when they had kindled a fire in the midst of the hall, and were set down together, Peter sat down among them" (22:55). It is always chilly at night on the Judean hills in the month of Nisan. Peter carefully insinuated himself among them, sat down, and stretched out his hands to their cheerful fire.

The usual chatter doubtless continued as people swapped ideas about the arrest of Jesus. Few, if any, said anything that might compromise them. They gossiped about Jesus, reflecting the views of the Establishment. Peter sat tongue-tied. What he could have told them had he dared!

Before long, "a certain maid beheld him as he sat by the fire, and earnestly looked upon him, and said, This man was also with him" (22:56).

Now is your chance, Peter. Tell her about your mother-in-law. Tell her about the little lad's lunch. Tell her about Malchus, half an hour ago. Go on! Tell her what He's really like, who He really is. Instead, "he denied him, saying, Woman, I know him not" (22:57). Denial number one.

"And after a little while another saw him, and said, Thou art also of them. And Peter said, Man, I am not" (22:58). Now he denied not only the Lord but also the Lord's people. Denial number two.

Still Peter stayed where he was, afraid to get up and leave. "And about the space of one hour after another confidently affirmed, saying, Of a truth this fellow also was with him: for he is a Galilaean" (22:59). We learn from the other Gospels that this time Peter reinforced his denial with curses. After that, the world was satisfied. No true disciple of Jesus would talk like that.

c. Peter's tears (22:60b–62)

"And immediately, while he yet spake, the cock crew" (22:60b). At once! While the dreadful words of denial were still ringing in the listeners' ears. The call of a rooster from some nearby garden was a wake-up call. Peter was suddenly awake to where he was and to what he had said and whom he had denied. And at that very moment "the Lord turned, and looked upon Peter. And Peter remembered the word of the Lord, how he had said unto him, Before the cock crow, thou shalt deny me thrice. And Peter went out, and wept bitterly" (22:61–62). The last vision that poor Peter had of his Lord as he crept away was of the Lord still in His festal garb, surrounded by enemies, His hands bound, and all alone.

So Peter crept away as the morning broke. Perhaps he tried to hide himself down some back lane. Perhaps he went to Gethsemane. Satan doubtless had a field day with Peter over the next three days. "You're finished, Peter. That man Jesus, even if He manages to get off, will never speak to you again. Peter the rock! Peter the pebble, more like. And you telling James and John that you were going to be the greatest! What were those curse words, Peter? Full of burning brimstone no doubt. Choice specimens from my own dictionary! You must have picked them up in your fisherman days. Well, you might as well keep using them. You're through. Don't you think it would be a good idea for you to commit suicide?

Ah no! Jesus had prayed for him that his faith might not fail. He probably was praying for him right then.

2. Jesus is derided (22:63–65)

In short, swift, stabbing statements, Luke now takes us from the courtyard to the courtroom. He shows us, through his Gentile eyes, how the religious elite of the Hebrew people mauled and then murdered their Messiah.

We see Him *badgered* by the men of Israel: "And the men that held Jesus mocked him, and smote him" (22:63). Mark and John fill in the details of this phase of the trial (Mark 14:55–64; John 18:13, 19–24). Caiaphas was present at this Hebrew trial and took a prominent part. It began, however, with Annas, the former high priest. Annas looked with dislike and disdain on Jesus. He saw an annoying Galilean carpenter whose activities had begun to imperil his position, prosperity, and power. Jesus looked into this man's withered little soul and saw a poor, lost man who needed a Savior.

Annas passed the case to Caiaphas, the official high priest. The priests sought out false witnesses. It is a sad commentary on the wickedness of men that they found plenty of people who were willing to toady to them and give false witness, but they were unable to squeeze a cohesive story from any of them. Throughout these highly irregular and criminal proceedings, Jesus remained silent. Finally, Caiaphas stood up, put Jesus under oath, and asked Him if He was the Son of God. His obvious goal was to get a whole roomful of people to witness the answer. He knew that Jesus' response could be construed as blasphemy. Jesus broke His silence. He affirmed His deity and warned them that one day they would be exposed to His unveiled glory. The high priest rent his clothes and appealed to his fellow conspirators, who agreed that Jesus was a blasphemer and worthy of death.

It was important now to get a quorum of the Sanhedrin. While the place was filling up with members, those already present beguiled the time by mocking Jesus. The word for "mocked" includes the ideas of derision, trickery, and deception. That this Galilean peasant, born and bred in the despised town of Nazareth, a village carpenter, indeed, should claim to be God struck these men as not only blasphemous but also very funny. So they mocked Him.

"And the men that held Jesus . . . smote him" (22:63). Oh, how the watching angels must have tightened their grip on their swords! These common men, taking their cue from their leaders, actually smote the Lord of glory. They roughed Him up as a pastime while waiting for the proceedings to begin.

But there was more: "And when they had blindfolded him, they struck him on the face, and asked him, saying, Prophesy, who is it that smote thee?" (22:64). Of course, He knew who smote Him. If these brutal men were not numbered later among those who were subsequently saved and added to the church, they will find out at the Great White Throne judgment that He knows perfectly well who smote Him. But at the time, He said nothing. He had come to save them, not to smite them.

Luke summarizes this sorry farce of a trial. "And many other things blasphemously spake they against him" (22:65). This trial before His fellow countrymen became an arena of hatred. The robed elders, priests, and scribes vied with each other to see who could say the vilest, most vicious things about Him, slapping Him, spitting on Him, and scoffing at Him. The Holy Spirit says that *they* were guilty of blasphemy.

3. Jesus is divine (22:66–71)

"And as soon as it was day, the elders of the people and the chief priests and the scribes came together, and led him into their council . . ." (22:66). The previous night, those members of the Sanhedrin who were in the clique of Annas settled on the charge that would most impress the full Sanhedrin. They had doubtless decided which witnesses they would call to substantiate their charge. Now they were ready for Him.

Luke shows us the various members and groups of the Sanhedrin taking the appointed places. They were going to deal with this troublesome Galilean Messiah once and for all. The hubbub died away. The horseplay stopped. The prisoner stood in their midst. He had been up all night. He had been buffeted and bullied for hours. Now the trial could begin.

"Art thou the Christ? tell us." They came straight to the point.

"If I tell you, ye will not believe," He replied. "And if I also ask you, ye will not answer me, nor let me go" (22:67–68). He had already answered their question and their response was visible in the bruises and blood that covered His face. He had been instantly and incessantly subjected to verbal and violent abuse. As for letting Him go, not on their life! After all of the trouble it had taken to seize Him? Now that they had Him, they intended to kill Him.

Having told them that it was pointless for Him to answer their question, He answered it anyway. "Hereafter," He said, "shall the Son of man sit on the right hand of the power of God" (22:69). They knew that the title "Son of man" was a messianic title (Ps. 8:4–6; Heb. 2:5–8) and that He frequently adopted it as His own. But they wanted something more explicit than that. Had He said simply that the Messiah would sit enthroned at God's right hand or that He Himself would be so enthroned? They pressed Him for a statement before which there could be no quibbling: "Then said they all, Art thou then the Son of God? And he said unto them, Ye say that I am" (22:70).

What we have here is a Hebraism denoting strong and positive affirmation. The Lord used a form of reply familiar to the rabbinical mind by which He accepted the question put to Him as His own affirmation: "It is as you say," or "what you say is so. That is what I am." He was the Son of God, entitled to sit upon God's throne, where indeed He would sit one day.

That settled it! "And they said, What need we any further witness? for we ourselves have heard of his own mouth" (22:71). The trial was over. From Dan to Beersheba, from the sea to beyond the Jordan, for three and a half years He had set before one and all countless demonstrations of His deity. They had ignored them all. The Hebrew trial was over. Caiaphas and his crowd, almost to a man, pronounced Him guilty of death. Caiaphas stood among his cronies receiving their congratulations for his masterly handling of a difficult and potentially highly explosive case. But an even harder case was ahead. They would have to handle Pilate with kid gloves.

    B. The trial before the heathen procurator (23:1–25)
        1. Pilate's political dilemma (23:1–12)

When Pilate visited Jerusalem, he most likely stayed in the magnificent palace built by Herod the Great. Pilate had very high connections in Rome. He had been nominated to his governorship by Sejanus, the powerful man who stood behind Tiberius and directed his power. Pilate's wife was Claudia Procula, a granddaughter of the great Augustus, and the Jews knew it. Pilate did what he pleased. Moreover, he had no love for Jews and specifically disliked Caiaphas and his crowd.

Pilate likely conducted the trial of Jesus in the praetorian of the castle of Antonia, which frowned upon the temple court. It seems likely that he was kept informed about the conspiracy. The Sanhedrin would not be so foolish as to try to keep him in the dark. He was the one who would ultimately decide what would happen to Jesus. According to John, the Roman who led a detachment of men to Gethsemane was a military tribune, the commander of a thousand men, a Roman cohort. An officer of such rank was constantly in touch with the Roman garrison in Jerusalem. It was an important city and one that often was in turmoil. The Jewish conspirators were afraid that Jesus might use His miraculous powers to resist arrest, even to launch a revolution. Their fear prompted them to request a Roman guard, and Rome took it seriously enough to send the tribune personally to ensure that things did not get out of hand. The tribune was the only Roman of Pilate's social class who was resident in Jerusalem. He surely told Pilate what was going on. Pilate, too, doubtless had an army of spies, prying into every corner of his realm. Nothing but good characterized the reports that he received about the Lord's activities. Probably he knew more about Jesus than Caiaphas did. It is likely, too, that Pilate wanted to keep his options open. He would not be averse to going along with the Sanhedrin, perhaps, to rid the troublesome province that he ruled of a potential Messiah and insurrectionist—until he met Jesus. Then he would have gladly backed out of the whole affair.

All of this lies behind the simple statement "And the whole multitude of them arose, and led him unto Pilate" (23:1).

First, there was a *lethal lie* (23:2–5). They said to Pilate, "We found this fellow perverting the nation, and forbidding to give tribute to Caesar, saying that he himself is Christ a King" (23:2). They had found Him doing nothing of the kind. Only recently He had told them to render unto Caesar the things that were Caesar's.

A king was He? Pilate would sit up and take notice of that. "Perverting the nation" no less. No more lethal charges could have been brought. The Jews had evidently decided to keep their charge of blasphemy in reserve. Pilate would be far more galvanized to action on a political charge than he would on a religious charge. The emperor Tiberius was a suspicious, filthy man. Pilate knew that the Jews of the Diaspora had people in high places everywhere. They would only have to get the attention of Tiberius for a few minutes, and Pilate would be banished or killed. The Jews had already reported him to Rome for offending their religious susceptibilities. Yes, indeed, Pilate would have to act with care.

Pilate turned to Jesus. "Art thou the King of the Jews?" he asked.

Jesus answered at once: "Thou sayest it" (23:3). Again, as before the Sanhedrin, Jesus used the same familiar idiom. "Yes," He said, "It is as you say. I am the King of the Jews." Pilate's scribes could have confirmed that fact from the temple records across the way. Jesus had nothing to hide. He was the last, rightful bloodline heir to the throne of David. His pedigree could be traced through a thousand years.

Pilate was puzzled. Nothing in the accused's appearance was striking. He was wearing a festive but homespun robe. He obviously had been abused. He certainly did not look, act, or talk like an insurrectionist. But He showed no fear, no servility. And an aura of regal dignity and power was about Him. The Sanhedrin probably had trumped up the charge.

"Then said Pilate to the chief priests and to the people, I find no fault in this man" (23:4). He should then have declared, "Case dismissed," but he didn't. He was frightened of not only what Caesar might do but also what the Sanhedrin might do. He did not have long to wait. "And they were the more fierce, saying, He stirreth up the people, teaching throughout all Jewry, beginning from Galilee to this place" (23:5). They saw that Pilate was skeptical. All of their plots might come to nothing. They grew stronger, more vehement, and more violent. They said, "He stirreth up the people." The word they used means "to shake up." It paints a picture of someone shaking to and fro the contents of a bottle. They pictured Jesus as being a political agitator. "All of the way from Galilee to here," they cried.

But they had gone too far. Pilate saw *a legal loophole* (23:6–12) because when Pilate heard of Galilee, he asked whether the man were a Galilean (23:6). Jesus had attracted vast crowds. People had flocked from all over to hear Him. Much of His time had been in Galilee. Pilate knew about Galileans. He had already killed some of them (13:1–2), but this Galilean had not caused any trouble. Indeed, Pilate, fully aware through his spies of the general nature of Christ's activities, knew that he had nothing at all to fear from Him. So he never bothered about Him. Besides, Jesus was not a Galilean but a Judean. At this juncture, however, Pilate was not interested in such fine points. Galilee? The very thing! That called for a change of venue. "As soon as he knew that he belonged unto Herod's jurisdiction, he sent him to Herod, who himself also was at Jerusalem at that time" (23:7).

Back in the fortress, Pilate doubtless congratulated himself on a very clever and convenient end to his troubles. He must have laughed up his sleeve at the fury and frustration of the chief priests at this turn of events. Herod Antipas had already murdered John the Baptist and had been troubled by his conscience ever since. Just the same, perhaps he would embroil himself in the plots of the Jews over Jesus.

So the Jews hauled Jesus to Herod. "And when Herod saw Jesus, he was exceeding glad: for he was desirous to see him of a long season, because he had heard many things of him; and he hoped to have seen some miracle done by him" (23:8). So Herod looked eagerly and expectantly at Jesus.

And Jesus looked at Herod. Before Him sat the man who had murdered John, His cousin, His dear friend and forerunner. The man was as weak as he was wicked. He was wrapped in the outward trappings of royalty, but he was as sly as a fox, a man who had no scruples. To him, Jesus had nothing to say.

But Herod had plenty to say. "Then he questioned with him in many words; but he answered him nothing" (23:9). Question after question! Silence! Herod suddenly realized that he was talking to himself. He was being ignored completely. But if Jesus was silent, His enemies had plenty to say. "And the chief priests and scribes stood and vehemently accused him" (23:10).

Herod looked from the silent Christ to the screaming priests and scribes. Of the two, Jesus annoyed him more. So! This was the King of the Jews! No wonder the Sanhedrin wanted to get rid of Him. What was it that He had publicly called him? A fox? That was it, a fox (13:2). So "Herod with his men of war set him at nought, and mocked him, and arrayed him in a gorgeous [splendid] robe, and sent him again to Pilate" (23:11).

This action produced an unexpected by-product: "And the same day Pilate and Herod were made friends together: for before they were at enmity between themselves" (23:12). Both men had faced the awesome holiness of Jesus and His formidable silence in the face of their weakness and wickedness. They had something in common at last—their rejection of Christ. They became good friends as a result. As the Lord draws His own people together in a common bond of love, so He draws His enemies together in a common bond of hatred.

> 2. Pilate's personal dilemma (23:13–25)
>   a. Roman justice demonstrated (23:13–15)

"And Pilate, when he had called together the chief priests and the rulers and the people, said unto them, Ye have brought this man unto me, as one that perverteth the people: and, behold, I, having examined him before you, have found no fault in this man touching those things whereof ye accuse him: no, nor yet Herod: for I sent you to him; and, lo, nothing worthy of death is done unto him" (23:13–15).

Well done, Pilate! Spoken like a Roman! Fair and fearless! Pilate was known to be stubborn, haughty, and impatient. He it was who had marched his men into Jerusalem and, in defiance of the religious sensibilities of the Jews against graven images, had set up the gleaming standards and eagles right where their presence would most offend the Jews. He it was who decided to improve Jerusalem's water supply and who seized consecrated money from the temple to pay for those improvements. He it was who did not hesitate to turn his troops loose to crush rebellion. He it was who, having tried Jesus, found Him to be innocent of all charges. Both he and Herod were agreed on that point. And so he told his old foes, the Jewish chief priests and rulers.

b. Roman justice distorted (23:16–21)

Had Pilate dismissed the case and freed the innocent Man at that point, he would have gone down in history as a hero. But that is just what he failed to do. The very next words that he uttered branded him as both weak and wicked: "I will therefore chastise him, and release him. (For of necessity he must release one unto them at the feast)" (23:16–17).

What a perversion of justice! To pronounce a man guiltless and then to scourge him before releasing him. A Roman scourging was a fearful ordeal. Men died beneath the terrible strokes of the flagellum, a short whip with multiple leather thongs weighted with jagged metal fragments. This cruel instrument of torture tore away flesh, exposed bones, and shredded the vital organs. "The man is innocent; scourge Him!"

In addition, Pilate invoked a tradition—the annual custom of releasing a prisoner each Passover. Pilate decided to kill two birds with one stone. He would release Jesus and satisfy the annual requirement, and he would release Him, justified and innocent as He was, and satisfy the demands of the Law. But the Jews were not fooled. Besides, if a captive was to be released, they certainly did not want it to be Jesus. They had someone else in mind. "And they cried out all at once, saying, Away with this man, and release unto us Barabbas: (who for a certain sedition made in the city, and for murder, was cast into prison)" (23:18–19).

By now, a crowd had gathered. The Sanhedrin evidently had its men mingling with the mob, carefully planted to ensure that the voice of the mob would be the voice of the chief priests and the scribes. They were to shout for Barabbas. Barabbas was a colorful character who had made insurrection against Rome. That was the kind of messiah the Jews wanted, someone who would rid them of Rome. The name Barabbas means "son of a father." Origen (A.D. 186–253) refers to him as "Jesus Barabbas." The choice would be clear—Jesus Barabbas or Jesus Christ.

The convict Barabbas was brought in. "Pilate therefore, willing to release Jesus, spake again to them. But they cried, saying, Crucify him, crucify him" (23:20–21). Pilate put the two men up for the crowd to see. On the one hand stood Barabbas, a bold enough ruffian by all accounts. On the other hand stood Jesus, much the worse for wear at the hands of the Jews and Herod and bone weary from a sleepless night. He faced the mob as Pilate tried his best. And the mob shouted one word, full of menace and synonymous with torture, agony, and bone-wrenching, bloodshedding, heart-stopping pain— *"Crucify!"*

c. Roman justice denied (23:22–25)

Then came Pilate's last stand: "And he said unto them the third time, Why, what evil hath he done? I have found no cause of death in him: I will therefore chastise him, and let him go" (23:22). This was Pilate's last feeble struggle with his conscience and with the terribly adamant Sanhedrin. The Jewish leaders were not interested in the guilt or innocence of Jesus; they wanted Him crucified. "And they were instant with loud voices, requiring that he might be crucified. And the voices of them and of the chief priests prevailed" (23:23). No doubt, the members of the Sanhedrin took malicious delight in the knowledge that the opprobrium for the death of Christ could be shifted from them to Pilate and that Jesus would not only die an excruciatingly painful death but also die under the curse of the Mosaic Law (Gal. 3:13). The fact that Jesus died on a tree and was therefore accursed ought to put an end to any lingering popular belief in His deity.

The yelling, shouting mob, goaded on by the Sanhedrin's agents, won the day: "Pilate gave sentence that it should be as they required. And he released unto them him that for sedition and murder was cast into prison, whom they had desired; but he delivered Jesus to their will" (23:24–25).

Pilate went home to his wife, who only that morning had shared with him a dream and a warning. Barabbas went back to his brigand's den. Caiaphas and his cronies hurried off to Calvary to enjoy the sufferings of Christ.

Roman justice had been shamed. An innocent man—and more than a man—was to be put to death on a hill of shame. The Jews had chosen a thief and a murderer rather than the Lord of glory. Thieves and murderers have pursued them ever since, all down the long reaches of time and in every land where they have sought to reside. Thieves and robbers will pursue them until they fall into the merciless hands of the Antichrist.

Section 4: The Tree (23:26–49)
　　A.　Jesus on the way to the cross (23:26–33)

First, we get a glimpse of *the foreign conscript:* "And as they led him away, they laid hold upon one Simon, a Cyrenian, coming out of the country, and on him they laid the cross, that he might bear it after Jesus" (23:26). A condemned man was required to carry his own cross. Jesus tried bravely to carry His cross. He staggered a little way, then fell beneath its weight. And no wonder! A sleepless night! The agony in the garden! The beatings and bruisings that He endured in the high priest's house! Hauled off to Pilate, sent on to Herod, brought back to Pilate! Scourged to the bone! And then out into the sunshine, dragging His cross. Then, down He went, exhausted. Even the callous Roman guards could see that He could carry that cross no more.

They spied a man coming toward the city. They conscripted him. "Here, you! Get busy and carry this cross!" A burly soldier shoved the rough-hewn wood onto the man's shoulders. And the doleful procession moved on. Angrily, unwillingly at first, the man bore the weight of the wood. He must have thought, *What will people say? If I meet anyone I know, they will think that I am the criminal.* But before the terrible journey was over, the man's thoughts surely began to change. His eyes were opened. This was Jesus of Nazareth. He had heard of Him. Around the prisoner's neck dangled a placard that proclaimed Him to be Jesus of Nazareth.

The man's name was Simon, a Cyrenian (23:26). Mark tells us that he was the father of Rufus and Alexander, who had become disciples of Christ. Cyrene was an important North African city with a large Jewish colony. Some people have linked this Simon with Simeon that was called "Niger" (a black man), who was prominent in the church at Antioch and one of the elders there who "laid hands" on Saul and Barnabas and sent them forth as the church's first foreign missionaries (Acts 13:1). Simon, of course, would have had no inkling of any of these yet future events. But Jesus did! When He went back home to glory, we can well picture the Lord Jesus saying to the Holy Spirit as He was about to invade this planet, "Don't forget Simon the Cyrenian!"

In any case, the Romans pressed Simon into service. So Jesus, despite Peter's denial and flight, had a man named Simon to carry His cross for Him after all. Poor Simon Peter!

Next, Luke shows us the *fickle crowd:* "And there followed him a great company of people, and of women, which also bewailed and lamented him" (23:27). Truly, the Lord Jesus had touched many hearts during His years of ministry. We see His heart going out for the poor, the deaf, the dumb, the possessed, the maimed, the widow, the orphan, the aged, the guilty, and the lost. Luke's gospel is full of women's portraits—Elizabeth and Mary, Martha and her sister Mary, Mary Magdalene, Joanna, and Susanna. We meet the widow of Nain, the woman who was a sinner, the woman who was bent, and the woman who was sweeping her house.

The women! Note that no gospel records any instance of any woman who opposed Jesus. The word *woman* occurs thirty times in Matthew, nineteen times in Mark, and nineteen times in John—but it's found no less than forty-three times in Luke.

Among the Gentiles, women were often degraded. Among the Jews, the rabbis in their liturgy actually thanked God that they were not born women. It is Christ who gives women dignity.

Jesus had a word about a *future calamity* for the women who wept and wailed as He wended His way to the place where He was to die: "Daughters of Jerusalem, weep not for me, but weep for yourselves, and for your children. For, behold, the days are coming, in the which they shall say, Blessed are the barren, and the wombs that never bare, and the paps which never gave suck. Then shall they begin to say to the mountains, Fall on us; and to the hills, Cover us. For if they do these things in a green tree, what shall be done in the dry?" (23:28–31).

This prophecy has a twofold fulfillment. Verses 28–29 refer to the time of the coming war with *Rome.* Conditions in Jerusalem at that time rapidly became terrible indeed. Famine raged, and desperate people devoured their own children. Plagues swept the city. Rival gangs fought each other and roamed the streets spreading terror. The suffering was beyond endurance. It would have been a blessing to be childless and a mercy to have the hills fall on them and bury them.

The rest of the prophecy refers to the days of the *Antichrist.* Never in all of their long and tear-drenched history have the Jews ever had so terrible a time of persecution as will be theirs in the Great Tribulation. It will last for three and a half years and will be terminated only by the coming of Christ in glory and power.

The story turns for a moment to the *friendless convicts:* "And there were also two other, malefactors, led with him to be put to death" (23:32), thus fulfilling Isaiah's ancient prophecy, "He was numbered with the transgressors" (Isa. 53:12). These two criminals who accompanied Christ to Calvary likely were companions of Barabbas. What did they think, we wonder, when they saw the living Christ of God crucified on the cross that was made for Barabbas, dying in his room and stead. Within a verse or so, Luke will let us catch a glimpse of what they said and did. Meanwhile, they stood there shrinking from the torture that would leap upon them soon. They were forsaken of men, friendless, and alone—unless perhaps Barabbas ventured to pass by. More likely, he was already over the hills and far away. But Jesus was there, and His heart went out to them. They were men for whom He was about to die.

Then came *the fearful crime:* "And when they were come to the place, which is called Calvary, there they crucified him, and the malefactors, one on the right hand, and the other on the left" (23:33).

Luke tells the story of the actual Crucifixion in four words: "there they crucified him." First, the *place.* That place, the place called Calvary, had been in the mind of God before time ever began. Then, in the unfolding drama of Creation, when God the Son was at work on this world, we can picture a pause. There it was—a skull-shaped hill amid the mountains. "Father," He might well have said.

"Here am I, My Son."

Behold, the place, now ready and waiting the coming dread day. Abraham, too, saw the place. David, likewise, came to the place and, as some people believe, planted Goliath's gory head right there—*the place.* Just across from the temple. There they crucified Him.

Then there were *the people*—the Hebrews, the Greeks, and the Romans were all there. The worlds of religion, culture, and power united to endorse His death. Jews, especially, were there in great numbers. Probably a million of them were around town for Passover.

Then, too, we note *the penalty*—they crucified Him. No crueler death was ever devised—a long, slow, agonizing death.

And, finally, *the Person*—Him! The Lord of glory! The Son of God! The One whom angels worshiped! The Creator of heaven and earth. There they crucified *Him.* It was the crime of crimes. No darker deed has ever been done. Human sin could go no further than that. The only reason God did not stamp flat the high hills of Judah, turn to blood the waters of the seven seas, and unleash on this planet twelve legions of outraged angels was because that crime—the high watermark of man's guilt—was going to become the high watermark of God's grace (Col. 1:20–22).

> B. Jesus and the work of the cross (23:34–49)
>   1. The Mediator (23:34)

Not for a single moment did Jesus give way to the excruciating pain that now assailed every nerve and fiber of His body. His first thought, however, was for others. He was the Mediator, the Daysman for whom poor old Job so greatly longed (Job 9:33), the God-Man go-between. Even as the soldiers seized hammer and nails to smite Him to the tree, He cried out—for them! "Father, forgive them; for they know not what they do" (23:34). This amazing prayer averted the instant judgment of God for this dreadful and diabolical crime—to lay their impious hands upon His immaculate person with such outrageous intent. Different from all others, Jesus had no need to ask forgiveness for Himself. He did not pray, "Father, forgive Me." He had nothing that had to be forgiven. He prayed, "Father, forgive *them*." In His sinless soul was no rancor, no resentment, and no desire for revenge—just love.

> 2. The mockers (23:35–38)

First, He was mocked by *the Hebrews*. They mocked Him as *Savior.* Having nailed Him to the cross, the soldiers seized the booty, callously casting lots for what they could not divide, indifferent to the chorus of cries and calls that swept and swirled around that central cross. They were more intent on the roll of the dice than on anything else. The horrific screams of anguish and the fearful curses were all in a day's work for them.

But it was something far worse with the Jews: "And the people stood beholding. And the rulers also with them derided him, saying, He saved others; let him save himself, if he be Christ, the chosen of God" (23:35). Imagine! The Jewish religious leaders actually took the lead in mocking the Messiah Himself. Yet, what they said in their blind hatred was literally true: He could have saved Himself; twelve legions of angels (seventy-two thousand of them) would have made short work of Jew and Gentile alike had He so desired. Those iron bolts of Rome that were in His hands and feet could have become thunderbolts for Him to hurl at His foes. He could have saved Himself! He could have saved Himself by going home to heaven from the Mount of Transfiguration. He could have saved Himself in Gethsemane; in the house of Annas; or before Caiaphas, Pilate, or Herod. But then, farewell to all hope of salvation for us.

Moreover, He was mocked by *the heathen.* They mocked Him *as Sovereign:* "And the soldiers also mocked him, coming to him, and offering him vinegar, and saying, If thou be the king of the Jews, save thyself" (23:36–37). Some people have pointed out that this incident took place about the time of the midday meal and that some of the soldiers mockingly invited Him to share some of their sour wine. Also, picking up the ribald shouts of the Jews, they mocked His claim to be King of the Jews.

Then, too, there was the mocking Latin title that they nailed to His cross: *REX JUDAEORUM HIC EST,* "THIS IS THE KING OF THE JEWS." The words were translated into Greek and Hebrew. Pilate had some excuse. After all, he was a Roman and could not be expected to know the Hebrew Scriptures. The Jews, however, rejected Him as their King, and along with Him they rejected the Word of God, which proclaimed Him as King (Isa. 9:7). They were without excuse. They were angry with Pilate for putting up the title, but they got nowhere with him. The placard was Pilate's sardonic way of showing his disdain for Caiaphas and his crowd. The Jews demanded that he change the title, but Pilate remained firm, refusing to do so. And Pilate, pagan that he was, wrote words of truth, for this Man was indeed the King of the Jews—and He will be owned as such one of these days (Rev. 17:14).

3. The malefactors (23:39–43)

"And one of the malefactors which were hanged railed on him, saying, If thou be Christ, save thyself and us" (23:39). Luke takes special delight in his gospel of emphasizing the truth of salvation. In Matthew, Jesus is the Sovereign; in Mark, He is the Servant; and in John, He is the Son. But in Luke, He is the Savior. In recording the taunts aimed at Jesus, Luke shows the rabble, the rulers, the Romans, and the robbers all making fun of Jesus' claim to be Savior (23:35, 36, 39). His gospel contains the word *sinners* more than all of the other Gospels combined (Matthew five times, Mark five times, John four times, but Luke sixteen times). Luke was also fond of such words as *salvation, grace,* and *Savior.* He also emphasized the universal significance of the gospel (2:14, 32; 3:6).

When the two malefactors were first nailed to their crosses, they both reviled Jesus. This second outburst of abuse by one of the malefactors, however, was much worse. This time, Luke used the word *blasphemō* which means "to blaspheme, or to revile." The man began to use insulting language. The word emphasizes speaking amiss of sacred things. Luke says that he kept it up; it was a litany of irrational hate. It sealed his eternal doom.

The other malefactor came to his senses. He rebuked his cursing companion: "Dost not thou fear God, seeing thou art in the same condemnation?" (23:40). He recognized the deity of Christ. He was the most unlikely person in the most unlikely place for the most unlikely purpose! One hanging on an accursed cross in excruciating pain, uncomplaining, freely forgiving—who could He be but *God?* It was a marvelous confession—God! In the same condemnation! It was incredible—but it was true. There was no other explanation. Who but God manifest in flesh could exhibit such triumph in the face of such torment?

"We," he continued, "receive the due reward of our deeds: but this man hath done nothing amiss" (23:41). He confessed his own guilt and the Lord's complete innocence. Then he spoke to Jesus. And, again, his grasp of truth was astounding: "Lord, remember me when thou comest into thy kingdom" (23:42). All appearances to the contrary, that Man was on His way to receive a kingdom. Nothing seemed more unlikely. The only crown that this world had for Him was a crown of thorns. The only tribute that it would pay Him was a mocking title nailed to the most hideous tool of torment ever devised by fallen man. The only homage it would offer was to accept Him as King if He would come down from the cross. With eyes wide open now, the dying thief's faith soared: "Lord," he said (putting Him on the throne of the universe), "remember me" (putting Him on the throne of his heart) "when thou comest into thy kingdom" (putting Him on the throne of David).

Just over yonder, on the other side of death, awaited the glorious kingdom of God. Oh, if only there was some way to enter there! Well, this Man Jesus was King of that place. Maybe He would take pity on him! So, greatly daring, he said, "Lord, remember me when You come into Your kingdom."

Nor did the answer tarry. The response was immediate: "Verily I say unto thee, Today shalt thou be with me in paradise" (23:43). On the other side, not long afterward, the Savior met the dying malefactor and took him with Him into Paradise—the first fruits of Calvary.

4. The miracles (23:44–49)

Luke records three miracles, the first of which had to do with *the sun:* "And it was about the sixth hour, and there was a darkness over all the earth until the ninth hour. And the sun was darkened" (23:44–45a). The Lord was crucified at nine o'clock in the morning. The supernatural darkness began at high noon. It lasted until three o'clock in the afternoon, six dark and dreadful hours. For three hours, He suffered at the hands of men; now He must suffer at the hands of God. It was not the torment of those first three hours that brought the bloodlike sweat to His brow in Gethsemane; it was the terror of the last three hours. It was then that He who knew no sin was made sin for us (2 Cor. 5:21). God pulled the blanket of night over the whole scene so that no prying eyes might gaze upon His agony. Darkness paralyzed the whole land and doubtless terrorized everyone.

The second miracle had to do with *the sanctuary:* "and the veil of the temple was rent in the midst" (23:45b). The inner veil of the temple separated between the Holy Place and the Holy of Holies itself. No one was allowed in the Holy of Holies except the high priest once a year on the Day of Atonement.

The veil was made of costly linen, heavily embroidered. It was sixty feet high; it spanned the temple from wall to wall and was as thick as a man's hand. No human hand could have torn that veil. It was torn by God's own almighty hand from top to bottom to signify the end of Judaism and the end of an age.

The third miracle had to do with *a soul,* with the souls of the centurion and his men: "And when Jesus had cried with a loud voice, he said, Father, into thy hands I commend my spirit: and having said thus, he gave up the ghost. Now when the centurion saw what was done, he glorified God, saying, Certainly this was a righteous man" (23:46–47). The Lord began His ordeal by addressing God as His Father. During the hours of darkness, that relationship seems to have been suspended. Christ, as the sinbearer, addressed God as Elohim. Now that the ordeal was over, He again addressed God as His Father. His spirit He commended to His Father's care. His body was buried by His friends. His soul went down to hades to proclaim His triumph there and to seize the keys of death and hades (1 Peter 3:19; Rev. 1:18).

Little or nothing did these Roman soldiers know of these things. But one thing they did know. They had seen people crucified many times and knew the full horror of it, but they had never seen the likes of this. This man had prayed for His enemies. He had cared for His mother. He had sublimely ignored every insult that His foes had hurled at Him. He had accepted the homage of a dying thief and comforted him, assuring him of happiness beyond the bounds of death. He had been clothed in darkness out of which darkness had come a mighty shout. Then He was gone, sovereignly surrendering His spirit to God. Those soldiers left Calvary believers, their thoughts full of One who was mighty to save.

"And all the people that came together to that sight, beholding the things which were done, smote their breasts, and returned. And all his acquaintance, and the women that followed him from Galilee, stood afar off, beholding these things" (23:48–49). The darkness had silenced and sobered the sightseers. They had come to witness the crucifixion of the Nazarene. They had witnessed, instead, a convulsion of nature itself. The crowds melted away, many of the people beating their breasts.

His closest friends stayed to the end. "They stood afar off," Luke says. Perhaps that was why Peter was so readily received back into the fellowship. He had followed afar off; they stood afar off. How could they cast stones at Peter? He had denied Him. They had not confessed Him. There was not so much difference between them after all.

Section 5: The Tomb (23:50–56)
    A.   The sepulcher prepared (23:50–54)

Our attention is now drawn to a very special man: "And, behold, there was a man named Joseph, a counsellor; and he was a good man, and a just: (The same had not consented to the counsel and deed of them;) he was of Arimathaea, a city of the Jews: who also himself waited for the kingdom of God" (29:50–51). This good man was a member of the Sanhedrin. He dissented, however, from the evil plots of the others. He simply went about quietly making his own secret plans. He could not stem the tide of wickedness all about him. It would end with Christ's death. Beyond that, there was no knowing what Caiaphas and his crowd would do. They were quite capable of desecrating the body of Christ. That was possibly their next order of business. These men were capable of anything. He could visualize their dumping the body of Jesus in a common grave or—perish the thought—denying it any burial at all by having it thrown into the ever-burning fires of Gehenna. He could put a stop to any such thing if he acted swiftly and secretly.

The moment he heard that Jesus was dead, Joseph acted. "This man," Luke says, "went unto Pilate, and begged the body of Jesus" (23:52). He was just the man for the job. Joseph of Arimathea was an aristocrat and a gentleman. Moreover, he was rich and a Sanhedrinist. Pilate had no hesitation in granting Joseph's request. Pilate must have been feeling shabby about his compromise. This generous response to Joseph of Arimathea made him feel better about himself. And it would be another stab at Caiaphas and the iniquitous Annas. He had already gotten in one good thrust at the Jews by the wording of the title for the cross. He'd be able to get under their skins again by giving the body of Jesus to the gentleman. Thus, God provided a Joseph to superintend the birth of His Son and a Joseph to superintend His burial as well.

So Pilate gave instructions for Joseph to have the body: "And he took it down, and wrapped it in linen, and laid it in a sepulchre that was hewn in stone, wherein never man before was laid. And that day was the preparation, and the sabbath drew on" (23:53–54). From that time, only loving hands touched Him. Now it was to be nothing but the choicest and the best—costly linen, rare spices, and a brand-new, rock-hewn tomb.

So the Lord was crucified on the preparation day of the feast, the fourteenth day of Nisan. He was buried in haste about six o'clock in the afternoon before the "high day," the first day of the feast, began. Everything had to be done in haste. The linen was torn into strips and wound, limb by limb, around the body between layers of myrrh and aloes, the head being wrapped separately in a napkin. Then the body was laid to rest in the niche of the tomb. The great stone that served as a door was rolled heavily and securely into place. The Passover Lamb was dead—and the Jewish Passover was now obsolete.

B. The spices prepared (23:55–56)

Before turning from the Lord's death and burial, Luke recorded a further item of interest regarding the women (23:55–56). They *watched:* "And the women also, which came with him from Galilee, followed after, and beheld the sepulchre, and how his body was laid." They took it all in with tearful but watchful eyes. They could have recounted every detail. And they *worked:* "They returned, and prepared spices and ointments. . . ." Two Sabbaths were involved in the events relating to the burial and resurrection of Christ. There was the "high" Sabbath, the fifteenth of Nisan, the first day of the feast. There was also the regular weekly Sabbath, the seventeenth day of Nisan, the third day of the feast. On the day in between, the women had to bring the spices needed for the completion of the embalming (Mark 16:1). They all believed Jesus to be forever dead. Yet, He still reigned in their hearts.

Then they *waited:* "and rested the sabbath day according to the commandment." This was the last Sabbath of the old economy. Soon they would be celebrating the first day of the week. They waited. And, being human, they were probably consumed with impatience to get back to the tomb and finish their task.

Section 6: The Triumph (24:1–49)
    A.   Events at the empty tomb (24:1–12)
        1. The vacant tomb (24:1–3)

The story now moves from gloom to glory. Luke takes us to the empty tomb, to the Emmaus road, and to the Upper Room. "Now upon the first day of the week, very early in the morning, they came unto the sepulchre, bringing the spices which they had prepared, and certain others with them" (24:1). Love is the greatest force in the universe. Doubtless, all of the Lord's disciples loved Him, but they did not love Him as much as these women did.

The men were still sleeping, hiding from the authorities, keeping a low profile. But these noble women were up at the crack of dawn and on their way to the tomb. Not a man in the city dared accompany them; not one was brave enough to carry a lantern before them or go on ahead to see if the coast was clear. But these women! Bravely they fought down their fears, heading in the gloom to a lonely garden and a guarded tomb. And the stone? Would love also find a way to break the governor's seal and chase away the guard? Well, that was one worry that was soon resolved. The guards had already gone, frightened out of their wits by an angel of God.

Boldly the women "entered in, and found not the body of the Lord Jesus" (24:3). They were suddenly full of doubts. Who had tampered with the tomb? Who had removed the body? Was it the priests? Had they taken that blessed body away to desecrate it?

        2. The vital truth (24:4–8)

Then they saw they were no longer alone: "And it came to pass, as they were much perplexed thereabout, behold, two men stood by them in shining garments" (24:4). Their reaction was immediate. "They were afraid, and bowed down their faces to the earth" (24:5a). It was the clothing of the visitors that struck awe into their hearts. The word for "shining" means "flashing like lightning." As for the angels, they looked like men and spoke like men. The women were afraid and full of awe.

The angels spoke to them: "Why seek ye the living among the dead? He is not here, but is risen: remember how he spake unto you when he was yet in Galilee, saying, The Son of man must be delivered into the hands of sinful men, and be crucified, and the third day rise again. And they remembered his words" (24:5b–8). Surely the thing about the people of our planet that must perplex the angels more than anything else is their chronic unbelief. How could anyone forget such truths as He had taught His own?

There they sat, two angels from high heaven. They must have looked around them with the liveliest curiosity. The land from whence they came had no tombs. They inspected the walls of naked rock, examined the empty grave clothes, peered out at the beauty of the garden. That men should have murdered heaven's Beloved was beyond all thought. That He should rise through the grave clothes, walk out through the wall, and vanish from view was all to be expected.

But where were the crowds? Surely on this day of days the disciples should have been there long before now. And where were the Jewish leaders and the Roman rulers? They sat down to wait. Voices! Women's voices! What was this, a handful of women with more grave clothes? What were they doing in a tomb anyway? Seeking the living among the dead! What folly! "He is not here, but is risen!" the angels declared. So *that* was why the tomb was empty! The truth dawned on the women at last.

3. The verbal tidings (24:9–11)

The women hurried back to tell the disciples. Luke says, "[They] returned from the sepulchre, and told all these things unto the eleven and to all the rest. It was Mary Magdalene, and Joanna, and Mary the mother of James, and other women who were with them, which told these things unto the apostles. And their words seemed to them as idle tales, and they believed them not" (24:9–11). Such is the entrenched unbelief of the human heart. If such is the case with "believers," those who in some measure know and love the Lord, how much more so, indeed, it must be with the ungodly. Nothing is more remarkable in this narrative than the utter inability of the believers to convince even other believers by their own personal testimony.

They would not believe the women. Thomas would not believe the united testimony of the other ten (John 20:25). The disciples would not believe the testimony of the two who met the Master on the Emmaus road (Mark 16:12–13). No wonder Mark adds, "Afterward he appeared unto the eleven as they sat at meat, and upbraided them with their unbelief and hardness of heart, because they believed not them which had seen him after he was risen" (Mark 16:14). The disciples were powerless to witness. Not until after Pentecost and the baptism and filling of the Holy Spirit were the disciples able to pass on the verbal tidings with effective, convicting, and converting power.

When the women came with their news, what they had to say to these defeated and demoralized men seemed to be "idle tales." The word used occurs only here. It means literally "silly nonsense." How frustrating that must have been to the women.

4. The visual test (24:12)

The insistent witness of the women finally got through to Peter. He decided to go and see for himself. "Then arose Peter, and ran unto the sepulchre; and stooping down, he beheld the linen clothes laid by themselves, and departed, wondering in himself at that which was come to pass" (24:12). John tells us that the napkin that had been around the Lord's head lay by itself (John 20:7). The evidence was conclusive. The spice-laden strips of linen that had been wrapped limb by limb around the body lay there just as they had been when Joseph left the tomb and closed the door, except that now they were hard and solid. The Lord's body had risen through them. They still retained the shape of the body. Lazarus had not been able to rise through his grave clothes (John 11:43–40), but Jesus rose through His. Peter went away wondering but not convinced.

B. Events on the Emmaus road (24:13–35)
1. The two disciples and their blighted hopes (24:13–24)

The long eventful first Easter Sunday was drawing to a close. Two of the disciples were heading home from Jerusalem. One of them was named Cleopas, and the other one was probably his wife. Luke says, "And, behold, two of them went that same day to a village called Emmaus, which was from Jerusalem about three score furlongs [seven or eight miles]" (24:13).

They left Jerusalem by the Western Gate. A little less than half an hour's walk brought them to a plateau with the guilty city behind them. Another half an hour and they could pause and look back and see the wide view back as far as Bethlehem.

Before long, they left the paved Roman road and headed up a lovely valley with Emmaus in view above and beyond them. The whole scene was idyllic.

The couple talked together. They had so much to discuss—the treachery of Judas and his subsequent suicide, the plots and guilt of the Sanhedrin, the weakness of Herod and Pilate, the terrible crime of Calvary, and, today, rumors of Christ's resurrection and the solid fact of an empty tomb.

"And it came to pass, that, while they communed together and reasoned, Jesus himself drew near, and went with them. But their eyes were holden that they should not know him. And he said unto them, What manner of communications are these that ye have one to another, as ye walk, and are sad?" (24:15–17). It was evident from their tearful faces, the droop of their shoulders, and the melancholy tone of their voices that something was seriously wrong.

The two travelers probably were only too glad to have this polite stranger give them an outlet for their perplexities and woes. Just to share their sorrow would be a relief. So they poured out their hearts. Cleopas spoke up: "Art thou only a stranger in Jerusalem, and hast not known the things which are come to pass there in these days?" (24:18). How could anyone be in Jerusalem and not know about the events of the past few days. "Art thou a stranger?" he asked. He was indeed a Stranger in this world. He thus described Himself (Matt. 25:35–46). Paul, in describing the wisdom of God, said that none of the princes of this world knew it "for had they known it, they would not have crucified the Lord of glory" (1 Cor. 2:8).

"What things?" Jesus asked. Then out came the story of their crucified hopes. "Concerning Jesus of Nazareth," they said, "which was a prophet mighty in deed and word before God and all the people" (24:19). What miracles He had performed! What messages He had proclaimed!

But where had it all ended? With a coronation? No, with a crucifixion! "The chief priests and our rulers delivered him to be condemned to death, and have crucified him" (24:20). If He had died a natural death, that would have been bad enough. If the Romans had instigated this horrible crime, it would have been a terrible thing. But it was not a natural death, and the Romans had not instigated it. Our own religious leaders had put Him to such a painful and shameful death.

"We trusted that it had been he which should have redeemed Israel," they said (24:21). The Lord did not reply, although His heart must have burned within Him at those words. The sad story continued. "Yea, and certain women also of our company made us astonished, which were early at the sepulchre; and when they found not his body, they came, saying, that they had also seen a vision of angels, which said that he was alive. And certain of them which were with us went to the sepulchre, and found it even so as the women had said: but him they saw not" (24:22–24).

Cleopas came to the end of the story. Obviously, he placed little, if any, credence in the witness of the women. A vision of angels indeed! All that the men had seen was an empty tomb and an empty linen chrysalis.

2. The two disciples and their burning hearts (24:25–27)

Now it was the Lord's turn to speak. "O fools [foolish ones], and slow of heart to believe all that the prophets have spoken: Ought not Christ to have suffered these things, and to enter into his glory?" (24:25–26). How typical of the Lord. He based everything on the inspired, inerrant, infallible Word of God. His first and final court of appeal was the Bible.

Their problem was that they had a lopsided view of Scripture. They wanted a militant Messiah. They read all of the Scriptures that spoke of a conquering Christ, One who would smash the power of Rome and make Jerusalem the center of a global, glorious empire based on liberty and justice for all. They read Scriptures that foretold a golden age when swords would become plowshares and spears would become pruning hooks. They had visions of an Edenic earth, filled with bountiful harvests, a world in which the lion would lie down with the lamb and where a person would still be young at a hundred years old.

Their problem was that just as many Scriptures spoke of a meek Messiah, One who would come to redeem us to God by His blood—such Scriptures as Psalms 22 and 69; Isaiah 53; and Zechariah 14. The Lord now gave them a balanced view of the prophetic Scripture: "And beginning at Moses and all the prophets, he expounded unto them in all the scriptures the things concerning himself" (24:27). What a Bible survey lesson *that* must have been! There were the great truths proclaimed by the prophets and the great types hidden in many a historical passage! There were Abel's lamb, Noah's ark, and the stories of Joseph, Moses, and David. There were the sacrifices and the feasts. Page after page of prophecy focusing on a Christ who was coming to redeem and to reign.

3. The two disciples and their blessed home (24:28–32)

The miles melted away, and, before they knew it, they had entered Emmaus and turned toward the street where they lived. "And they drew nigh unto the village, whither they went: and he made as though he would have gone further.

But they constrained him, saying, Abide with us: for it is toward evening, and the day is far spent. And he went in to tarry with them" (24:28–29).

They did not want to see Him go. They had never been so blessed by this survey of the Old Testament Scriptures. They wanted more. Would He stay the night? They were insistent. The word for "constrained" suggests entreaty or compelling force. He responded at once.

"And it came to pass, as he sat at meat with them, he took bread, and blessed it, and brake, and gave to them. And their eyes were opened, and they knew him; and he vanished out of their sight" (24:30–31). He took His place at the table. It only seemed natural that He should act as Host. He reached out for the bread, broke, and gave it to them with His blessing bestowed upon it. So simple! So sublime! They had seen Him do it before—when He fed the hungry multitudes. He had done this very same thing in the Upper Room. Perhaps that was what opened their eyes. Or was it that as He broke the bread, they saw the print of the nails in His hands?

As quick as a flash, they knew Him! And as quick as a flash, He was gone! It was the Lord! "And they said one to another, Did not our heart burn within us, while he talked with us by the way, and while he opened to us the scriptures?" (24:32). He had not only melted the miles on the road to Emmaus but also melted their hearts.

4. The two disciples and their breathless haste (24:33–35)

They had no thought now of going to bed. They must go back to the Upper Room. "They rose up the same hour, and returned to Jerusalem" (24:33). Back down the hill, over the bridge, and past the fork in the road. Back along the paved Roman road to the spot where they could see Bethlehem. On into the city by way of the Needle's Eye in the Western Gate—all seven or eight miles of it on feet that flew. Back to the house, up the stairs, and in at the door—"We've seen Him!" They "found the eleven gathered together, and them that were with them." The word used suggests that the place was packed. They had to compete with their news. "The Lord is risen indeed, and hath appeared to Simon." That was what greeted them. And Simon would have to tell all about it, laughing and crying at the same time. But part of the story he would tell no one as long as he lived. But he knew that he was forgiven, and he had worshiped the Lord. And he knew that Jesus was alive.

Then the Emmaus disciples had their turn: "And they told what things were done in the way, and how he was known of them in breaking of bread" (24:35).

302 Exploring the Gospel of Luke

C. Events in the Upper Room (24:36–53)
1. Jesus in the midst (24:36–49)

Amid all of the clack and clatter of tongues, suddenly Jesus was in their midst. "And as they thus spake, Jesus himself stood in the midst of them, and saith unto them, Peace be unto you. But they were terrified and affrighted, and supposed that they had seen a spirit" (24:36–37). He did not come up the stairs and knock on the door; that would have frightened them because a knock on the door at night was likely to be the Sanhedrin police. Or if they opened the door and saw Him standing there in the shadows, they might have screamed. By far the simplest thing was to come in through the wall or just materialize in their midst— which is just what He did! The Lord's "Peace be unto you" did not allay their alarm. And who can blame them?

The Lord made allowance for their fears. He gave them *bodily proof* (24:38–43). He said, "Why are ye troubled? and why do thoughts arise in your hearts? Behold my hands and my feet, that it is I myself: handle me, and see; for a spirit hath not flesh and bones, as ye see me have. And when he had thus spoken, he showed them his hands and his feet" (24:38–40). Here was tangible evidence. This was no phony spirit body made out of ectoplasm. This was a real, solid body—His body, the body they had last seen being taken down from the tree to be placed in the tomb (1 John 1:1).

They were still not fully convinced. "And while they yet believed not for joy, and wondered, he said unto them, Have ye here any meat? And they gave him a piece of a broiled fish, and of an honeycomb. And he took it, and did eat before them" (24:41–43). So much for vegetarianism! His resurrection body was real enough. He was able to sit down to table and eat solid food. What more positive, prosaic proof could anyone want?

He then gave them *biblical proof* (24:44–49). "And he said unto them, These are the words which I spake unto you, while I was yet with you . . ." (24:44a). After Peter's great confession at Caesarea Philippi, He had repeatedly told them exactly what was going to happen to Him. Every detail had been fulfilled over the past week.

Furthermore, He reinforced His teaching in the Upper Room by pointing them back to the Bible, the written Word: "that all things must be fulfilled, which were written in the law of Moses, and in the prophets, and in the psalms, concerning me" (24:44b). This was the threefold division of the Hebrew Bible. The whole Jewish Bible spoke of Him. He endorsed each and every part of it.

"Then opened he their understanding, that they might understand the scriptures" (24:45). They needed that spiritual enlightenment because "the natural man receiveth not the things of the Spirit of God: for they are foolishness unto him: neither can he know them, because they are spiritually discerned" (1 Cor. 2:14).

The task that lay before them was daunting. They were to be His ambassadors in a hostile, unbelieving world: "And [he] said unto them, Thus it is written, and thus it behooved Christ to suffer, and to rise from the dead the third day: And that repentance and remission of sins should be preached in his name among all nations, beginning at Jerusalem. And ye are witnesses of these things" (24:46–48). Their task? To evangelize the world!

He looked at them. What an unlikely group of people! A few fishermen, a former tax collector, a onetime zealot—mostly people from Galilee, a despised part of the country where the accent could be cut with a knife. There was not a scholar among them, not even a trained rabbi. This collection of nobodies was to preach in defiance of the Sanhedrin and in the face of the intellectual Greeks and the all-powerful Romans. The disciples contemplated all of this with stunned disbelief. Why, only an hour earlier they had found it virtually impossible to make Christ real to each other.

The Lord, however, was not quite through. "And, behold, I send the promise of my Father upon you: but tarry ye in the city of Jerusalem, until ye be endued with power from on high" (24:49).

So that was it! The second person of the Godhead was going home to heaven, but the third person of the Godhead was coming down to earth to take His place. The Lord had no intention of leaving it up to His disciples to formulate the plan and carry it out to earth's remotest bounds. The Holy Spirit would enlighten them and enable them. He would reveal truth to them, superintend the writing of the New Testament, supernaturally open blind eyes and deaf ears, and raise from spiritual death people who were held in the bondage of sin. All they had to do for now was wait. It was just past Passover. They would need to wait until Pentecost, a period of fifty days. Then the Holy Spirit would come, and the church would be born. They were to depend on Him. Luke would have to write another book!

2. Jesus on the mount (24:50–53)

Jesus stayed in the environs of earth, appearing here and there for a period of forty days. Then He took these people to Olivet, out "as far as to Bethany," where

He had spent some of His happiest times. There was the house of Martha, Mary, and Lazarus. There was where Simon the leper lived. The Lord took a last look around, "lifted up his hands, and blessed them," and stepped into the sky. "And it came to pass, while he blessed them, he was parted from them, and carried up into heaven. And they worshipped him" (24:51–52a). The last they saw of Him, He was blessing them. The last He saw of them, they were worshiping Him. And it has been like that ever since—Jesus blessing us; we worshiping Him.

As for the disciples, they "returned to Jerusalem with great joy: and were continually in the temple, praising and blessing God" (24:52b–53). The Jewish leaders did not like it, but what could they do? The extraordinary things that had happened must have given them pause. They would wait and see.

Meanwhile, a ten-day countdown began. Then, with a mighty rush and roar, with a "mighty rushing wind," and with "cloven tongues like as of fire," the Holy Spirit arrived, the church was born, and things would never be the same again (Acts 2:3).